50

4th and GOAL

Also by Monte Burke

Sowbelly: The Obsessive Quest for the World-Record Largemouth Bass

Leaper: The Wonderful World of Atlantic Salmon Fishing (co-editor)

4th and GOAL

One Man's Quest to Recapture His Dream

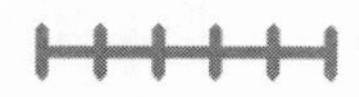

MONTE BURKE

GRAND CENTRAL PUBLISHING

NEW YORK BOSTON

Grand Central Publishing
Hachette Book Group
237 Park Avenue
New York, NY 10017

www.HachetteBookGroup.com

Printed in the United States of America

RRD-C

First Edition: September 2012
10 9 8 7 6 5 4 3 2 1

Grand Central Publishing is a division of Hachette Book Group, Inc.
The Grand Central Publishing name and logo is a trademark of Hachette Book Group, Inc.

Library of Congress Cataloging-in-Publication Data
Burke, Monte.
4th and goal : one man's quest to recapture his dream / by Monte Burke. — 1st ed.
p. cm.
Includes index.
ISBN 978-1-4555-1404-5 (hardcover)
1. Moglia, Joseph H., 1949- 2. Football coaches—United States—Biography. 3. Businessmen—United States—Biography. I. Title.
GV939.M58B87 2012
796.332092—dc23
[B] 2012008284

To Harper and Dylan,
team players

Contents

"What happens to a dream deferred?
Does it dry up/Like a raisin in the sun?"

—Langston Hughes

"Don't do it. Don't go into coaching unless you absolutely can't live without it."

—Paul "Bear" Bryant

INTRODUCTION

Storage Room

It's a frigid early Sunday morning in the late fall of 1983. Joe Moglia, the thirty-three-year-old defensive coordinator of the two-time defending Ivy League champion Dartmouth Big Green football team, lies awake in his bed in an unheated storage room located on the top floor of the Davis Varsity House, an old, red brick building on the school's Hanover, New Hampshire, campus. During daylight hours, from the room's huge circular window, one can see the green grass of the football field, encircled by a vermilion running track that's pinstriped with white lane lines. But it is now 4:00 a.m., that dark, unsettling hour when the racing minds of the sleepless become easy prey for creeping anxieties.

Joe's back nearly touches the icy cement floor, the springs on his single bed having long since surrendered to the fatigue of three decades of use. He watches his vaporized breaths blow into a thin slice of streetlamp light pouring in through the uncurtained window. His shirts hang from the room's exposed water pipes like laundered ghosts. A half-dozen pigeons, sleepless themselves, are perched on the ledge outside his window, trilling softly.

To stave off the cold, Joe is wearing a gray sweat suit, the hood pulled over the ski hat on his head. He's also wrapped four old Army blankets—providing all the suppleness of steel wool—around his body. Joe is fighting the urge to urinate. He doesn't want to break the seal of warmth that his body has taken hours to create—the bathroom is down two flights of stairs, in the football team's locker room.

The previous afternoon, Dartmouth had tied Columbia to remain undefeated in the Ivy League. They are very much in contention for their third straight league championship. For the past three seasons Dartmouth has been led by Joe's defense, one of the best in college football. Though they are an undersized, slow-footed group, he has somehow managed to convince them that a football game is won as much with their heads and hearts as it is with their bodies.

It's not unusual for a football coach to be awake at this hour. Sleeplessness is a common malady among this particular fraternity of men, who are judged, fairly or unfairly, by a single metric: whether they win or lose on Saturday afternoons. Nights after games are the worst. Brains hum, exulting in a victory or stewing over a loss or, perhaps, already fretting about next week's opponents.

But Joe has something bigger than a football game on his mind. Since he was a teenager, he has worked toward his one abiding dream, his lifelong obsession: He wants to become the head coach of a college football team.

But he has decided on this early morning in Hanover—well into the second year of his ascetic, solo existence in this musty storage room—that his dream must die.

Technically, Joe is still married, though that will not be the case in a few months. His separation and subsequent divorce from the woman he married at age nineteen will be, always, what he counts as his greatest failure. Together, he and Kathe have four children: three elementary school–aged girls and a five-year-old boy. But Joe's current salary is $33,000. He has decided that he can no longer patiently work his way up the football-coaching ladder and still provide for his family.

His main objective now will be taking care of his family. Making this choice will require an almost unbearable sacrifice. He will have to lose his dream. But he will also lose something much more important. In order to take care of his family, Joe has decided, he must leave them. He will regret the consequences of this decision for the rest of his life. But he will always believe he made the right choice.

Two months later Joe will be offered a job on the defensive staff of the defending national champion University of Miami Hurricanes, with a promise that he will soon become the team's defensive coordinator. It is exactly the right job for this point in his career, a high-profile chance to position himself, eventually, for a head-coaching gig.

But Joe will decline the offer. Instead, he will follow through on his new life plan. Joe has his sights set on Wall Street. He has decided that if he is going to lose both his career and everyday contact with his family, he is going to make a lot of money doing so. Somehow, he hopes, it could ease the pain.

But neither a Wall Street job nor the money that comes with it is guaranteed. He is fantastically unqualified for employment in one of the most competitive industries in the world. In his professional life, he has known only the world of football. He is rolling the dice, betting on himself.

On that cold morning in that storage room in New Hampshire, Joe believes his coaching career—the sole ambition of his professional life—is now over, forever. The Yogi Berra–like maxim tossed around by the salty old-timers in the profession, Joe knows, is true: the only way to get back into coaching is to never leave it.

Unless…

Twenty-eight years later, now sixty-two, Joe Moglia is standing on the sidelines of a football field in Nebraska, wearing a headset and a white polo shirt with the words "Omaha Nighthawks" stenciled over the left breast. It is a Thursday night in the fall of 2011, chilly and sprinkling with rain. The stadium lights are aureoled in the mist. Joe can see the vapor from his breath.

Joe has become the head coach of the Nighthawks, one of four franchises that constitute the United Football League, a professional minor league in only its third year of existence. Constantly teetering on the brink of obsolescence because of financial troubles, this is a league made up of football players and coaches who, for one reason or another, are currently either National Football League castoffs or wannabes. The UFL provides them with a chance to get back into the biggest, most powerful sports league in the world, or to make it there for the first time.

The league provided Joe an opportunity, too. In a life filled with overcoming challenges, he has sought out yet another in his quest to become a coach again. He had been born and raised in a rough-and-tumble inner city New York neighborhood from which half of its kids never made it out. He was an audacious young football coach who scratched and clawed his way up the profession for sixteen years. After leaving coaching in 1984, he embarked on one of the most remarkable—and unlikely—business careers of the last half century, one that was completely self-made. With no experience or pedigree, he somehow willed his way into a new career on Wall Street. In his seventeen years at Merrill Lynch, he rose quickly to a top management position and, along the way, actually changed the way Wall Street does business.

In 2001 Joe remade himself again, shocking the financial world when he left his very comfortable and highly lucrative post at

Merrill to take over a money-losing, left-for-dead online broker. In his eight years at TD Ameritrade, he rescued the company from the bursting of one financial bubble, helped it to completely sidestep another, and in the process created one of the strongest financial services firms in the country.

Then, at the top of the financial game, he walked away. Voluntarily. He was almost sixty. Deep inside, Joe knew there was one more life task left undone, one more challenge to face. He never had become the head coach of a college football team, and now, he decided, the time had come.

This guy is totally insane, said members of both the financial and football worlds, as Joe embarked on his dream chase. When he couldn't find a job right away, he became, at age sixty, an unpaid intern for the University of Nebraska's football team to regain the football experience, the brushing up, he believed that college athletic directors required to take a chance on him, to prove that he wasn't some rich Wall Street kook. He did this for two seasons, working eighty hours a week at Nebraska. But it wasn't enough. Joe got five coaching interviews, and had some nibbles at a few other places. But, in the end, no athletic director was willing to stick his neck out to hire a sixty-year-old man who had not coached in a quarter of a century. After all, athletic directors are naturally nervous critters, their own job security hinging on the success of their hires.

For nearly three years, Joe looked for a college-coaching job to no avail. Then came the offer from the UFL. True, it was not a college job, but it was the only job he'd been presented. It would give him the opportunity to prove himself. It was a risk he had to take. If he succeeded here, he believed, then those skittish athletic directors would find themselves out of excuses.

That's how Joe has found himself standing on the sidelines on this fall evening in Omaha. Tonight is Joe's first time coaching a football team in twenty-eight years.

It is also his first game as a head coach for any team above the level of high school.

And what he's facing isn't exactly high school competition. Across the field from Joe, on the opposing team's sideline, is Marty Schottenheimer, the coach of the UFL's Virginia Destroyers, and the sixth-winningest coach in NFL history. He is one of the three marquee-name, former NFL coaches who lead teams in the UFL (the others are Jim Fassel and Dennis Green). Schottenheimer, tall, toothy, and sixty-eight years old, looks younger than he did during his last coaching stint in the NFL. He is rejuvenated, no longer under the intense and confounding burden of coaching in a league that fired him after a 14-2 season with the San Diego Chargers, a league that deemed him a failure for winning countless games, but never the most important one: the Super Bowl.

With the UFL's Destroyers, Schottenheimer has inherited an experienced quarterback (thirty-five-year-old Chris Greisen) and team, one that in its previous iteration as the Florida Tuskers had advanced to the UFL championship game in the league's first two years. Schottenheimer runs a prototypical pro offense: drop-back quarterback, lots of I-formation sets, lots of runs on first down.

Conversely, Joe has a team that he himself has hastily assembled just in the last few months. Most of them, players as well as coaches, are new to each other, as well as to him, with very little team practice time under their belts.

Joe does not run a prototypical pro offense. He's installed a no-huddle, spread option offense that incorporates the quarterback in the running game, a strategy more commonly found in the Canadian Football League or the college ranks. To run the offense, Joe has chosen to split snaps between two quarterbacks who are by no means typical NFL drop-back passers: Eric Crouch, the thirty-two-year-old former University of Nebraska star and 2001 Heisman Trophy winner, who has never before played the quarterback position in an American professional game; and Jeremiah Masoli, a rookie who, during his two years at the University of Oregon, had run an offense similar to Joe's plan for Omaha. Joe succeeded in business by differentiating himself from his contemporaries. With this offense, he's attempting that again in the UFL.

He also has an ultra-aggressive plan for his special teams. Most professional and big-time college teams do not put much effort into blocking kicks, preferring instead to set up for a return (on punts) and to avoid incurring a "roughing the kicker" penalty (on both punts and field goal attempts). Joe has the Nighthawks doing just the opposite. They rehearse and study the art of blocking kicks—of onrushing wingmen making themselves "skinny" by turning their torsos sideways as they came through the line—for hours every week at practice. Joe believes the blocked kick is the most psychologically devastating play in football.

And Joe has one more thing he thinks will differentiate him from the other UFL coaches: the quarter of a decade he spent out of the game. He believes that experience—contrary to conventional wisdom—will make him a *better* football coach, one with wisdom about life both on and off the field. Football, he tells his players and staff, is just a game. Nothing more, nothing less. But everyone on the team—himself included—has chosen to be a part of it. Thus their actions within the game, how they choose to practice for it and play it, are manifestations of the way in which they choose to live their lives. "Be a man," he reminds them at least once a day. Stand on your own two feet. Accept responsibility for yourself and your actions.

Joe runs a seminar for his players every week called "Life after Football," in which he talks about résumés, job interviews, and financial planning. He tells them that their careers in football will end someday, and they should start planning for that right away.

It all seems a little college, or maybe even high school, and, indeed, it is how Joe coached in both of those places. But it is also how he ran businesses. Joe believes that "being a man" is the fundamental principle of life. It's why he left football in the first place. And it's why he wants to return. And it is self-serving, in a way: he also believes that responsible people make for better football players.

Before the game, Schottenheimer seems utterly relaxed. He's on the field, talking, smiling, and shaking hands with players and coaches from both teams, many of whom he knows or has worked with during his thirty-one years as a coach in the NFL. Asked what he thinks of facing Joe, the former CEO, Schottenheimer curtly answers: "I cannot place any judgments on someone I do not know."

Joe, on the other hand, is nervous. So much so that, a few hours before kickoff, he cannot sit still in his cell-like office in the bowels of this baseball ballpark in Omaha (home to the College World Series) that's been temporarily converted into a football stadium, crusty infield dirt included. So Joe decides to go for a walk outside of the ballpark to visit with some of the thousands of tailgaters in the parking lot who are listening to loud heavy metal music and getting properly buzzed before the game. He stops first at the tailgate party hosted by his second wife, Amy, to whom he has been married for fifteen years. With her are twenty of their friends from Omaha, the Midwestern city that Joe, Amy, and her two sons have lived in ever since he took over what was then known as Ameritrade in 2001. It is a town they have all grown to love and where they have planted deep roots. Joe feels both comfort and pressure at the thought of coaching his hometown team. Warren Buffett is just one among many friends who are in the stands tonight to watch his debut, and Joe wants not to fail in front of them.

After giving Amy a hug and kiss, Joe works through a few more tailgate parties, shaking hands, patting backs, smiling, and thanking the fans for coming out. He stops just short of kissing babies.

And then it's game time.

Twenty-eight years ago Joe Moglia was lying in a cot in that unheated storage room. It seems a lot like yesterday. It seems a lot like forever.

What happens to a dream deferred?

CHAPTER ONE

The Intern

Reclaiming a deferred dream requires sacrifice. Which explains what Joe Moglia was doing with his life two years before he found himself hired on as head coach for the UFL's Nighthawks....

At 6:30 on an early winter morning in 2009, Joe exited the revolving doors of the Embassy Suites hotel in Lincoln, Nebraska, hugging a University of Nebraska football playbook to his chest. Outside, the biting prairie wind cuffed him, ruddying his cheeks and watering his eyes. Through the blear he saw the sun breasting the flat horizon. It didn't make him feel any warmer. That winter would go down as one of the coldest ever recorded in the state. Joe pulled the collar of his jacket up to his throat, leaned into the wind, and hurried the three hundred yards from his hotel to the Osborne Athletic Complex, home to the school's football facility.

Joe looks like a football coach. His body is big in the shoulders and chest, tapers a bit through his torso and upper legs, then swells again into cantaloupe-sized calves. It's a body made for wearing gray sweats. His hair is the color of rust. His brow furrows easily over his clear, alert, blue eyes that never miss a thing. His nose can quickly turn pugnacious—like a bulldog's—when he gets worked up. He even shouts well, in short, declarative barks spiced with traces of an inner-city New York accent that's easily discernible above nearly any din. He has a presence that commands attention.

However, Joe was not a football coach. Not then, in 2009. He was one once, long ago. But in 2009 he was a sixty-year-old grandfather trying to somehow retrace the steps back to that place where the road forked, to find that other path, the one that leads to a dream unfulfilled. Since there didn't seem to be any shortcuts to that path, Joe was in Lincoln now serving as an unpaid intern—officially, the "executive advisor to the head coach"—for the University of Nebraska football team. That frigid winter day would be just one of the hundreds he spent with the team over the next two years. Fourteen hours a day catching up on half a lifetime away from the game. Film study. Practices. Meetings with coaches and players. Legal pads filled with his scribbled notes. Two years living in a hotel room. Four thousand hours of work.

Typically Joe wouldn't return through those revolving doors at the Embassy Suites until midnight, when he would go to his room, make a brief call to Amy back in Omaha, then plunk down in a chair with a Bible-thick book of the plays that he had decided he needed to understand completely if he were to return to coaching. Later, a few hours of sleep would end with a 6:00 a.m. wake-up call, starting the whole cycle over again. For his efforts, he would be paid exactly $0.00.

He did it all with a huge smile on his face. Joe wanted to be a football coach again, and this, he thought, was the first step he needed to take to get there.

Joe had done something extremely rare in the world of American business: he left at the absolute pinnacle of his career. There was no Securities & Exchange Commission investigation, no personal scandal, no precipitous drop in stock price, no shareholder revolt. Very simply, he took over a company, led it through one of the stormiest periods in the financial world's history, then left it a much stronger and more profitable place than it was when he started.

In the summer of 2008, Joe voluntarily walked away from the CEO post at TD Ameritrade. In just eight years, Joe had transformed the company, first by saving it from the disastrous pop of the dotcom bubble, then by building it into one of the most complete financial services firms in the world. Under his watch, TD Ameritrade not only completely skirted the 2008 financial crisis, it actually posted big profits.

Joe left because there was really nothing else to prove. He was presented with a huge challenge when he took over the company in the spring of 2001. By 2008, he'd exceeded the goals he set out to reach. He'd been in the business world for twenty-five years, and before that in an intense sixteen-year coaching career. Joe had worked since he was ten, when he started doing shifts in his father's New York City fruit store. Since boyhood, he'd never had any extended time off from work. Now, he had certainly earned it.

And that was what he thought he'd be getting, some serious time off. When Joe stepped down from his position as CEO in the summer of 2008, he became TD Ameritrade's chairman, which came with some responsibilities—mainly board meetings—but was a cakewalk, time-wise, compared to his previous job. So Joe played golf and read books. He went to the gym and kept detailed logs of his workouts and weight loss. ("He was starting to get chubby," says his wife, Amy. "I told him, 'You can be old or fat, but not both.' And, well, he wasn't getting any younger.")

The professional world didn't leave him alone, though. Within weeks of his resignation, he'd had a half-dozen inquiries from folks in the financial and media worlds. (Joe had spent some time guest-hosting CNBC shows during his TD Ameritrade stint.) He responded to all the calls with polite but firm *no thank yous*. Amy really believed that after what amounted to half a century of hard work, her husband was finally ready to take a breather. "I was really excited," she says. "Look, I don't want a guy who's following me around all the time and asking me what we're going to do today. But I wouldn't mind a little of that. I was ready for at least a year of relaxing a bit. He'd worked so hard. We've been really lucky. I wanted to enjoy it for a little while."

Joe's daughter Kim also thought that a break would be good for him and the entire family. "He was always driving himself so hard," she says. "Now he was financially set. I wanted him to exhale. I wanted him to spend more time with us." Even Joe signed on. "I was in no hurry to do anything. I was ready to try to relax."

At least that was the plan. Two months after he left his job, Joe and Amy went to Vermont to visit Joe's oldest child, Kelly. One night Joe and Amy were in their hotel room getting ready to go to a party at Kelly's when Joe's phone rang. It was Charles Johnson, chairman of the mutual fund company Franklin Resources. Joe thought this was just another guy calling to try to woo him back to finance. But Johnson also happened to be a major donor to the athletic program of his alma mater, Yale. He told Joe that the school's football head-coaching job might be available at the end of the year. He wondered if Joe was interested... *in coaching*.

Joe was stunned almost to the point of incoherence. He eventually mumbled something about being flattered that Johnson would even think about him as a potential candidate, especially since he'd been out of the game for so long. He told Johnson he'd think about it.

"Who was that?" Amy asked after Joe had hung up. They were late for the party.

"Uh, Charlie Johnson. He wanted to know about a coaching job," Joe replied. He was still dazed.

Amy thought little of it. They went off to the party. Joe didn't tell anyone else about the call.

But as days went by, Joe began to think about it more and more. The nights were the worst. "I literally could not sleep," he says. The call had stirred something within him that he thought he had repressed and walked away from forever.

Joe spent the next few months sitting alone in the office in his Omaha home for hours at a time, thinking about coaching and writing down thoughts and notes on legal pads. He wanted to be completely honest with himself in answering two questions: Was he qualified to coach again? And did he really want to? "The answer to the first one was an overwhelming yes," says Joe. After all, he'd been a coach before. And he was a leader. He'd managed teams in business that numbered in the hundreds, even thousands. His football-coaching career had been a huge asset to his business career. And now he had twenty-five years of managing, of decision making, of leading in business. How could that not be an asset on the field?

Answering the second question, however, was a bit more complicated. Joe knew that during the football season, he would end up working even harder than he did at Merrill and TD Ameritrade. Coaches routinely put in ninety to one hundred hours a week. What would Amy think of that? And there would be serious personal and reputational risks involved. Coaches are judged by wins and losses. No extra credit is given for all of the hard work put in. He could fail. He could certainly get fired.

As he sat in his home office and furiously scribbled notes (he would eventually fill five legal pads), a feeling began to overwhelm him: "It became clear that I couldn't really live with myself if I didn't give this a try."

Joe reached out to friends to get their opinions, just to make sure he wasn't totally crazy. One of those friends was fellow Omahan Warren Buffett. Joe asked him to dinner one night. It turned out that he was hugely supportive. "I always tell college students how lucky I was to find my passion very early in life and that they shouldn't give up until they find theirs," says Buffett. "Joe's dream obviously was to coach a top-notch football team and there is no question he would be terrific at it. So I encouraged him to do it."

By December 2008, Joe had made up his mind. He was going to attempt to land a head job at a Division I school, at either the FBS or FCS level. (Simply put, the FBS—Football Bowl Subdivision—is populated by the big-time football schools and conferences. The smaller schools and conferences make up the FCS—Football Championship Subdivision. The biggest difference: FBS schools have more scholarships and more money for those scholarships.)

He broke the news to Amy and the rest of the family. "He just looks at me one morning and goes, 'You know, I don't think I can let this go,'" says Amy. "I'll admit I was a little disappointed that he wasn't going to take some time off. But he told me that this was his passion now, that he was really feeling it. I wanted him to be happy. So I was like, 'Okay, here we go.'"

His kids had mixed reactions. "I just asked him, 'When will it all be enough?'" says daughter Kim. "But he explained it to me and he said, 'I feel like this was something I never really finished.'"

His youngest daughter, Kara, says with a knowing sigh: "He is who he is."

His youngest child and only son, Kevin, who bears a striking resemblance to him, says: "I was too young to remember his earlier coaching career, so I was pumped. I wanted to see him out there."

No one in the family should have been surprised that Joe was unable to remain idle for long. It was in his genes. His father had worked until he was eighty-two years old and stopped only when his Alzheimer's disease had become completely debilitating.

When he told his old colleagues about his decision, they were flabbergasted. John Bunch, who had worked closely with Joe since 2005 as TD Ameritrade's president of retail distribution, remembers thinking: "Are you crazy, man? Go do something fun with your money!" Ed Sheridan, Joe's old Merrill teammate, was skiing in Telluride, Colorado, when he got the call while riding a chairlift. "I initially thought, *This dude has lost it*. But he explained it to me. By the end of the lift ride, I was sold."

Joe called Yale about the job. They never called him back. It didn't matter. The fire was lit.

Joe went after a coaching job the same way he'd gone after a Wall Street job as a thirty-four-year-old, divorced father of four—with everything he had. He first hired an agent. He then put together a detailed spreadsheet of college football teams, focusing in particular on losing programs with coaches who had expiring contracts. He started sketching out his plans for recruiting and researching the potential names of his coaching staff. He networked, making four to five calls a day—many of them cold—to conference commissioners, athletic directors, and coaches. Whenever anyone agreed to a face-to-face meeting, Joe jumped on a plane. He met, in person, with the commissioners of the Big Ten Conference, the Missouri Valley Conference, and the Colonial Athletic Association, and the athletic directors at West Point, Fordham (his alma mater), Northwestern, Duke, and East Carolina. He figured he was not a candidate for a big-time FBS program like Notre Dame or Tennessee. Not yet, anyway. But he decided that he did not want to coach anything lower than a Division I team and that he was going to be a head coach or nothing. He didn't want to take the more traditional route and start as a coordinator and work his way up again. "There was no time for that," says Joe. And anyway, he was a manager, a leader. That was where his skill sets lay. Joe believed that with his background, he was a perfect candidate for a job at an Ivy or Patriot League school, someplace where a kid desired an education to go along with his football.

He had his doubters. "A reasonable amount of people told me I had no shot at a job," Joe says. "But people also told me that when I applied to Merrill. Most of my life people have told me that. I've never used that as a motivating factor. I just never agreed with it."

But he also had legions of admirers. His quest—the seeming impossibility of it all, the determination to not go gently into that good night—struck a chord with some people, particularly those for whom middle age was in the rearview mirror. *They* might not be able to throw caution to the wind at age sixty and chase a dream. But it was extremely important—vital, really—to know it could be done. "It's just such an example," says Rik Bonness, an Omaha lawyer and former linebacker for the Oakland Raiders in the 1970s who had become friends with Joe. "I mean, he didn't have to do this. He could have retired. But he *did* do it. It's a reminder that if you want to stay energized, you have to commit to something and do it full speed and not be afraid of failure."

For Bill Campbell, the former CEO of Intuit (and now the chairman) and a member of Apple's board, Joe's quest resonated deeply. Campbell had been the head football coach at Columbia before he embarked on his own starry business career. "People ask me why I left football for a career in business," says Campbell. "And my answer is always the same: 'Did you see my won-loss record?'"

In six years as the head coach at Columbia (1974–1979), Campbell never had a winning season, finishing with a 12-41-1 overall record. He says once he left football, he never seriously considered going back. "But if I'd had more success, I probably would have stayed in the profession," he says. "It was a hard thing to give up, and I still have pangs."

Joe reached out to Campbell for advice when he decided to go back to coaching. Campbell is a big fan of Joe's, but even he had his doubts about Joe ever finding a college job. "The problem is that as good a manager as he is, an athletic director still has accountability, to his trustees, his alumni, the players, the students. All these groups will say to the AD, 'You took a guy who hasn't coached a game in twenty-plus years?' Joe is fighting long odds. Someone will have to see how energetic, bright, and enthusiastic he is. Someone will have to overcome fear and take a chance on him."

Joe knew all of this. He realized he could fail. "Doubt isn't the opposite of faith; it is an element of faith," wrote the theologian Paul Tillich.

When Joe met with the coaches, athletic directors, and conference commissioners, he told each of them his personal story, starting with his inner-city childhood, then his coaching career, then his painful decision to leave the football field, then his business career. (Rare is the occasion when a conversation takes place with Joe when he *doesn't* tell a story. He is a natural storyteller. But as they say, stories happen only to those who can tell them.) Joe made it very clear to everyone he talked to that he was dead serious about this. He was well aware that his money, instead of being an asset in his search, could instead make it harder for people to take him seriously.

Most important, though, Joe sold himself, trying to turn his quarter century away from the game from a potential negative into a positive. He gave all of these football people his pitch: A head coach *is* the CEO of his program. He's the leader. He's a recruiter of talent. He's organized. He's an ambassador for the program and the school. Joe had run teams at Merrill for seventeen years. He'd run an *entire company* for eight years. Ameritrade, when he got there, was no different from the type of foundering football program that needed a coach like him. *And look what he'd done there!* He knew how to lead, how to delegate, when to coddle and when to castigate. And imagine the sway he would bring to recruiting, especially with Ivy League kids. He could appeal to the kids' own sense of their future, and to the parents' hopes and dreams for their children, too.

With the kid—and his parents—sitting right there, Joe said, this is what he would tell them. "I will help you stand on your own two feet and accept responsibility for the consequences of your actions. I will help you be a man. At some point in time—next year, after college, after ten brilliant years in the NFL—your football career will come to an end. What will you want to do? Become a doctor? A lawyer? A businessman? Chances are that I can provide greater insight on that, on your future career, than any other coach in the country."

Then Joe would end his sales pitch with what he believed to be his clincher. His voice would inevitably rise a notch or two in volume. "And the bottom line is that I know my football! I was a coach!"

Someone out there had to give him a chance.

As it turned out, only one school did. The University of Massachusetts, in need of a new coach, called in late 2008. Joe flew in for an interview with the athletic director, John McCutcheon. But right away he could tell that the interview was really more informational than serious. UMass ended up hiring someone with more recent coaching experience.

By the following February, the college football hiring window had closed. Joe was jobless. He'd heard the same thing from nearly everyone he'd talked to: *Great story, Joe. Really inspiring. But after so long out of the game, no one is going to hire you as a coach. No one.*

The problem was with the athletic directors, who, as Bill

Campbell had anticipated, were naturally risk-averse. After meeting Joe, Terry Holland, the AD at East Carolina, said: "He is an impressive leader and would have all the skills necessary to be a head football coach at the college level, except for his lack of recent experience actually coaching a team. But I could not hire him here as our football coach. The number one rule for athletic directors is to 'at least win the press conference.' It would be difficult for any AD to make a hire that would be likely to generate more questions than it answers."

Kevin White, the AD at Duke University, a college not known for its football excellence, also met with Joe in early 2009. "He would be a non-traditional hire. A university would have to see him as a risk that makes sense to take."

And none of them did.

Clearly, as Terry Holland noted, the lack of recent experience was crippling Joe's job search. He would have to find a way of getting that experience in order to buff up his résumé.

Tom Osborne is a demigod in the state of Nebraska. He'd coached the University of Nebraska Cornhuskers for twenty-five years—during the football program's glory days—and won three national championships. He later served for six years as a U.S. congressman for the state. Then, in 2007, with the football program in disarray, Osborne was called back to the university, this time as the athletic director, where his sage-like, grandfatherly presence eventually righted the ship.

Osborne and Joe were casual acquaintances. Nebraska is a small state, population-wise, and most of its movers and shakers have run into each other at one time or another. Osborne had been one of the people Joe had talked to right after he made his decision to try football again. "At first I thought he wasn't thinking very clearly," says Osborne. "It was a very unusual move. But he gradually convinced me that he was dead serious. And he sure did have a lot of passion for it."

When Joe didn't find a job in 2008, Osborne came up with a suggestion: why didn't Joe do an internship as a "shadow coach" with the Nebraska football team? Osborne said he'd have to clear it with the fiery, young head coach, Bo Pelini. Joe was game. So, it turned out, was Pelini: "I was like, 'Why the hell not?' The guy obviously had organizational skills and knew how to run a team."

Joe joined the Cornhuskers as an unpaid intern in July 2009. By NCAA rules, he couldn't actually coach (thus his official position: "executive advisor to the head coach"). "I will always be grateful to Tom and Bo," says Joe. "They gave me a chance." As part of the deal, Joe agreed to be a "life coach" to the entire athletic program. Joe ran seminars for student athletes, counseling them on personal finance and job seeking, similar to what he would later do with the Nighthawks players. But what he really did at Nebraska was concentrate on reacquainting himself with a game he had left two and a half decades before.

Joe spent the first few months with the team acting like the proverbial "good child." He was seen—at every practice, meeting, and film study session—but he was not heard. "I didn't make a peep there for a little while," he says. Instead, he soaked up every detail he could. He noted where the different coaches arrayed themselves at staff meetings; the order in which the playbook was put together; how the team lined up for the national anthem on the sidelines; even how Nebraska fed its players.

At Pelini's suggestion Joe concentrated on the defense, which made sense given Joe's history with that side of the ball. In doing so, though, he would also gain insight into the multiple offenses Nebraska would face during the year, which ran the gamut, from the pass-happy pro style of Oklahoma to the run-first philosophy at Colorado. Nebraska that year had a dominating defense, led by future NFL star tackle Ndamukong Suh. The only offenses that really gave Nebraska trouble were the spread option ones, which is one of the reasons Joe grew so fond of the style, and later decided to use it with the Nighthawks.

Joe started off studying with the linebackers, the position from which the Nebraska defense flowed. "He was just there all the time," says Blake Lawrence, a linebacker on the team in 2009. From there Joe moved to the defensive backs. Soon he was shadowing Carl Pelini, the defensive coordinator (and brother of Bo). During games Joe sat in the coaches' box above the field with the defensive staff. He listened in on the play calls and the back-and-forth between Bo Pelini and his coaches.

As the season progressed, Joe started to feel more comfortable. But the coaches remained a bit wary. Coaching staffs are like close-knit families. They work grueling hours in an intense atmosphere and in very tight quarters. Outsiders are usually iced out. "There was sort of a sense of *Who is this dude?* when Joe first got here," says Doug Colman, then the quality control coach for the Cornhuskers.

Joe kept his head down, but was present for everything. If the coaches were dealing with a problem at 1:00 a.m., Joe was right there with them. Gradually, they began to realize that he wasn't some weird old wealthy guy just getting his kicks from hanging out with a football team. He was a guy who was there to learn.

By October Joe had been accepted as part of the team. Because of the NCAA rules, he couldn't actually run players through drills during practice. He was just supposed to observe. But, gingerly at first, he started to become more vocal, on the field and in the meeting rooms. "He just eventually became 'Coach Joe' to us," says Blake Lawrence.

In late October of that year, Nebraska, then 4-2, hosted Iowa State, one of the weaker programs in the Big 12, and a team that Nebraska had not lost to at home in thirty-two years. But Nebraska had eight turnovers in that game, including four within Iowa State's 5-yard line. The Cornhuskers lost, 9–7. "That was the first time that season that I felt incredible pain from a loss," says Joe. "That night I had flashbacks to the horrible games I'd had as a coach. Then I said, 'Hold it. I don't want to feel like this.' So I challenged myself and asked myself, had I not learned anything in the past forty years that would help me handle this?" Joe says he stayed up most of the night thinking it through, and eventually felt at peace.

The next day he went to the team's football offices. Pelini walked in, looking like he hadn't slept at all. "Bo just looked at me and said, 'I can't believe that you want to do this,'" says Joe. "I told him I had a thought for him."

They went to Pelini's office. Joe explained what he had wrestled with the night before. And he reminded Pelini that 300 colleges had played football that Saturday, 150 of whom had lost. "We're not trying to cure cancer here, we're not protecting democracy and capitalism. We're playing a football game. And, yes, we love the game and we want to win, but it's just a football game, and once in a while we are going to lose and we've got to keep it in perspective. It's not the end of the world."

Says Pelini: "Joe just always had great perspective after a tough loss or a big win, and those conversations were really beneficial for me."

Joe also started to help with recruiting. Although the NCAA didn't allow him to visit recruits off campus, when potential recruits came to the university, they all met with Joe, who talked to them about his life and told them why he had chosen the program to help reboot his career. "He really helped with these kids," says Megan Rogers, Nebraska's director of on-campus recruiting. "A lot of these kids came from rough backgrounds like he did."

Joe did all of this while living in a room at the Embassy Suites hotel in Lincoln six days a week, away from Amy and their home in Omaha. He drove the fifty miles back to Omaha on Thursdays to have dinner with Amy. On Friday mornings, he went into the TD Ameritrade offices, then drove back to Lincoln in the afternoon, either to catch the charter flight for games that were played away, or to spend the night in the hotel where the entire team stayed for those that were played at home. He was a sixty-year-old man busting his ass. "I was a bit surprised at how hard he went at it," says Osborne. But Joe knew he had to prove how serious he was.

Nebraska, behind its defense, rebounded from the loss to Iowa State to qualify for the Big 12 Championship game, where they lost by a point to then-number-one-ranked Texas. In the Holiday Bowl, the Cornhuskers crushed Arizona, 33–0.

Joe learned a lot that season. Yes, the game had changed since he last coached: it was faster, especially with increased use of the no-huddle offense; it was more specialized, with each side of the ball having essentially fifteen "starters"; and there was more emphasis on schemes and less on the fundamentals of tackling and blocking.

But he felt the game had not passed him by. "I mainly had to adapt to the faster pace," says Joe. The specialization wasn't that hard to master: it was just different players in the same old roles. And the emphasis on schemes? Joe believed that there was an overreliance on them. The fundamentals still mattered. "Out of old fields comes all the new corn," Chaucer once wrote.

Joe went back out on the job hunt. This time, he came equipped with some heavy-hitting references—Osborne and Pelini. By now, having watched what Joe brought to the game, both on and off the field, Osborne had become a big fan. "I thought he'd make a great college coach," he says. When he called fellow athletic directors on Joe's behalf, Osborne broke down Joe's candidacy to its bare essentials. "I told them that coaching is not rocket science, it's not some mystical endeavor.

If you work hard, are a good communicator, are well organized, and hire a good staff, you can do it. I told them that Joe had all of those ingredients in spades," he says. "But I didn't get anywhere with a lot of them."

As an athletic director himself, albeit one with a little more job security than most, Osborne says he somewhat understood their reticence. "If you go out on a limb and it doesn't work out, you are *really* out on a limb," he says. "Still, someone should have given him a shot."

Joe did get a little more traction this go-around. He landed an interview at Cornell, exactly the kind of place he believed would be a perfect fit for him. But they ended up hiring a coach who'd been an assistant at Ole Miss. He had interviews with Princeton and Richmond. The former hired an assistant with the Cincinnati Bengals, the latter an assistant from the University of Virginia.

Like Osborne, Joe understood the predicament he put athletic directors in—to a point. "I knew that the typical AD wasn't going to hire me. I needed to find one who could make a true risk-reward decision and figure out that the risk in hiring me wasn't that huge and the reward would be great."

But folks weren't buying it. Most of them told Joe that his mission was nearly impossible to accomplish. Mike Bohn, the Colorado athletic director, loved Joe and his story, and had a coaching vacancy. But he couldn't pull the trigger on hiring Joe. Instead he hired an NFL assistant, and floated the idea of Joe's taking a "head of football operations" position at the school, where he would have responsibilities for both on- and off-the-field sides of the program (akin to what Bill Parcells had done with the NFL's Miami Dolphins). Joe wasn't interested. He wanted to be the one on the sidelines.

Meanwhile, he was attracting a fair amount of national press for his quest to get back into coaching. It was a great story: Man at pinnacle of his career steps down from powerful CEO position to seek college football job a quarter of a century after coaching his last game. ESPN did a few segments on him. Spots aired on CBS, ABC, and CNBC. *Sports Illustrated* ran a long story on its website. *Forbes* ran a feature piece (written by this author). "I would get my hopes up every time one of these stories would hit," says Joe. "I was hoping some athletic director or some college president somewhere would see it and realize how serious and how qualified I was."

But every time, those hopes were dashed. Nobody wanted to take the chance.

Then in late 2009 Walter O'Hara, a managing director at the investment bank Allen & Co., called Joe to talk to him about the Williams College coaching job, which was vacant. (Though O'Hara didn't go to Williams, he had fallen in love with the school and was well connected to its influential alumni.) Williams was a Division III school, which Joe had decided early on he didn't want any part of. Football just wasn't taken seriously enough at those small schools. Plus the recruiting was brutal: there were no scholarships, and chances were that if you ever did find a really good player, he'd be snapped up by a Division I school before he enrolled.

But O'Hara worked on Joe, selling him on what a special place Williams was. Chuck Johnson, the coach at Ridgewood High School, a perennial New Jersey prep powerhouse, also called Joe to talk up Williams. Johnson sent a lot of his players there and loved the school, which he said actually did take its football seriously. The two men eventually persuaded Joe to pursue it. "I didn't want to act like I was too good for this," he says. "At the time, I didn't have anything." O'Hara and Johnson made calls to the school on Joe's behalf. So did Fay Vincent, the former commissioner of Major League Baseball and a Williams alum. Joe followed up with a note and a packet of his credentials.

But he never heard from Williams. He followed up again. He never got a response. The message couldn't have been clearer: not even a Division III school wanted him.

That year, Joe sent his résumé to sixteen different colleges that had head coach job vacancies. Only three of them had the courtesy to respond with a "no, thank you."

Joe was left completely stymied.

Faced with no job, Joe went back to Osborne and Pelini. He was not quite ready to give up. One more year at Nebraska, he thought, would do the trick. It had to. He had no idea what to do if it didn't. Amy wasn't surprised. "Once he puts his mind to something, he doesn't give up easily," she says. He went through the entire process of shadow coaching again: the playbook, the note taking, the meetings, the film study, the practices, the games, and the cookie-cutter hotel room. Nebraska had another good year, buoyed again by their stellar defense. Joe ingratiated himself with the team even more that season. After it ended, the players voted to give him the Admiral U. S. Grant Sharp trophy for leadership and service, an annual award usually given to a player or coach who has demonstrated unselfish commitment to the team. It was an unusual gesture to give it to someone who was not even an official coach.

As the season neared its end, Joe started his job search once more, still hopeful, if a bit unnerved by his previous two unsuccessful attempts. Kent State called. So did the University of Buffalo. But they ended up going with younger guys who had more up-to-date credentials. It was all happening again.

Joe grew frustrated. He was accustomed to working hard toward a goal, then actually achieving it. He called friends and vented. "I have exactly what it takes to be a head coach," he told them in the fall of 2010. "I have the skill sets. I've demonstrated myself on the field and in the business world. At this point in my life, I could do whatever the hell I want. But I've chosen to become a football coach. I've spent four thousand hours at Nebraska. I don't understand why these folks don't see that."

But he never let his frustration show publicly. "What is stunning about him is that he always 100 percent checked his ego at the door," says Charlie Besser, a TV producer who had followed Joe's story. "He pitched these guys like his life depended on it and took their 'I would never hire a guy like you' in stride. Most CEOs would have had three advance people fly in before the interview and would have made a huge deal about it all. Joe didn't. He called them himself. He went to them himself. He had this unusual combination of drive and humility, never letting his ego get in the way of his desire to accomplish the goal."

Despite this ego check, despite the determination and the four thousand hours at Nebraska, Joe still had nothing to show for it. Zero.

He had no idea what to do now. He couldn't go back to Nebraska again. What was a third year as a volunteer going to do, anyway? He thought he had failed. He thought his dream was now officially dead.

Then in November, he finally got a job offer. It wasn't from a college. It was from a man named Michael Huyghue (pronounced "hewge"), the commissioner of something called the United Football League.

CHAPTER TWO

Life in the Little Leagues

Joe was originally contacted by the UFL—basically a minor league for the NFL—not as a possible coach but as a potential investor in the Omaha franchise. He politely demurred, telling them he was only interested in being on the sidelines.

Michael Huyghue, a former NFL team executive and sports agent, did some research on Joe and his story and came away intrigued. Maybe this guy was a coaching candidate, he thought. At the time Huyghue had a head coach vacancy with the Virginia Destroyers, based in Virginia Beach. It was called an expansion team, though it was, in reality, the remnants of the Florida franchise, which had been successful on the field but not off it. He flew to Lincoln a few times to meet with Joe. "I grilled him," says Huyghue. "I asked him what type of offense he planned on running, how he would handle time-outs with two minutes remaining in the game, what type of quarterback he would want." He was basically making sure Joe had the chops to actually coach.

During one interview, Huyghue brought along Eric Crouch, the former Nebraska star and his former client during Huyghue's sports agency days, to help suss Joe out. Crouch told Huyghue later that he would "definitely play for that guy." (No one knew at the time, of course, that Crouch actually *would* end up playing for that guy.)

Huyghue was sold. He offered Joe the job in November 2010, and Joe accepted. "The UFL was the best opportunity for him," says Huyghue. "He needed a bridge to cross for his coaching career. That was very hard because most people rely on a set of standard coaching credentials that he didn't have. For us, we didn't have any of those obstacles."

Still, it was an unusual hire, even for the UFL, which had prided itself on the big-name coaches it had been able to attract since its inception. In late 2010, the league boasted an all-star roster of coaches: Jim Fassel, Dennis Green, Jay Gruden (Jon's brother), Jerry Glanville, and Jeff Jagodzinski.

And now they had a former CEO.

Coaching professional players was something Joe hadn't even considered when he decided to reclaim his dream. Not that he had a problem with the pro game, but college was clearly where his heart was. He believed his skills fit best there, with the recruiting, the kind of loyalty incumbent upon both the player and the coaching sides in a four-year commitment, the molding of eighteen- to twenty-two-year-olds into men.

Professional players were more or less already men. They were not wooed the way recruits were. They were designated to teams through the draft or picked up off the free agent market. The pro game, on the personnel side, was a mercenary one, more of a true flesh trade. Pros played for money. And when they got hurt or underperformed, they were swiftly jettisoned and another body was brought in as a replacement. That part of the game didn't fit Joe's sensibilities. But Joe was open. He had to be. The truth was, he had nowhere else to go.

There was just one issue about the job that gave him pause: The UFL was losing serious money, to the tune of almost $100 million in its first two seasons. Start-ups, he knew, were precarious entities. When Joe joined the league, he quickly found out that the owners had some financial issues to resolve before the 2011 season could even take place. But he was assured that the problems would be taken care of in time for the start of the season eight months later. Joe didn't fully realize it at the time, but one of the reasons the UFL had hired him was precisely because of his financial background. They wanted—and needed—his business expertise to help them carry on. The UFL would end up leaning on him for this advice more than he could have ever imagined.

But despite the risks, despite the extra work he would have to take on, Joe gratefully took the job. It was his only chance.

The United Football League was a "league of opportunity" in more than one sense. The opportunity it offered began with the entity of the league itself, which was trying to prove that there was indeed a market in the United States for a high-quality alternative to the $9 billion beast that was the NFL. At the beginning of 2011, the UFL believed it had what was a rare chance to gain some traction and raise its low profile. Because of the expiration of the NFL's collective bargaining agreement, that league looked headed for labor trouble. There was talk of a shortened or even canceled NFL season. With $9 billion at stake, most observers concluded that the chances of that happening were very slim. But it was there. And if it happened, the UFL would be the only professional football in town.

But part of the very reason for the existence of the UFL was as a talent pool and proving ground for the NFL, for many of its players and coaches had been in the NFL and were looking for a way back in. Others had never gotten the chance and were hoping to get into the big league for the first time. The same was true for the front office and personnel staffs, the trainers, the equipment managers, and even the interns in the league. The UFL's real opportunity came from what it provided to its players and team staff members.

For Joe, the opportunity provided by the league was a bit different. If he succeeded in the UFL, especially against the caliber of coaches he would face, then those risk-averse college ADs would find themselves out of excuses. They could win their damn press conferences.

After Joe was named the head coach of the Virginia Destroyers, he planned to rent an apartment in Virginia Beach for the five-month duration of training camp and the eight-game season. Amy would join him when she could. But before he could even start his apartment search, Jeff Jagodzinski, the head coach of the league's bottom-dwelling Omaha Nighthawks, was fired by the UFL. And suddenly, Joe was tapped by the UFL brass to be his hometown team's new head coach.

Joe was happy to be home (and Amy was happy to have him around for a change). But coaching in Omaha came with some added pressure. He would be putting his reputation on the line in a very public setting, as well as in front of family and friends. He was also inheriting a paradox: The Nighthawks were far and away the worst team in the league. But they were also the most popular.

The paradox was easily explainable: that which made the Nighthawks so popular off the field was exactly what made them so terrible on it—their 2010 team headliners, the former NFL stars Jeff Garcia (quarterback) and Ahman Green (a running back who had attended Nebraska). That year, the team had started the season 3-1. Then they completely fell apart, losing their last four games in spectacular fashion, by an average score of 31–9, and finishing last in the league in points scored *and* in points allowed. Their ineptitude could be traced in large part to Garcia, 40, and Green, 33, who completely ran out of gas in the middle of the season. Garcia started throwing multiple interceptions. Green's average dropped to a measly two yards per carry.

And yet the Nighthawks sold out every home game—even when they were losing big—to the twenty-four thousand fans who filled their stadium to capacity. People came out to see Garcia and Green. They bought their jerseys (the best-selling ones in the league). They didn't seem to care about the final score.

But now these fans had a new coach, a hometown boy, a former CEO, a minnow in a sea of former NFL whales who would be assembling a team basically from scratch. It was anyone's guess how that would all pan out.

For Joe's first staff hire, he turned to his old friend Tom Olivadotti. The two men first met in 1971 when they were both high school coaches in Delaware. Joe, then twenty-two, was working at his first head-coaching job, at a small private school—Archmere Academy—with a terrible football program. Olivadotti was on the opposite end of the spectrum, the head coach of Salesianum School, a prep powerhouse that would win the state championship in 1972. The duo attended the same coaching clinics around the state and hit it off.

Olivadotti, now sixty-six, is a big bear of a man who walks with the bobbling gait of someone who has spent a lifetime on his feet. He has perpetually bloodshot eyes, a snow-white goatee and mustache, and wears two huge rings on cigar-sized fingers on each hand: a national championship ring from the University of Miami and a Super Bowl ring from the 2000 New York Giants team that lost to the Baltimore Ravens. "I don't have a safe, so I keep them on me," says Olivadotti. Given his size and countenance, the rings will be just fine where they are.

Joe and Olivadotti stayed in touch after they both left Delaware. Olivadotti went on to a long and impressive career as a defensive coach. In 1976, he moved from Salesianum to Princeton, where he coached the linebackers. After a brief stint as the defensive coordinator at Boston College, he moved into the same position with the University of Miami Hurricanes under Howard Schnellenberger. While he was with the Hurricanes they won the 1983 national championship against Nebraska, whose coach was none other than Tom Osborne, who was right in the middle of his long tenure there. That victory was one in which Joe had actually played a role.

In the winter of 1983, when Joe was in his last year as the defensive coordinator at Dartmouth, he went on a recruiting trip to Florida. While there, he visited Olivadotti, who was just a few days away from coaching in the national championship game. After dinner, the two retired to Olivadotti's study to look at Nebraska game film ("This is what coaches do for fun," says Olivadotti). Olivadotti had been worried about defending Nebraska's two-point conversion, a play that they had been wildly successful at converting all year, thanks mainly to their three offensive superstars Turner Gill (quarterback), Heisman Trophy winner Mike Rozier (running back), and Irving Fryar (receiver). Olivadotti showed Joe Nebraska's play, which involved Gill rolling out and either running or passing. Olivadotti had planned on going into tight man-to-man coverage to shut down the throwing lanes. Joe watched the play a few times, and then suggested that Olivadotti bring pressure on Gill with two linebackers coming from each edge of the line of scrimmage, which would inhibit his ability to run. It was one of the strategies Olivadotti says he was considering, "but Joe's reaffirmation sealed the deal."

In the 1983 national championship game, the Miami Hurricanes were huge underdogs, not yet the powerhouse program they would eventually become. "We were just so undersized compared to them," says Olivadotti. His players were very nervous. He tried to calm them down in the locker room before the game. "I'll never forget, I told them, 'Hey, they put their pants on just like we do.'" And Rodney Bellinger, who was one of my cornerbacks, said, 'Yeah, but it takes them a lot longer to reach their waist.'"

The title game went back and forth until the very end. Nebraska scored a touchdown with forty-eight seconds left in the game. All they had to do was kick what was almost a sure-thing extra point to tie the game and, most likely, win the national championship. (Nebraska came into the game undefeated, Miami had one loss, and there was no overtime back then.) But Osborne bravely decided to try to win the game for the Cornhuskers with a two-point conversion. Olivadotti called the defensive play that he and Joe had discussed. The linebackers got just enough pressure on Gill, whose pass was tipped away at the last second by Miami safety Kenny Calhoun, giving Miami the win and the national championship.

After that season, Olivadotti offered Joe a job at Miami as a defensive assistant—with either the linebackers or the secondary—with the agreement that he would eventually run the entire defense. That was the offer Joe declined because he'd come to the conclusion that he had to leave coaching in order to provide for his four young children after his divorce.

As Joe worked his way through his business career, Olivadotti moved into the NFL. He started as a defensive assistant with the Cleveland Browns under Marty Schottenheimer, then spent nine years as Don Shula's defensive coordinator at the Miami Dolphins. Later, he held assistant positions at the Minnesota Vikings, under Dennis Green; the New York Giants, where he went to the Super Bowl with Jim Fassel; and the Houston Texans. (In other words, he had in fact worked for all three of the big-name UFL coaches whose teams Joe would be competing against, and Tom knew their styles well.) Olivadotti himself became the foremost practitioner of a defensive style known as "pattern read," which is essentially a scheme in which the linebackers and the defensive backs start in zone coverage, then switch to man-to-man once the patterns of the receivers express themselves. John Fox, the current coach of the Denver Broncos, has run versions of the pattern read throughout his career. So has Alabama coach Nick Saban. Olivadotti says his defense is really just a mass accumulation of his forty-one years of coaching experience. "When you forget where you got something, it's yours," he says. Olivadotti had been in semiretirement, running a few football clinics at home in south Florida, when Joe called about the Nighthawks.

Olivadotti's vast experience has given him a very laid-back mien and Zen-like attitude. While he expects much out of his players and coaches, he rarely raises his voice to get his points across. A simple shake of the head or a raised white eyebrow usually does the trick. He tends to view his profession in simple, aphoristic terms. The essence of coaching, he says, is "getting good players and not screwing them up." Throughout the Nighthawks season, Olivadotti would fill the role of Joe's consigliere. Joe would lean on him for advice and counsel. The two share the same philosophy when it comes to coaching, chewed over during their four-decade friendship. Olivadotti's calm demeanor and vast experience also help, as does his straightforward style. "Joe knows I'll never bullshit him," says Olivadotti.

Next Joe went shopping for an offensive coordinator. What he had in mind was a progressive, attacking plan for offense. Although Joe had been a defensive coach during his career, he had thought a lot about offense. In fact, while coaching the defense at Dartmouth, he had penned a book about the offensive strategy he believed was best suited to attack his own defense.

For the Nighthawks, Joe wanted an up-tempo, no-huddle scheme that would tire out defenses, something akin to what the University of Oregon had been running in recent years. This offense would be his differentiator, he believed, as the other coaches in the UFL, given their histories, would probably be running more conventional pro offenses, with drop-back passers and a steady dose of I-Formations.

Joe found his man in Bart Andrus. The fifty-three-year-old native Californian wears his dark hair slicked back, starting from his high hairline. He has a patrician nose, downward-pulling lips, and a prominent chin. With a powdered wig, he'd make a spot-on George Washington impersonator. Andrus had played quarterback at the University of Montana, and had been coaching in the collegiate and professional ranks since 1984, the year Joe left the game. He started as a graduate assistant for the Brigham Young team that won the national championship under coach Lavell Edwards, one of the early implementers of the pass-happy attack that would later become known as the West Coast offense. Andrus went on to tutor Steve McNair as the quarterbacks' coach of the Tennessee Titans from 1997 until 1999, when the Titans lost the Super Bowl to the St. Louis Rams. He then coached the Amsterdam Admirals in NFL Europe for seven years, winning the 2005 World Bowl.

In 2009, however, Andrus's coaching career took a nosedive. He became the head coach of the CFL's Toronto Argonauts, but had trouble adjusting to the strange Canadian version of the game, which included 110-yard fields, three downs instead of four, and receivers who could get a running start at the line of scrimmage before the snap. Under Andrus, the Argos had a disastrous season, finishing 3-15. His unemotional style never meshed with his team. After the season, one of his players told the *Toronto Star* that Andrus treated the CFL "like a summer beer league."

Andrus had been out of football for a year when Joe called. He offered Andrus a shot at redemption. Andrus was game.

What Andrus and Joe worked out for the offense was the first of its kind in American professional football: a read-option, no-huddle spread attack in which the quarterback, contrary to the current prevailing NFL style (Tim Tebow excepted), was actually encouraged to run as much as he passed. Based on his read of the defense before the snap, he could either run or pass on any given play. (Thus, the "read-option" moniker.) Andrus had once gotten Jeff Fisher, his head coach at the Titans, interested in this offense. Fisher ran it a few days during training camp one year, but eventually lost his nerve and went back to a more traditional style. Joe's rationale for running this offense with the Nighthawks was fairly simple: In the NFL, most offenses are designed to protect the quarterback, who is generally one of the highest-paid players on the team. That offense made total sense if you had a quarterback, like Tom Brady or Aaron Rodgers, who was worth the money and thus the protection. But, as Joe reasoned, how many teams have a truly elite passer in the NFL? Five? Seven, maybe? He certainly wouldn't have one in the UFL, where quarterbacks, though they were the highest-paid players, still made only $7,500 a game.

So, Joe figured, why not find a quarterback (or preferably two, because of the higher chance of injury from the hits taken while running) who could throw *and* run and play to those strengths? After all, those were the types of quarterbacks who had given Nebraska's great defense fits. If he executed well, this type of quarterback could do the same to the UFL's pro-style defenses, which were more accustomed to traditional drop-back passers.

To the naked eye of even the most hardcore football follower, the most startling part of this offense was the line. Joe and Andrus would require their linemen to maintain three- to four-foot gaps between them at the line of scrimmage. What these pronounced splits did, at least in theory, was spread out the defensive line, thus creating big passing and running lanes. "In the NFL, everyone is so tight on the line. You could blow up an entire offense with one grenade," says Andrus. "With this offense, we will create space all over the field."

At first blush, the offense would look fairly easy to attack—just send a defender right through the splits. "The defense will try that at first, for sure," says Andrus. But it's not quite as easy to shoot the gaps as it seems. Offensive linemen can quite simply pinch any rusher. Andrus knows that these professional defenses, run by experienced coaches, will eventually make adjustments. But they will have to get out of their base formations to do so. "And that's half the battle," says Andrus. "We want them to be uncomfortable. We want them to have to practice something entirely new the week before they play us."

Joe had one more wrinkle he wanted installed in his offense. It was something he called "powerball." Unlike the spread offense, which was a relative novelty, powerball harkened back to football's origins as a running game. These days in football, the first step made by offensive linemen is usually a lateral one, in which they pass block to a designed side, or block to where a running back is supposed to run (known as "zone reads"). In powerball, the offensive linemen blast straight into the defense with angled blocks, double teams, traps, and cross-blocks. (It would still be run from the wide splits.) The advantage of powerball, Joe believed, is that it would have the same effect as a baseball pitcher's changeup. A defense that was constantly being shown a read-option offense would, all of a sudden, face something completely different. It would be useful on the goal line and in other short-yardage situations. But it could be used at any spot on the field to keep the defense guessing.

In late January 2011 Joe was asked to coach a team in the Eastham Energy All-Star Game in Arizona, an end-of-the-year showcase game for draft-eligible collegiate players. (Former Texas Tech and current Washington State coach Mike Leach interviewed him for the gig. Leach, an offensive innovator, loved Joe's proposed scheme on that side of the ball.) Joe jumped at the opportunity to do what in effect would be a one-game coaching dry run for the Nighthawks season. It also enabled him to stage a tryout for his coaching candidates for both the offensive and defensive lines. Don Lawrence, a seventy-four-year-old who had been the head coach at the University of Virginia and the tight ends coach of the Buffalo Bills back in the 1990s when the team went to four straight Super Bowls, was the potential offensive line coach. He'd been in pro football for fifty-two years, most recently in NFL Europe. The defensive line candidate was Brandon Noble, a big, blue-eyed thirty-eight-year-old who was a former defensive lineman in the NFL (Cowboys and Redskins) and, at the time, the coach of that position at West Chester University, a Division II school in Pennsylvania. Though Joe's side lost the all-star game by six points, he was impressed with both Lawrence and Noble. He hired both of them.

On the player personnel side, Joe kept Rick Mueller, the Nighthawks' 2010 general manager and a former talent evaluator for the New Orleans Saints. Mueller assembled his own staff made up of seasoned NFL scouts: Matt Boockmeier, Byron Ellis, and Greg Mohns.

⊢+++⊣

Starting in late March, the Nighthawks hosted a series of national tryouts for the team, in Omaha, Jacksonville, and Dallas. A couple hundred wannabe players showed up at each spot and forked over sixty dollars each to show their stuff. No attendee came close to making the team's training camp roster. But that was okay with Joe. The tryouts had to be done, just in case the next Lawrence Taylor was out there on the street.

Joe had another purpose in mind for the tryouts anyway. By then, he had pretty much filled out the rest of his coaching roster. He wanted to use the tryouts to see how his staff meshed. He had assembled a mix of youth and experience. For his chief of staff, Joe had hired a sixty-nine-year-old named George Glenn, an old friend going back to his Delaware high school coaching days. Brock Olivo, a former running back and special teams maven for the Detroit Lions, was the running backs coach. (The squat and muscular thirty-five-year-old had the added bonus of looking like he could still play the position in a pinch.) Robert Hunt, a big, bald thirty-six-year-old former NFL offensive lineman, was brought in to assist Don Lawrence at that position. Kevin Daft, a studious-looking thirty-five-year-old who was the third-string quarterback under Andrus at the Titans, was the wide receiver coach.

To coach the secondary, Joe chose Marvin Sanders, forty-three, an outspoken man who had been in that position at the University of Nebraska. Pete Kuharchek, a pot-bellied, longtime NFL Europe head coach, was the linebackers coach. The sixty-three-year-old had developed many current NFL players while in Europe, including the Pittsburgh Steelers' tempestuous star linebacker, James Harrison. Lastly, for what Joe considered one of the most important positions on his staff, he chose Richard Kent—a skinny, fidgety fifty-five-year-old Southerner with an ever-present pinch of Copenhagen snuff tucked in his lower lip—to coach the special teams.

Working for Joe at the Nighthawks was a big opportunity for each of these men. Andrus had the chance to redeem himself after the CFL fiasco, and to try his offense on a professional stage. Olivadotti would finally be able to work with a longtime friend, closing a loop that had opened in 1984, when he'd offered Joe a job with the Hurricanes. And for the younger staffers, most of whom were hoping to get into big-time college programs or even the NFL, the Nighthawks job enabled them to bulk up their résumés.

There was also something else, another chance that these coaches and even the front office staff members had with the Nighthawks, something that was left unsaid but was nonetheless true: if the team had success, all of these men would be able to boast to a potential employer that *they had helped a friggin' CEO beat some NFL coaching legends*.

They would look like geniuses.

Besides wanting to see how well his new team would work together, Joe saw the tryouts as an opportunity for a bit of mischief—and to test his staff to make sure they would stand up to him. Joe's stepson, Jeff Jardine, had asked if he could intern for the team during the upcoming season. The twenty-one-year-old had just graduated from Southern Methodist University. Joe said he could, but he needed a favor from him first. Joe wanted Jeff to secretly try out for the team in Dallas, not letting any of the other coaches know about their family connection. Their different last names provided the necessary cover. Jardine agreed and decided he'd go out for quarterback. "I thought I might as well aim high," he says. Though he'd last played football as a sophomore in high school (as a backup offensive guard on the junior varsity), and is maybe a tad short for the position, Jardine did sort of look the part. He's a good-looking, sturdy kid with thick, sandy blond "high school quarterback" hair.

Jardine showed up on the day of the Dallas tryout. He and Joe didn't share so much as a glance during the entire day. Jardine informed Mueller and Andrus that he was there to play quarterback, then proceeded to choose the very un-quarterback-like number 91 for his tryout shirt.

Like a method actor, Jardine totally dove into his role. “He was running around like a chicken with no head, slapping high-fives with the other players and some of the coaches,” says Andrus. Jardine lined up for the forty-yard dash. He finished it in a glacial six seconds, then, huffing and puffing, jogged up to Andrus and explained that a huge gust of wind had blown against him right as he started running. Then Jardine hopped into a drill where the quarterback is supposed to throw simple ten-yard “out” patterns to wide receivers. His throws went nearly everywhere but their intended targets. “And he had absolutely no zip on the ball,” says Andrus. But his lack of throwing success didn’t dampen his spirits. “He never stopped running around, slapping guys on the butt and yelling, ‘C’mon, guys, let’s get it!’” says Andrus.

Meanwhile, Mueller, who’d been watching Jardine, turned to his personnel guys: “Man, there is something really wrong with that guy.”

Then he watched as Jardine launched himself into a big blue pad at the bottom of the goalpost.

“I think that guy is on drugs,” said Mueller.

Andrus dutifully made a note on Jardine. (“I think I wrote down ‘no freakin’ way,’” he says.) Then he moved on to evaluating the other guys at the tryout. But number 91 refused to relinquish the stage. He kept yelling; he kept asking Andrus how he was doing. When the final whistle blew and the tryout ended, Jardine delivered his coup de grâce. As the 150 or so players started to make their way off the field, Jardine played sheepdog and rustled them all together, arranging them in a circle around him. “All right guys, good workout,” he yelled. “On three, ‘Nighthawks’... *one, two, three, ‘Nighthawks!’*” By that time, more than a few of the other players were looking around, confused.

"I really think this guy is on drugs," said Mueller again.

In the van on the way back to the hotel, Joe asked Andrus if he saw any quarterbacks he liked. Joe was sitting shotgun. His coaches were all in the back. No one could see his face.

"No, but we might have found our mascot in that squirrelly white kid, number 91," Andrus replied.

At the hotel, the coaches met to go over player evaluations. They went around the room to each coach, going over the positions one by one, and finally came to the quarterbacks. Andrus said they were all terrible.

"I kinda liked that squirrelly kid. I liked his leadership," said Joe. "And it looked like he could run."

Andrus looked at his sheet. "He ran a 5.9, Joe."

"But how much experience does he have? Maybe we can work with him?"

Andrus looked at his sheet again. "It says here—and these are his words—'To tell the truth the last time I played organized football was in JV, as a backup guard. But the last few weeks I've been throwing the ball around with my buddy, Robbie.'"

There was a round of dismissive laughter from everyone in the room—except for Joe.

"I kinda liked him," said Joe, sounding insistent.

Andrus says now that at that moment, a cold fear began to creep up the back of his neck. He worried that he had signed on as a first mate on a ship that was going to sink before it left the harbor, that Joe really had been out of football too long and had no idea what he was doing.

"He can't play football, Joe," Andrus said, pleadingly.

"Yeah, but he had spirit," Joe said. "He really led those guys out there. I think we need someone like that on the team." At this point Joe was biting hard into his knuckle to keep from laughing.

"There was something really, really wrong with that kid," came Mueller's voice from the back of the room.

"But Joe, the guy couldn't play! At all!" said Andrus. He felt like putting his face in his hands and weeping.

Joe couldn't hold it in any longer. He finally 'fessed up. The room rocked with relieved laughter.

"Well, at least you know I'll always be honest with you," Andrus said.

"I still think there's something wrong with that kid," said Mueller.

Jardine would join the team as an intern during training camp a few months later. Mueller would eventually admit that he was actually "somewhat normal."

In April, Joe and his staff started to work on the team's roster. They quickly made the decision not to invite Garcia and Green back, despite their ongoing popularity with the fans. "They were both pretty done," says Mueller. The staff combed through the rest of the roster to see who they did want to keep.

Despite being the worst (and oldest) team in 2010, the Nighthawks did have some high-quality players, especially on the defensive side. Dusty Dvoracek, the former Chicago Bear, was a very good nose tackle. Ricardo Colclough, the former Pittsburgh Steeler, was an athletic cornerback and kick returner. Stuart Schweigert had been a four-year starter for the Oakland Raiders at safety. The long snapper, Matt Overton, was proficient.

On the offensive side, George Foster was a big and physical left tackle. Running back Shaud Williams, a former Buffalo Bill, was a solid runner and pass catcher. And Joe wanted to bring back another running back, the troubled former Ohio State star, Maurice Clarett. D. J. Shockley, the team's third-string quarterback in 2010, would serve as a good backup.

But that was pretty much it. In all, Joe and his coaches decided to keep just sixteen of the fifty-one players from the 2010 squad. Mueller and his staff had some work to do. Most important, they needed to find a quality quarterback. It turned out they had one right in their backyard.

⊢+++⊣

Eric Crouch had been out of football for three years. He'd become a medical supplies salesman and also ran a playground construction firm in his hometown of Omaha, where he was born and raised. The former Heisman Trophy–winning (2001) option quarterback from the University of Nebraska had endured a checkered professional football career. The St. Louis Rams had drafted him in 2002...as a wide receiver. Then he was injured in training camp and never played. He'd later been in camps with the Green Bay Packers and Kansas City Chiefs, but didn't make the final rosters. He'd played in NFL Europe as a safety. He'd tried to play quarterback in the CFL but was injured after only three games. After seven years of bouncing around (and getting operated on—he'd had eight surgeries on his shoulders, knees, and legs), Crouch had seemingly retired for good.

But in the spring of 2011 Crouch got a call from Joe, who wanted to know if he had any interest in playing for the Nighthawks. For Joe, the move was risky (Crouch's rust and injuries), but it also made some sense: if Crouch could still play, his ability to run and throw would be a perfect fit for the Nighthawks offense. And if he made the team, the hometown hero—who'd gone to high school at Omaha's Millard North—would put some butts in the seats, potentially even more than Garcia and Green ever could.

Crouch didn't immediately say yes. But the more he thought about it, the more the idea intrigued him. He'd liked Joe a lot when he'd met him with Huyghue the previous fall. Crouch no longer harbored dreams of playing in the NFL, which would make him a rarity in the UFL. But he did feel like he still had something to prove, to himself and to others. Like Joe, he had not quite finished what he'd started when it came to football. Crouch also wanted to set an example for his children, a twelve-year-old daughter and a seven-year-old son. "I wanted to show them that I don't give up," he says. And he wanted to have them see him play in an actual game, now that they were old enough to understand and remember it. "I certainly wasn't going to do it for the money," says Crouch.

He called Joe back and said he was interested. He came in for a tryout in front of Joe and Andrus. "He looked good," says Andrus. "He threw the ball well. He just had to get that burst back in his legs. But he had time for that." The Nighthawks signed him shortly thereafter.

In late April, the NFL was still locked in its labor battle. The big league did, however, go through with its annual collegiate draft hullabaloo. The event, held at Radio City Music Hall, is spread over three days and is nationally televised from start to finish.

Just two days after the NFL's draft, it was the UFL's turn. Things are a bit different for them. There were no ESPN cameras present at the UFL draft, no helmet-haired Mel Kiper Jr. breathlessly obsessing over the forty-yard-dash times of the prospects. There wasn't even a central place where the teams gathered to do their picks. It was all done remotely, and the picks were announced as they happened on Twitter.

The UFL draft presents a difficult conundrum for UFL general managers like Mueller. While the Nighthawks obviously want to draft the best players available, they don't want them to be *too* good. If they actually do have true NFL-level talent, they probably won't sign, preferring instead to wait and try to make an NFL team as a free agent. If they even *believe* they have NFL-level talent (or have an agent telling them so), they may not sign, either. No UFL draftee jumps out of his chair and tearfully hugs his grandmother upon seeing his name attached to a UFL team.

Complicating everything even more this year was the NFL's labor situation. With no new collective bargaining agreement in place, no players—rookies or free agents—were allowed to sign with NFL teams. The problem was, once a player signed with the UFL, he couldn't sign with the NFL (unless he was released by his team). So most of the players who would be drafted by the UFL were waiting out the NFL drama.

Still, the UFL draft goes on. The Nighthawks took Reynaldo Hill with their first pick. Hill, twenty-eight, had been out of football for two years, but he was once a starting cornerback for the Titans. He wanted to work his way back to the NFL. Mueller had watched him work out and liked what he saw. Perhaps more important than that, Hill seemed very likely to sign with the Nighthawks. NFL teams don't generally sign guys who have been out of the game for two years.

Later in the draft the Nighthawks selected Jeremiah Masoli, a quarterback. At the University of Oregon, Masoli had run an offense very similar to the one Joe and Andrus were planning to install with the Nighthawks. In 2009 Masoli had led the Ducks to the Rose Bowl (they lost to Ohio State), throwing for 15 touchdowns and running for another 13 that year. He made the cover of *Sports Illustrated*. But just as his football career was beginning to take off, he ran into trouble. He and a teammate got caught stealing some laptops and a guitar from a fraternity. Then he got busted for possession of marijuana. He was kicked off the Oregon team. He transferred to Ole Miss, where he didn't quite replicate his Oregon success, throwing for 14 touchdowns but also 13 interceptions. Masoli had played against Joe's team in the college all-star game. Joe had liked what he saw of him on the field. Both he and Andrus believed Masoli was a perfect fit for their system. And his off-the-field troubles at Oregon could even work to their advantage: they might scare off potential NFL teams.

As feared, the 2011 UFL draft amounted to merely a perfunctory act. Only three of the twelve players the Nighthawks chose actually ended up on the team—Hill, Masoli, and tight end/long snapper Kyle Nelson. The others either went to the NFL, failed to report to camp, or didn't make the final roster.

CHAPTER THREE

Nightmares

For its headquarters, the Nighthawks use the Kroc Center, a lavishly endowed Salvation Army community center located in south Omaha, a predominantly Hispanic section of town that was once home to the city's famous stockyards. (The area's past is never far from mind, however: even the slightest breeze from the north carries with it the scent of kibble from a pet food plant that's strategically located near one of the few remaining animal rendering plants.) The Kroc, as it's known, is surrounded by small boxy houses and is across the street from the Davis Erection Company, a crane sales and service concern that proudly and somewhat profanely displays its name in large letters on the side of an old, out-of-service tractor trailer.

The first thing a visitor notices about the artificial turf football field in front of the Kroc is that it is visibly slanted to the north. This is for drainage purposes. Most football fields are slightly crowned for this same reason, but because the Kroc was built on former stockyard land—where decades of animal waste have been (one hopes) buried—digging more than five feet deep into the earth requires special permits that can take years to procure. Slanting the field a bit solves the bureaucratic problem and doesn't seem to affect the players much.

It's not quite an NFL setup, but the Nighthawk facilities stack up with any midlevel college program and are far and away the best in the UFL, with everything a football team could need: modern weight room, locker room, basketball courts (for indoor walk-throughs), a vast dining area, and plenty of meeting rooms.

The entire team—seventy players, and all of the coaches and staff members—reports to the Kroc on July 13, 2011, two days before training camp is set to begin. There had been a three-day minicamp in June, and the coaches had been together for most of that month, but the real work would start now. Training camp is supposed to be a month-long preparation for an eight-game season that begins in late August and runs through late October.

Joe huddles with his coaches that night to reiterate the plans for the offense, defense, and special teams and to reiterate his general philosophy. This is worth doing: after all, it's an entirely new staff and, save for sixteen players, a brand-new team. He tells the coaches that he does not want them to be at the Kroc at all hours of the night and day. "Get some sleep during camp and the season," he says. "Exhaustion gives you no advantage, especially at critical moments in games and in practice, when I want you cool and sharp." The way to do this, he says, is to keep things simple, to concentrate on a few crucial things and to do them extremely well. It is, he says, the best lesson he learned during his business career.

At the end of the meeting Joe asks some of the interns to stand up and introduce themselves. Chris Parker, a twenty-four-year-old who will be helping out with the secondary, ends his introduction with his voice coming to a crescendo: "And I want to bring home a championship. I want to get a ring!" Then he stops and turns to Joe with a questioning look. "If they do that kind of thing here," he says in a lowered voice. He means the league, which sort of seems like the NFL but isn't.

"Rings? Are you crazy?" Joe says. "Chris, do you know how much money this league lost last year?"

The coaches erupt in laughter. But the merriment won't last long.

The Nighthawks already have some fairly serious issues to deal with. First and foremost, Masoli hasn't reported to camp. He's holding out hope that he will land in an NFL training camp, if and when the lockout lifts. The team has brought in former Penn State quarterback Daryll Clark, another run-pass threat, to compete with Crouch and Shockley. A possible fourth quarterback has broken his hand in a bar brawl and won't be showing up.

But there is a potentially bigger problem with the league itself. Rumors abound that the NFL lockout is about to end, which would leave the UFL and its players in a state of uncertainty. The UFL would lose players just as its training camps were beginning. But more important, the league had gone all-in with the bet that the NFL would miss at least some games, and had structured the season around taking advantage of that circumstance. The UFL doesn't seem to have much of a backup plan if the NFL resolves its issues and plays all its games, as it now appears will happen.

The next morning, one day before camp is to begin, Joe calls an emergency meeting with the coaches. They gather in the defense's meeting room. Joe is sitting on a table when they walk in, his back against the wall, his arms resting on his knees. It's a relaxed, confident pose, but with a tip to either side, it could easily become the fetal position, which might better reflect how he feels at this moment.

The coaches gather around him, most of them standing. Joe tells them he's been on the phone all morning with the commissioner and owners of the league. He has disturbing news. No one is allowed to take the practice field. No players, no coaches. On any team. The issue is with worker's compensation—which pays an employee who is hurt on the job in exchange for waiving the right to sue. Needless to say, it's an essential thing for a professional football league to have. Though the league has had months to do it, they have not fully paid the 2010 bill for worker's comp, and thus cannot even begin paying it for the 2011 season. Joe's face is taut. The league's owners are scrambling to find some liquid capital to pay the bills, he says. Everything will be in limbo for a few days. If they fail to do so, there will be no season. "And there is a decent possibility that they won't figure this out," says Joe.

Audible sighs fill the room. The coaches look at each other, raise their eyebrows and shake their heads. Joe scans the room, his eyes flaring. His voice becomes sharp and louder. "Guys, we need to make this a positive. Let's not complain about it. The players will respond to the way *we* handle this. Set a good example. The measure of a coach, the measure of a man, is how you handle stuff when your back is up against the wall."

Joe later addresses his players in the Kroc's chapel, telling them that there is a chance the league will fold. They won't know anything for a few days. He says they will all make the best of this time. They will spend extra time in the classrooms learning the playbook, will use the gym to walk through plays, and will hit the weight room hard and get stronger.

He doesn't show it in front of the players or his staff, but Joe is as heartbroken as anyone else at the thought of not playing the season, maybe more so. First of all, he feels responsible. After all, *he* is the one who hired all of these coaches and staffers. Some of them left other jobs to come to the Nighthawks. All seventy players came to play on *his* team. What would they do without a season? He even took on a dozen interns, some of whom passed up other internships to work for the Nighthawks.

Then, of course, there's his own dream, which, ironically, might be done in by just the sort of business mistakes that he himself would never have made or tolerated in the career he had left behind.

The players spend the next four days shuffling from the meeting rooms to the gym then to the dining hall, all in that slow-gaited, toe-stubbing manner typical of seasoned athletes, as if they are perpetually sore or trying to save energy. They look antsy and bored out of their minds, like kids in a driver's education program stuck in the classroom, waiting to get behind the wheel. "I want to do some hitting," says Dvoracek, the nose tackle. The players are not optimistic about the UFL's chances. Resignation swiftly settles in. After all, these are players who have had their football dreams crushed before, many very recently. They've been booted out of the big show, or, after stellar college careers, they never made it there in the first place.

Joe updates the team every day. "In times of crisis, the rule is 'meet more,'" he tells them. Out of his own pocket, he continues to give the players their meager $50 per diem, which is usually paid for by the league, but had been cut off due to the delay. "If the league doesn't like that, screw 'em," says Joe.

Then, finally, on the nineteenth there is some news. The league has decided to push back the start of the season by thirty days. Presumably the extra time will allow them to come up with some money and, with the NFL lockout all but over, rejigger the season schedule. To many outsiders, it all seems like merely a postponement of the UFL's inevitable death, useless life support for a league that is showing no vital signs. The Nighthawks' coaches and players believe that as well.

In his last address to the players before they leave, Joe tells them that he does believe the league owners will do everything in their power to keep the league afloat. "They've put so much money into this league so far," he says. "I don't think they want to just walk away from it." But he admits that he is not totally sure they will pull through.

"You guys are free to do whatever you want," Joe says. "You can join an NFL team, you can stay here and train, you can retire, you can go work. Anything. But we are going to plan as if training camp starts in a month. If you want to play, please do all you can to stay in shape. I promise you this: if you want to come back, we will honor that and welcome you back and give you a fair shot to make the team." He even offers to put up, on the team's dime, the players who want to stay in Omaha and train. Around twenty of them will take him up on the offer.

Then Joe bids them—and maybe his dream—adieu.

CHAPTER FOUR

His Mother's Son

Joe Moglia was born on April 1, 1949, in the Inwood section of Manhattan, the first child of John and Frances Moglia. He was baptized Giuseppe Hugo Moglia, in the Italian tradition of naming a firstborn son after his paternal grandfather.

Joe's mother, Frances, was Irish. While she conceded the naming of her baby to her husband's homeland tradition, she did decide that there was no way in hell that she was going to call her son "Giuseppe." And she knew that using the English version, "Joseph," wouldn't work—John's Italian relatives would just translate it and call him "Giuseppe" anyway. She needed something completely different. Fortune smiled on her in that regard. Joe's paternal grandfather, for reasons unclear, had always been called "Jim." So Joe's mother decided to call her son by the same name. By doing so she would still, technically, be hewing to the Italian tradition.

It worked. Everyone in the family—aunts, uncles, cousins—called Joe "Jim" or "Jimmy." His three living siblings do so to this day.

As a toddler, Joe thought his name really was "Jim." He had no reason to believe otherwise. No one had ever told him his real name.

That is, until he went to school. When Joe was five years old, his parents enrolled him in kindergarten class in a little stone house on the grounds of the Payson Playground in Inwood. On the morning of his first day of school ever, Joe and his mother made the five-minute walk from their apartment to the playground. Streams of other kids were walking with their moms in the same direction.

When they reached the stone house, Joe and his mother went in and found a classroom filled with the clamor of small children. Joe's mother smiled and made small talk with some of the other moms. After a while she crouched down in front of her son. Joe started to feel nervous for the first time that morning. His mother patted his head and gave him a good-bye kiss on his cheek, then told him "I love you" in her mellifluous Irish accent and started to walk away. But she stopped suddenly in her tracks, whirled around and came back. "Oh, I forgot to tell you," she told Joe. "They're going to call you 'Joseph' here."

"Why?" asked Joe.

"Because that's your name," she said, then patted his head again and left.

Joe gave her what he now calls his "what the hell?" face. From that day on, the outside world knew him as "Joe." Within the family, he would always be "Jim."

"My cousins would always say, 'No wonder Jim's all messed up. He never knew his name,'" says Joe.

Joe's father, John, was born in Pessola, Italy, a small, valley-bound rural hamlet in the province of Parma. With tensions between the socialists and fascists in the country rising, and with rapid industrialization resulting in a scarcity of jobs outside of cities, the Moglias moved to the United States in 1927, when John was eleven. They lived in an apartment at 4535 Park Avenue, in the Italian section of the Bronx.

John never went to school in the United States. During the day he worked in his father's fruit store. In the evening he took classes in ballroom dancing. He became quite good at it and would eventually compete in national dancing events. He wanted to be a dance instructor when he grew up.

But John's father thought his son's dancing was utter nonsense and forced him to go to work instead and help support the family. In his early twenties, John opened his own small fruit store, Hillside Market, on busy University Avenue in the Bronx.

Then, as his new country entered World War II to fight against his old one, John was drafted. After basic training at Fort Bragg, he served as a sergeant in the 57th Quartermaster Sales Company in France, supplying the Allied forces with all of their basic material needs, save for ammunition and medical supplies. John's experience in the fruit stores prepared him well for the detail-oriented job. Relatively speaking, it was a good post to have during wartime: John did most of his work from well behind the frontlines.

Sometime after V-E Day, as the Allied war effort wound down, quartermasters were taken from their posts near the battlefields and dispersed across Europe to help supply the war-ravaged citizens. John was reassigned to Belfast, where he started the 58th Quartermaster Sales Company. An Allied quartermaster, because of his access to food and other basic goods, enjoyed a role of prominence in many of these destitute European cities.

Within the grounds of the Belfast Zoo, on the northeastern slope of a promontory known as Cavehill, there was an art-deco building named Floral Hall, which was built to host dances. It had opened just before the war but was only now being properly used, as American servicemen and local lasses were caught up in the ecstatic joy of the Allied victory. John Moglia still loved to dance, and fancied himself, in his dashing uniform, as a young Rudolph Valentino. He became a regular patron of

Floral Hall. So did a young Belfastian woman named Frances McLarnon.

One evening, as Frances was leaving the hall with some friends, John, standing outside, spotted her. She was singing along to a dance tune. She had a pretty voice. John was immediately smitten. He walked over and introduced himself. "I want to dance with the person who was singing," he announced.

Frances was hesitant. But the American serviceman eventually got his way. They met the next night at Floral Hall, and danced together for hours. "My mother was initially really reluctant to get involved with this guy," says Joe's sister, Mary. "But my father was pretty charming then, and he could dance well." Frances was relieved to find out that John was Catholic and not Protestant, which to her family—proud members of Northern Ireland's minority denomination—would have been a nonstarter. Their courtship in Belfast was chaste. "My mother was a good Catholic girl and my father respected that," says Joe's youngest brother, Paul. He believes that John may have endeared himself to the McLarnons by pilfering for them a few of the much-desired items they had lived without for years—like new undershirts and stockings—from the quartermaster store.

Just a few weeks after meeting Frances, John was sent home to the United States, and he went back to work at the fruit store. He was heartbroken but undeterred. When he got back to the Bronx, he unleashed a steady barrage of letters upon Frances. "He was a good letter writer. He expressed himself well," says Paul. John corresponded with Frances for the better part of two years before he asked her, via letter, to move to the United States and marry him.

According to family lore, the McLarnons studied the mailed proposal and weighed its pros and cons. They knew John was Italian. That was a mark against him. But he *was* Catholic, which was a good thing. And he was a business owner. Another check in the "pro" column. Then they examined the return address on his letters. It read "Park Avenue." The McLarnons asked their Irish friends who'd been to New York about Park Avenue. "That's where the millionaires live!" their friends told them. "Then my mother's parents said, 'You can't let this guy get away!'" says Joe.

Frances sailed to the United States without her family. There she discovered that John's "business" was a ten-by-thirty-foot fruit store on a busy, grimy street. She moved into John's two-bedroom apartment, which was indeed on Park Avenue, but the significantly less-gilded portion of it in the Bronx. The apartment overlooked the noisy, sprawling, industrial wasteland of a railroad yard. John had also failed to mention that he still lived with his mother, his sister, and two of his brothers. They spoke mostly Italian to each other, just as the rest of the neighborhood did, and rarely bothered to try to include Frances, who spoke no Italian, in their conversations.

Despite all these presumably unnerving departures from Frances's expectations, she and John were married almost right away. None of her family made the trip for the wedding. One of John's brothers (and her new apartment-mate) walked her down the aisle and gave her away.

As the story goes in the Moglia family, Frances wrote her parents a few months later and told them: "I have no idea why people here make such a big deal about Park Avenue." Though the entire story may be apocryphal, it does accurately convey her humor, good-natured disposition, and willingness to adapt. "She always told me that story with a huge smile on her face," says Paul. "She never said she was disappointed."

She did, however, have ample reason to feel that way. The young American serviceman whom she married—back home after the terrible war, struggling to make a living—was a lot less charming than she remembered. "All traces of that expressive man who loved to dance quickly vanished," says Paul. "He seemed angry about his lot in life, about the fact that he had to work grueling hours in the fruit store six days a week to make ends meet."

In 1949 John and Frances Moglia finally moved to an apartment of their own at 1825 Riverside Drive, a six-story, utilitarian, brown brick building in Inwood, a predominantly Irish neighborhood in Manhattan. The Moglias lived in a two-bedroom apartment on the building's uppermost floor, for which they paid a monthly rent of $88.

Inwood is the northernmost neighborhood in Manhattan. Legend has it that this is the place where the cunning director-general of the New Netherlands colony, Peter Minuit, "bought" the island of Manhattan from the native Lenape Indians for a few trinkets worth $24 in present-day terms. It was also the home neighborhood of Harry Houdini, Jim Henson, and Lew Alcindor (later known as Kareem Abdul-Jabbar).

The Moglias had five children: first Joe, then Johnny, Bernadette, Paul, and Mary. All seven of them were crammed into that two-bedroom apartment. The boys slept in one bedroom (Joe and Johnny shared a bed for a while) and the girls slept with their parents in the other one. In addition to the two bedrooms the apartment had one bathroom, a foyer, a kitchen, and a living room. "There was always a line for the bathroom, and the living room, which was the biggest room in the apartment, was off limits to the kids," says Paul. "But what strikes me now is that it didn't feel to us like we were all on top of each other. It didn't feel small. We didn't know any other way."

At the time Joe's father owned a fruit store on 181st Street in Washington Heights, the neighborhood just south of Inwood, called Cabrini Market. He worked six days a week, rising at 5:00

a.m. to go to the store to receive deliveries of fruit, and not returning home until 9:00 p.m. after closing up. Work was his life. Joe remembers only one family vacation during his childhood, when the Moglias went to Newburgh, New York. They were supposed to stay for a week on a lake and go horseback riding and boating. It turned out there were no horses, the only boat was a rickety rowboat, and the "lake" was really a pond that was, at best, thirty feet in diameter. After only three days Joe's father got restless and took his family home, while he went back to work at the store.

As soon as they were old enough to communicate with customers, all of the children worked shifts at the store. ("For my tenth birthday, my present was to work at the store from 8:00 a.m. to 8:00 p.m.," says Paul.) Occasionally a city inspector would visit the store and fine John for using child labor, even though they were his own kids. Sunday was the only day the store was closed. After 9:00 a.m. Mass, the Moglias would either visit John's relatives in the Bronx and sit through protracted, three- to four-hour lunches, or they would pack a lunch and picnic at nearby Dyckman Street Park on the Hudson River. And every Sunday John would take an extended afternoon nap that was not to be disturbed under any circumstances.

John Moglia had dark black hair. He was a hard, wiry man, nearly six feet tall and weighing two hundred pounds. His shoulders bulged with muscles developed from lifting crates of fruit every day. His hands were huge, knotty, and scarred—like a stonemason's—from yanking open boxes of fruit and trimming heads of lettuce. Joe's father was in every way the Italian *Il Padrone*, the unquestioned ruler of the family. He was the provider, and that alone commanded his family's respect. "When I was four, my mother would make us sing this song: 'Clap your hands, clap your hands until daddy comes home. Daddy has money and mommy has none,'" says Joe's brother Johnny.

"Once in my life I want to come home and be treated the way

Mr. Moglia was treated when he walked into the apartment from work," says Dave Hunt, a childhood friend of Joe's from Inwood. "Everything in the house just stopped and everyone snapped to attention." Frances and the children would all greet John at the door. One of the children would take the shopping bag—filled with fruit from the store—from his hands. Another would draw a hot bath. When John was done bathing, he would sit at the table—alone, since everyone else had already had their dinner—and eat the hot meal that Frances had prepared just for him. "They all appreciated how hard he worked," says Hunt.

Despite all the appreciation and attention, John was not particularly warm in return. While he was having his dinner, Joe would often grab his homework and come join his father at the table, but John would usually just continue to sit there in a sullen silence. "He wasn't exactly the kind of guy who asked you how school was that day," says Joe. He was also frequently ill-tempered. "When he got into one of his moods at the fruit store and started yelling, the guys who worked for him would just turn to each other and say, 'Uh-oh, it's gonna be one of those days,'" says Johnny. There were days like that at home, too. One freezing winter Sunday Joe and Johnny were in the apartment playing with toy guns they'd received for Christmas. The noise woke their father from one of his sacred naps. "He just walked out of the bedroom and took our guns and broke them in his hands," says Johnny. "It was terrible."

John frequently used physical means to get his message across. Back then, the beatings he administered to his children (mainly the older boys, Joe and Johnny) would have been considered somewhere on the extreme edge of normal. Today, they'd probably be over the line. John O'Leary, a family friend, remembers John Moglia once scolding Johnny for some transgression. "Johnny stared his old man right in the face and said 'You ain't so bad,'" says O'Leary. John hit him. Johnny pulled himself back up and repeated his defiant line. His father hit him again. Johnny got back to his feet and said it again. "Finally Joe stepped in and said, 'Johnny, just shut up or he's going to kill you,'" says O'Leary.

Another time, Joe was napping in his bedroom when Johnny came in and told him that their father wanted to see him. Joe walked into the living room and his father started hitting him. "What did I do? What did I do?" asked Joe. His father said: "I told you never to go down to the river."

"I had no idea what he was talking about," says Joe. Later, Johnny explained to Joe that he had just told his father about the time he and Joe had saved a baby pigeon that had been stranded on the banks of the Hudson. "My father was pissed because he thought I had risked my life and Johnny's to save a stupid bird," says Joe. "The thing was that it had been a whole year since we did it." Apparently his father's rage had no statute of limitations.

John's work seemed to be the main source of his anger. "I think he felt financially stuck in a business he'd grown up in. He owned his own store. Relative to many of his peers, he was financially successful. But I think he felt even more pressure because of that," says Paul. It didn't help that he was a drinker, too. Not exactly an alcoholic at the time, but somewhere close to it.

For the record, Joe has a slightly gentler view of his father than his siblings do. "Deep down, I really believe he was a good man," says Joe. "He was just self-absorbed and so focused on providing for us. He was definitely a 'glass half-empty' guy."

Joe's mother was the family's counterbalance, the "glass half-full" parent, the velvet glove to their father's iron fist. Frances was pretty, a stylish dresser who liked to sport flamboyant hats and big, dark sunglasses. "She was sort of like an Irish Jackie Onassis," says Joe's daughter, Kara. Says Hunt: "She was a knockout. In a neighborhood of somewhat plain and dowdy women, she really stood out. When she walked into a room, you knew it."

Her natural hair color was auburn, but she enjoyed changing

that, dyeing it various different shades. (She would open her own beauty salon in the 1970s when she and John moved to Yonkers after Mary, their youngest, went off to college.) Frances was always humming or singing. The Moglias had a small piano in the apartment, and Frances played it daily. One of her favorite songs was "When Irish Eyes are Smiling." Back in Ireland as a young girl she had sung the challenging *Adeste Fideles* solo in her church at the Christmas Mass. Always the first to dance at weddings, she was an animated woman who loved to tell jokes and laugh. She doted on her family and friends. "She had a way of making you feel like you were important," says Johnny.

She and her husband seemed to have little in common. They were not very affectionate. "They really didn't know each other that well when they married," says Paul. "But I never heard her complain about her marriage. The most she would ever say was, 'Marriage is not always a bed of roses.' But there was a lot of love and energy in the house and in the family, mainly due to her."

What Frances and John did have in common was a strong work ethic. While John spent his days and nights at the store, Frances occupied herself with raising her five children. She was fiercely protective of her brood, providing them shelter from both their tempestuous father and the world outside their doors, which, given their neighborhood, could sometimes be particularly tough on children who were as safeguarded as the Moglias were.

Inwood was, in many ways, a great place for a kid to grow up. It's bordered by the Hudson River on the west and the curling Harlem River to the north and east, and is home to two big wooded parks: Inwood Hill on the banks of the Hudson and Fort Tryon to the south. The parks and water give the neighborhood the feeling of being isolated from the rest of Manhattan. Inwood was loud and busy. On scalding-hot summer days, children swam in the rivers and families gathered on fire escapes to get away from the heat of their stuffy, un-air-conditioned apartments. In the winter kids went sledding on the steep slopes of Fort Tryon. "It felt like a small town to us when we were growing up," says Hunt.

But it was a small town with an inner-city edge, veined in concrete, menacingly shadowed by the elevated train tracks that ran right through the middle of the neighborhood and packed with tenement houses occupied by recent immigrants striving to find their way in the new world. The vibe on the pushy, busy streets was make-it-or-break-it. Some did. Others didn't. Paul Moglia estimates that 60 percent of the kids they grew up with never made it out of Inwood and instead settled for lives as "cops or criminals," amorphous demarcations in the neighborhood. While Inwood wasn't exactly a crime-war zone, it wasn't a place where you wanted to be on the streets at night, when trouble could be found in any darkened alley. (Jim Carroll, an Inwood native, wrote his bleak, drug-addled autobiographical book, *The Basketball Diaries*, about growing up in the neighborhood.)

Frances wanted something better for her children. She pushed them to study hard. She also did all she could to stave off the dangerous influences of the neighborhood. She didn't want her children to grow up too fast. For the most part she succeeded, sometimes only too well—especially in their younger years, when she managed to keep them in a state of innocence that might seem hard to imagine these days.

When Joe was ten he asked his mother where babies came from. He had no concept of what sexual intercourse was; he was just curious. Frances told him that God came down and planted a seed behind a woman's heart. That seed grew for nine months. Then the doctor took the baby out of her stomach. "That's why we have belly buttons," she explained.

Good enough for Joe, who gave no further thought to the matter.

By age thirteen, Joe was in a gang. While it wasn't exactly the Crips and the Bloods, Joe's gang, the Tiny Tots, did drink booze, commit minor acts of robbery and roll bums in the park. Some of them even carried knives. But mostly what they did was get into fistfights.

Inwood was divided, socially and economically, by three Catholic church parishes: St. Jude's (where Lew Alcindor went to school) was predominantly black and Hispanic. Good Shepherd (Jim Carroll's parish) was populated by the neighborhood's middle-class Irish. Our Lady Queen of Martyrs, the Moglias' church and the site of Joe's grammar school, was mostly lower-middle-class Irish.

Each of the parish's schools had its own "gang," and each gang had its own respective territory, determined by borders (usually cross streets) known only to the gang members themselves and not the adult world. If a member of, say, the Good Shepherd crowd crossed into Our Lady Queen of Martyrs terrain, a fistfight was usually in the offing. But, as might be expected in a group of high-spirited, prepubescent boys, much of the fighting took place within their own gangs.

Since most of the really bad stuff—the beat-downs that required hospitalization, the occasional stabbings—took place after school and at night, Joe didn't have much exposure to that. Athletics kept him off the streets after school. At night he was usually working in his father's store, and when he did have an occasional evening off, his parents held him to a very strict curfew.

But Joe did get into some bad scrapes, including a particularly nasty beating that occurred when he was thirteen—an unintended consequence of his mother's ardent desire to protect her son and his innocence. One afternoon as Joe and the Tiny Tots were leaving school, somebody in their group yelled the word *fuck*. The boys' teacher, a hard-bitten, streetwise-by-necessity nun, yelled back: "You don't even know what that word means."

The boys laughed as they ran to Fort Tryon Park, one of their main hangouts. On their way over, Ray Gonzales, a member of the gang, did the sometimes cruel calculus that young boys do, and got the sense that Joe actually didn't know what the word meant. He put Joe on the spot in front of the other boys. Joe said nothing. Gonzales told him: "It's how babies are made, you dumbass."

Joe, initially embarrassed, believed then that he had gained the upper hand.

"That's not how babies are made," he told Gonzales. Joe explained to the group what his mother had told him three years earlier, about God and seeds and belly buttons.

The boys, led by Gonzales, howled with laughter. Then, as if set off by some secret signal, they jumped Joe. They didn't put him in the hospital, but they gave him quite a beating. Blows to the face and the head were followed by kicks to the ribs and the crotch after he finally went down.

When Frances opened the door to let Joe into the apartment that afternoon, she gasped. He had a swollen left eye and dried brown blood around his mouth. Fresh, bright red blood dripped from his nose. Frances loathed fighting. Luckily for Joe, his father, who also disapproved of fighting, was still at work.

"Did you get into another fight?" she asked. She was visibly angry.

"Ma, I have one question for you," Joe said. His breaths whistled through his bloody nose. "Remember when you told me how babies are made? Remember? Was that true? Were you telling me the truth?"

Frances pursed her lips and looked down at her hands as she wiped them on her apron and said nothing. That was all Joe needed to see. He ran into his bedroom and slammed the door. He was not punished for fighting.

Joe may have lost that fight, but as he got older, the losses were few and far between. In his teenage years he was fairly big and strong, and very athletic. "He was a tough guy," says Hunt. "If you got into a beef with him, you had your hands full. But he was never a bully."

In fact, Joe couldn't stand bullies, and made a sport out of taking them down a notch. Hunt remembers one day walking up Academy Street toward Inwood Hill Park. He and Joe were going drinking (they began drinking at age eleven, and by thirteen Joe was drinking fairly regularly). Hunt was carrying a brown paper sack with a twelve-pack of beer in it. "For whatever reason, Joe was walking a block behind me," says Hunt. "And this older kid in the neighborhood, a well-known bully, comes up and just rips the bag out of my hand. Beer cans flew all over the place. But the guy didn't know that Joe was coming up behind me. When he saw him, his eyes got huge."

Joe chased down the bully and smacked him a few times. Then he made the kid get on his hands and knees and fetch all of the beer cans. "They were under cars, in the gutter," says Hunt. "But that guy got every last one of them."

Joe and his brother Johnny were quite the formidable duo. Just fourteen months younger than Joe, Johnny matured early ("I was sent home from school in the seventh grade to shave," he says) and was the bigger of the two. Both he and Joe suffered from a stutter, but Johnny's was much worse. "Johnny would just sit there, in front of all these tough guys and just blubber," says Joe. "It broke my heart every time I heard it."

But Johnny didn't need any help standing up for himself. He let his fists do most of the talking. Those big knuckles never had a problem with being misunderstood or mocked. Joe and Johnny started to establish a reputation in the neighborhood as a duo you didn't want to mess with. "We didn't lose many fights," says Johnny.

Johnny was the more feared of the two, and didn't mind putting a good licking on another guy. But Joe always held back a bit. Says Johnny: "Joe never crossed that line. He didn't want to really hurt anybody."

Fran Perdisatt, a classmate of Joe's at Our Lady Queen of Martyrs, says: "Joe was probably a little more sheltered than the rest of us. Johnny hung out with a tougher crowd. Joe knew them all, was friendly with them, but he never went in that direction. He would always go up to the point when he was going to get in trouble, then he'd back off."

As the kids in the Inwood gangs grew older, the level of violence and malfeasance rose. Some of the kids fell deeper and deeper into a more hardcore gang life and never got out. Just a few years after Joe got beaten up for not knowing how babies were made, the stakes rose considerably. Ray Gonzales would die of a drug overdose. Another Tiny Tot, John Spaulding, was shot and killed by two cops as he walked a crowded street waving a gun. Seven members of Joe's class of twenty boys at Our Lady Queen of Martyrs would not live to see the age of forty, due to drugs and violence.

But Joe was on another path, held back from the edge not just by the fact that, as Johnny says, he didn't really want to hurt anyone with his fists, but ultimately by his reluctance to do anything that would hurt his mother. Through two episodes during his eighth-grade year, Joe would learn this the hard way and, in the process, turn around a life that still hung in the balance.

Getting busted for having a couple of bottles of booze on a school trip might not sound like something that would alter a person's life. But because of what it did to his mother, it changed Joe's.

Every year Our Lady Queen of Martyrs hosted an annual

school trip to Rye Beach outside of New York City for the kids and some of the parents. Anticipating the outing during their eighth-grade year, Joe and his friends "got the bright idea to bring some booze along," as he recounts the episode, and to ask the girls, who were traveling on their own bus, to stash it for them. "We figured the nuns wouldn't check their bags," he says. They figured wrong. On the day of the trip, the nuns had all the boys open their bags. They found nothing. "We thought we were so clever," says Joe. But fifteen minutes later, the nuns came barging onto the boys' bus, holding bottles of liquor. They had checked the girls' luggage, too. "I was dead," says Joe.

The principal, a nun named Sister Mary Margaret, called Joe into her office. Then she called Joe's father at the fruit store. "My father did *not* like having to leave the store," says Joe. With the two of them standing there looking at him, Joe made up a story about how the booze actually belonged to a boy named Tommy Robino, who had been kicked out of the school the year before and was now in public school. Joe told the story well, complete with tears. "My father actually looked at the nun and said he was inclined to believe me," says Joe. Sister Mary Margaret knew better, though. She told John Moglia that the girls told her that Joe had given them the bottles.

"Is that true?" John asked Joe.

"I said 'yes,' and before I could get another word out of my mouth, he was smacking me all over the room," says Joe. "I deserved this one."

Joe was forced to work in the fruit store that day as his friends made their way to the beach. "I just remember being so sad, being stuck at the store," says Joe. It got worse for him when he went home and saw his mother. Much worse. She didn't yell at him. She didn't say anything, actually. She just cried. "She couldn't stop crying," says Joe. "I'd let her down. She knew she could count on me and I let her down."

Joe was not allowed to take part in the eighth-grade graduation ceremony. He worried that Fordham Prep, the Catholic high school he had worked so hard to get into, would find out and take away his admission. (Prep never found out.) The episode became the defining moment of his childhood, the turning point when he made the conscious decision to make something of his life. "It was the greatest single thing that made me grow up," says Joe. "I let my mother down. I spent a good portion of my life trying to make her proud of me again, trying to earn back her trust. From that point on, I became really focused."

Making her proud, though, was only part of it. Later that year, his father came home from work and told him that his mother had to have some sort of surgery and would be in the hospital for a few days. His father didn't tell him what kind of surgery it was (and to this day, Joe still doesn't know). John didn't betray any worry at that time, not that he was prone to showing his emotions, anyway. Joe shrugged it off. "Back then, I thought I was one of the toughest guys in the neighborhood," says Joe. "In fact, I *was* one of the toughest guys in the neighborhood." And being tough meant never showing emotions around his family, never letting down that wall.

But later that night, as Joe lay awake in bed, he heard a noise coming from his parents' room. He tiptoed down the hallway. Light was coming from the cracked-open door. Joe looked in and saw his father kneeling at the foot of his bed. He couldn't see his face. But his strong shoulders were heaving forward. He realized his father was silently sobbing. "I'd never seen my father cry before," Joe says.

He went back to his own bed and was suddenly wracked with fear about his mother. Then it hit him: though he'd made the pledge to make her proud, he'd been trying to be such a tough guy that he had never told this woman—whom he loved more than anyone in the world—how he felt about her. That night he prayed, asking God to save her so he could rectify his horrible mistake. He promised he would demonstrate his love for her every day, and would never take the love of others for granted.

His mother eventually recovered from the operation. Joe never forgot that night.

⊢+++⊣

Joe and his siblings all made it out of Inwood and into solid professional careers. Johnny has had his ups and downs in business, but he has been the owner of restaurants, nightclubs, strip clubs, and liquor stores. Before she died, Bernadette was a manager at Citibank. Paul is a clinical psychologist in Long Island, and Mary is a portfolio strategist in Rochester, New York. Given the temptations and pitfalls of their childhood neighborhood, their professional success is remarkable, a testament to their parents' strengths and their own ability to draw on those strengths. From John, they learned lessons about the ethic of work. And like Joe, they all desired to be worthy of their mother's unconditional love.

Joe's father may have been tough to live with, but his life can be considered a huge success because, among other reasons, he fulfilled the American immigrant dream of giving his children the ability to create lives better than his own.

His oldest son, in particular, outperformed any expectations his parents might have had for him. Joe worked hard at improving himself in all facets of his life. He participated in the athletics program at Our Lady Queen of Martyrs, which, though modest, had its share of successes. ("A lot of the guys I went to school with had been held back a year or two," says Joe. "That's why we were pretty good at sports.") Joe also sought out opportunities outside of school to brush up on his skills. He organized tackle football games in the park and constantly played stickball in the streets to hone his batting eye. He joined youth leagues in both football and baseball, and was on track to become a star in both sports. And despite his tough-guy façade, he studied very hard for school, fulfilling his mother's wishes. "Joe had, like, a 100 average in seventh grade," says Johnny. "I got really sick of the nuns asking me, 'Why can't you be like Joe?'"

He embraced a leadership role in his family as well, trying to make up for the attention and encouragement his siblings didn't get from their father. "We would all go to him for advice or if we had any problems," says Paul. Joe gave Mary a locket on her tenth birthday. He scolded Bernadette when she wore a dress that he thought was too short. He gave his parents a photo album for their fifteenth wedding anniversary that he worked on for months. And as Joe grew older, he especially loved to dote on his mother. Every few months he would give her a small present—a book, some flowers, a piece of jewelry. "It was like a competition," says Mary. "Like he wanted to show her how he could take care of her and how much he loved her."

Joe brought intensity to everything he did—including having fun. "I used to love working with him in the store," says Paul. "He was hilarious. He would keep up the patter with the customers, keep everything light and make jokes. Sometimes he would take me to a local Chinese restaurant for lunch and he would have me laughing through the entire meal."

As the children all grew into adulthood, Joe continued to take the lead when it came to family matters. He delivered the eulogies at the funerals for both of his parents, and later for Bernadette, his carefree and fun-loving sister who died in 2009 at age fifty-six after a long battle with various health problems.

Going to high school at Fordham Prep in the fall of 1963 was a huge deal for Joe. Academically, it was one of the best Catholic schools in the city. Located in the Bronx, an hour away by bus, it got him out of Inwood, at least during the daytime. And it had very good athletic teams.

Joe's father, who was quite bright but had never gone to school, was curiously suspicious of education. (Later in life, when his daughter, Mary, graduated from law school, John told her: "I'm proud of you, but don't go around thinking you're better than I am.") Frances, however, insisted that Joe and his siblings get the best schooling they could, even if it pushed the family's budget to its limits.

Joe earned good marks at Prep. He worked hard at it, as he did at everything. Paul remembers frequently waking up late at night and seeing his brother sitting on his bed with his homework papers in his lap, lost in deep concentration.

But playing sports was what Joe enjoyed the most. It was a release from studying and working at the fruit store. He was a very good outfielder on Prep's baseball team, with a strong arm and good discipline at the plate. He started as a sophomore and led the team in hitting all three years, batting over .400. He became the captain of the team his senior year.

He stood out even more in football. Joe made the varsity team as a sophomore, and he started on both offense (as a guard) and defense (as a linebacker). At just 180 pounds, Joe was undersized, thirty to forty pounds lighter than some of the other players. But he soon learned that he could use his mind as well as his body to get leverage over the competition. A quick study, he watched the players on the opposing teams, and turned their weaknesses to his advantage. He never missed a play in a game. In his junior year, he was viciously clipped on one of his ankles. That ankle never quite healed fully for the rest of his sports career, but he played through the pain. He wore the number 60, which seemed to be an appropriate one for an undersized, overachieving, two-way football player.

The football coach at Prep was a man named Joseph "Sammy" Ososki. He was famous for having played in the 1942 Sugar Bowl, in which he helped Prep's parent school—Fordham University—beat the University of Missouri 2–0 in a game that was played in a driving rainstorm. Ososki was the quintessence of old school. He'd grown up in coal mine country in western Pennsylvania and, as a Marine, had survived Iwo Jima. "He was a brutal man and a brutal coach," says Robert Sior, a high school teammate of Joe's. "He could have never coached today."

One of Ososki's annual traditions in training camp was to have the team practice for six hours straight in ninety-degree heat—with no breaks for water. He screamed and he threatened his players, and slapped them when he thought they needed it. He believed you didn't mold boys into men—you sandblasted them. Ososki was also famous for his theatrical halftime speeches. If his team was down, he would often shift the pipe in his mouth so that the smoke would waft into his eyes and make them water. He wanted the team to think that their tough old coach wanted to win so badly he was crying.

Joe knew from his experience at home how to deal with a man like Ososki. As a result, Joe thrived on the Prep team. He played hard, even when he was hurt. He was disciplined on the field and rarely made the same mistake twice. "Joe was easily one of the best players we had, a ferocious hitter," says Sior. "And he was a leader. He really naturally took on the role of getting the team in line." Ososki liked that.

As Joe entered his senior year at Prep, he started getting some attention for his play. Colleges around the northeast wrote him letters, mentioning athletic scholarships. "I really loved football," says Joe. "All I wanted to do was play the game in college." But his parents didn't want him to leave home.

It was pretty clear where Joe's father stood on the issue. He thought Joe's love of sports was childish and frivolous. Like his own father before him, he believed that doing anything but working for a wage and providing for one's family was a betrayal of masculine responsibility. He refused in any way to encourage Joe in athletics, and he let Joe know that he was angered by the fact that they took him away from the fruit store.

John never saw his son play a baseball game. And he went to exactly one of Joe's football games, the traditional Thanksgiving Day game that pitted Prep and Xavier High School during Joe's senior year, which would turn out to be the last football game Joe ever played. It so happened that the fruit store was closed that day.

Despite his father's resistance Joe was prepared to leave home and go to a college to play football and perhaps even baseball. But then the one person in his life whose wishes he could never ignore stepped in. As Joe was considering offers from different colleges, his mother sat him down one night and told him that his father was unwell and that he needed him in the fruit store. "I just couldn't say no to her," Joe says.

It turned out that Joe had one more reason for not enrolling in some college far from home to chase his football dreams: A pretty, five-foot-six, dark-haired girl named Kathe Lutz.

Just like his father, Joe met the first true love of his life at a dance. The circumstances were a bit different, however. "I introduced them, sort of," says Dave Hunt. Fordham Prep hosted a dance one night during Joe's sophomore year. The school was—and remains to this day—all male, so female dance partners had to be shipped in from all-girl Catholic schools in the area.

That night Joe and Hunt decided to leave the dance early. "We were probably going to try to find some beer," says Hunt. As they were walking out of the hall, they passed a group of older boys who had already graduated. Because of their ages, they weren't allowed into the dance. Apparently, they found this circumstance frustrating. "As we walked by them, one of the boys just stepped up and, without saying a thing, punched me in the nose," says

Hunt. "The punch pushed my nose back up into my face and knocked me down."

Joe went chasing after the boys while Hunt sat on the sidewalk with blood pouring down his face. "Out of nowhere, this very pretty young girl came up and asked if I was all right and gave me some tissues," says Hunt. It was Kathe. Joe returned to Dave after a few minutes, having been unsuccessful in trying to catch the older boys. Kathe caught his eye immediately.

The two began dating. Kathe lived in Yonkers, an hour-long bus ride away for Joe. Kathe liked Joe's confidence. "He seemed to be able to achieve whatever he set out to do," she says. The relationship got very serious right away. With a girlfriend he wanted to stay close to and a mother insisting he was needed at home, Joe decided to forgo his college athletic career. He enrolled at Fordham University. But he would not be playing football there. Fordham—Vince Lombardi's alma mater—had canceled its football program in 1954.

Instead, Joe buried himself in his studies and work. He majored in economics. He continued to do shifts in the fruit store. He drove a mail truck in Manhattan. He also drove a cab.

Near the end of his freshman year at Fordham, Joe began to seriously think about trying to play football again. He had pretty quickly realized that his father was not ill; his mother had just wanted to have her oldest child close and to preserve family harmony by keeping his father happy. In a rare moment of putting her own desires ahead of those of one of her children, she had misled him.

And things with Kathe, while serious, were also tempestuous. "They argued a lot," says Johnny. "I remember one time he was on the phone with her and they were yelling at each other. When Joe hung up he started punching the wall. I said, 'How can you let her make you get so upset?' Then he turned from the wall and started punching me."

Joe reached out to the colleges that had contacted him the year before. They all said he'd be welcome, but there would be no scholarships. Unfortunately, Joe couldn't afford to go without financial support. He was stuck at Fordham.

It hit him then that he would never play football again. So he began to think about coaching. He approached the new football coach at Fordham Prep, Bruce Bott (who had succeeded Ososki when he retired), and asked if he could become an assistant. Bott said yes. Joe started with the junior varsity team, coaching the offensive and defensive lines and making $800 a year. He discovered two things very quickly: He had an aptitude for coaching, and he loved it. The fact that he never got the chance to play sports in college would always gnaw at him. But he would eventually grow to love coaching even more than he did playing.

Then Joe's world changed. He and Kathe had been dating on and off for five years, alternating between being madly in love and never wanting to see each other again. In one two-week period in the fall of Joe's sophomore year, they broke up for what looked like the last time; then they got back together again. During that reconciliation—one of the many they'd had over the course of their relationship—they had intercourse for the first time.

Kathe got pregnant. They were both nineteen years old.

CHAPTER FIVE

Alternatives

Bill Hambrecht is a seventy-six-year-old Silicon Valley venture capitalist. During his long and lucrative business career, he helped take Apple Computer, Adobe Systems, and Amazon.com public, and pioneered the use of "open" initial public offerings, which make shares available to anyone and everyone who wants to invest. He is currently the chairman of W. R. Hambrecht, which invests in emerging technologies.

Like Joe, Hambrecht first caught the football bug in his teens and never seemed to quite shake it. Back in the mid-1950s, he played one season at Princeton as a blocking wing in the Tigers' single-wing offense. Then he got hurt and never played another down. But that didn't stop him from trying to get back into the game—on the ownership side.

Over the years, Hambrecht says, he has taken a look at various NFL franchises, but had never really believed he had a serious shot at owning one. The closest he came was in the mid-1980s, when he became an investor in the United States Football League's Oakland Invaders.

He eventually decided that if he couldn't own a team, he'd just start a league. Hambrecht says he first came up with the idea for the United Football League back in 1996. What he envisioned was something akin to an "off-Broadway" version of the

NFL's Broadway. He would put franchises in football-mad cities that did not have an NFL team. Ticket prices would be family friendly, in the range of $20 to $50. The players and coaches would be drawn from the vast pool of professional football talent that wasn't, for whatever reason, currently employed by the NFL. The new league would have some differences that, in theory, could make it a looser, more fun version of football than the NFL: On defense, at least four defenders would have to be on the line of scrimmage with at least one hand on the ground, and you could blitz no more than six people at a time (the idea being that these defensive restrictions would make the league more passer friendly); there would be no "tuck rule," that strange, hard-to-call rule that has caused controversy in the NFL (see: Tom Brady, New England Patriots, 2001 NFL playoffs); in overtime each team would get at least one possession; women would be included among the referees.

In rethinking the rules for the UFL, and by placing franchises in non-NFL cities, Hambrecht was looking to subvert an entrenched business model—just as he had done with his plan for open IPOs—and come up with something fresh and original. "No one believes me, but I started the UFL as a business decision," says Hambrecht.

The timing, he thought, was perfect. In 1996 CBS had just lost its NFL television rights. Hambrecht began talks with the network about airing the UFL. And though he says negotiations initially looked promising, CBS eventually balked. But over the years that followed Hambrecht didn't let his dream die.

In 2007 Hambrecht finally roped in some monied friends. Tim Armstrong, a former Google executive who is now the CEO of AOL, and Mark Cuban, the tech billionaire and owner of the NBA's Dallas Mavericks, helped with some seed money. Hambrecht's buddies Paul Pelosi, a California real estate investor (and the husband of Nancy), and William Mayer, a partner at Park Avenue Equity Partners and the former CEO of First Boston, came in later and bought pieces of franchises, to help defray the investment made by Hambrecht, who owned the majority of the league. Pelosi and Mayer each invested tens of millions of dollars.

And they started losing money right away.

The National Football League is a $9 billion behemoth that soaks up all noise that's not its own. No professional football league has ever truly competed with, or even managed to last very long beside, the NFL, not since the American Football League successfully forced a merger with its older contemporary in 1970. But that fact hasn't stopped wealthy men from giving it a shot.

The World Football League, backed in part by the Canadian movie producer John F. Bassett, folded partway through its second season in the mid-1970s. The United States Football League, despite procuring an actual television contract ($18 million for two years on ABC) and signing college superstars like Steve Young, Jim Kelly, and Herschel Walker, made it only three seasons. The XFL, a joint venture between the World Wrestling Federation (now known as "World Wrestling Entertainment") and NBC that featured miked-up players and stripper-like cheerleaders, lasted one season before running out of money.

Even pro football leagues that play a slightly different game have struggled for relevance. The Canadian Football League hasn't had any buzz since Doug Flutie left in 1997 to play for the NFL's Buffalo Bills. And the Arena Football League, that fast-paced indoor hybrid of the game, went bankrupt in 2009 before reconstituting itself a year later in stripped-down form.

The NFL has tried its own hand at an alternative league, too, and even *it* failed. The idea behind the World League of American Football, which eventually became known as NFL Europe, was to broaden the game's reach by playing in Europe, and to develop players for the American game. NFL Europe ceased operations in 2007 after fifteen money-losing seasons when NFL owners tired of putting up the dough to keep funding it.

Yet despite the decades of failures, there is still a fairly strong argument for an alternative league to the NFL, particularly one that's set up to serve a developmental purpose. Good rookie football players slip through the NFL draft and free agency cracks every year. NFL veterans often actually do have something left in the tank. What these players need is a place to attempt to prove themselves.

There's also the issue of injuries that occur during an NFL season. In 2010, 352 NFL players went on the season-ending injured reserve list, missing an average of nine and a half games, which is more than half the season. NFL teams have what's known as practice squads of up to eight players apiece. But that's not nearly enough to replace the injured. A developmental league would certainly help.

The list of marquee players who have played in developmental leagues—especially NFL Europe—and then gone on to become stars in the NFL is fairly impressive. Kurt Warner, a two-time NFL Most Valuable Player, played in both NFL Europe and the Arena Football League. James Harrison, the Steelers' All-Pro linebacker and the 2008 NFL Defensive Player of the Year, is an NFL Europe veteran. Fred Jackson, the star running back for the Bills, toiled in an indoor league and NFL Europe for years. Quarterbacks Jake Delhomme and Brad Johnson, offensive lineman Brian Waters, defensive lineman La'Roi Glover, and kickers Adam Viniateri and David Akers were just a few of the other 250-plus players who made NFL teams after playing in NFL Europe. It's very possible that these players would eventually have found homes in the NFL. But it's inarguable that the time they spent in NFL Europe gave them the time and place to further develop their skills.

Alternative leagues—and again NFL Europe in particular—have also served another crucial function: they act as training grounds for coaches and referees, and laboratories in which the NFL can test potential new rules. In 2011 the NFL had three head coaches who had been in NFL Europe: Chan Gailey, Steve Spagnuolo, and Hue Jackson (though the latter two were fired after the 2011 season). Scott Green and Alberto Riveron, NFL refs, started in Europe. The two-point conversion, the current playoff overtime rules, and one-way radio communication between players and coaches were all first tried in Europe (so was awarding four points for a field goal of fifty yards or longer, but that one didn't make the jump across the pond, much to Sebastian Janikowski's chagrin).

Without a league like NFL Europe, the NFL relies on the college game—which, to be sure, is one of the greatest and cheapest (read: free) farm systems in the pro sports world—for the vast majority of its players, coaches, and innovations.

Hambrecht and his friends were betting that the UFL could help fill a real void.

In 2007 the owners of the UFL hired Michael Huyghue to be the commissioner of the new league. Huyghue is a 1983 graduate of Cornell, where he was a wide receiver on the football team. (While there, he ran routes against Joe's Dartmouth defense three times. Cornell lost each game.) At age twenty-eight, he became the first black general manager in pro football history when he was hired by the WLAF's Birmingham Fire. He later moved into vice-president roles at the NFL's Detroit Lions and Jacksonville Jaguars, handling the team's salary caps. With the Jaguars in "near financial ruin" at $23 million over the salary cap, according to NFL reporter Adam Schefter, Huyghue left the team to start a sports agency. He represented, among others, Adam "Pacman" Jones, Vince Wilfork, and Eric Crouch.

Huyghue is a charismatic man, warm, thoughtful, and always impeccably dressed. To his detractors, his charms merely serve to mask his flaws, the main one being the sin of financial mismanagement.

Huyghue and the UFL owners had grand visions for the league. They started with a plan for eight initial teams and player salaries that ranged from $100,000 to $1 million. It wasn't NFL money, but it wasn't the chump change that the Arena League paid its players ($400 per game). There was even talk about quickly expanding into Canada and Mexico.

But the financial crisis of 2008 put an end to most of those dreams. The league postponed its launch to 2009, and scaled back to four teams—in Orlando, Las Vegas, San Francisco, and New York. By having teams in the latter two cities, which between them host a total of three NFL teams, it went against its own mandate to put teams only in cities that didn't have an NFL team. Those franchises were moved after the first season.

The product on the field was of some quality. It helped that the league was viewed as a last-chance ticket back to the NFL by some of the NFL's former stars. Simeon Rice, Daunte Culpepper, and Dominic Rhodes all found homes there, playing alongside a slew of hungry rookies, many of whom were last cuts in NFL camps. When asked if his team could compete with an NFL team, Jim Fassel, who has coached the Las Vegas Locomotives since the league's inception, claims that on his team's better days, they could indeed beat a lower-tier NFL team. "We'll never be better," says Fassel. "The NFL has the money and the picks of the litter. But we could compete. We're closer to the NFL than Triple-A baseball is to the major leagues."

The high quality of play has a lot to do with the coaching as well. And, as with the players, the quality of that coaching has a lot to do with the NFL. Going into the 2011 season, the league had a stellar lineup of former NFL coaches (plus one former CEO of course) for its five teams—Schottenheimer, Green, Fassel, and Glanville—who for one reason or another, sometimes not very good reasons at all, had been deemed no longer fit for the NFL.

Like Virginia's Schottenheimer, Dennis Green, the Sacramento Mountain Lions head coach, posted some superb regular-season records in the NFL, at least during his tenure in Minnesota. He led the Vikings to a 15-1 record one year and made the NFC Championship game twice, losing both times. His stint with his second NFL team, the Arizona Cardinals, is, for better or worse, remembered mostly for the nonsensical rant he delivered to the media after his team lost to the Chicago Bears on *Monday Night Football*. ("The Bears are what we thought they were... now if you want to crown them, then crown their ass! But they are who we thought they were!") The outburst probably sealed his fate as an NFL coach for good, but it did provide him with a presumably lucrative career as a pitchman for a beer company.

Jim Fassel, the Las Vegas coach, was with the New York Giants from 1997 to 2003. The former NFL coach of the year (1997) made the playoffs three times and went to the Super Bowl in the 2000 season, where his Giants were manhandled by the Baltimore Ravens. After a bizarre loss to the San Francisco 49ers in the 2002 playoffs (the Giants blew a 38–14 third-quarter lead) and a 4-12 season in 2003, Fassel resigned and has never gotten another chance to be a head coach in the NFL.

The Hartford Colonials' Jerry Glanville was the least accomplished of the quartet of former NFL coaches. During his nine-year NFL career with the Houston Oilers and the Atlanta Falcons, he was best known for his sidelines antics, all-black outfits, and for the fact that he frequently left game tickets at the will-call window for Elvis Presley. But even he made the playoffs four times.

Combined, these four men boasted fifty-four years of coaching experience and 431 wins in the NFL. That win total was greater than any single division of coaches in the NFL could claim at the start of the 2011 season. (Only the NFC East's four coaches—which included veterans Mike Shanahan, Andy Reid, and Tom Coughlin—came close, with a combined 408.)

The UFL has given these men the chance to continue to do what they love. Possibly, it even gives them a chance to burnish their reputations enough to get back into the NFL.

Joe, of course, is the outlier, the business guy with exactly zero wins as a head coach at the professional or even collegiate level. His last win as a head coach came back in 1977—as the head coach of a high school team.

Not surprisingly, his hiring raised a few eyebrows among the league's coaches. Fassel says his first thought upon hearing of Joe's appointment was: *What are we doing? If this guy is just doing this as a hobby, then I'm going to be offended. This is my profession.* But Fassel says he talked to Joe and learned about his background and came away impressed. "I loved his passion," he says. And he wasn't worried about Joe's coaching chops. "He's a proven leader." Fassel's assessment, even down to some of the words he uses, is similar to what Tom Osborne had said when trying to talk Joe up to college athletic directors. "Coaching isn't rocket science. You don't have to be a great tactician, you just have to hire the right people, give them the tools, and motivate them and push them to greatness."

Besides, there was some sound tactical logic behind hiring Joe. The league was a mess financially. With Joe, the UFL was getting a two-for-one deal. They got a coach. But they also got someone who could help them figure out how to clean up the finances of the Nighthawks (the team had lost $11 million in 2010)—*and* the league. "To me, that was the attraction of Joe, the financial stuff," says Hambrecht. He certainly needed the help.

⊢+++⊣

To be sure, any start-up venture—and especially one that is going up against an entity as powerful as the NFL—will incur losses, at least in the beginning. But the UFL's first two years seemed even rockier than might have been expected. The league overestimated revenues and underestimated expenses. They were late in payments across the board, from concessionaires to its players (a few companies claim that they've still never been paid for the work they did for the league). The UFL failed to secure national media rights for its games—the lifeblood for any professional sports league—instead opting to *pay* HDNet and Versus for airtime. And given that the league was essentially acting as a farm system for the NFL, having already supplied their teams with more than a hundred players by the end of 2010, getting some kind of support from the NFL, financial or otherwise, seemed like a natural step. But the UFL never succeeded at establishing a working relationship with the NFL. There also seemed to be a serious imbalance in the league's pay structure: the high-profile coaches made around $1 million for the season (Joe, not so high-profile, was being paid $400,000); player salaries, which started in the tens of thousands, had dropped to $5,000 per game (quarterbacks made slightly more).

At the beginning of its third season in 2011, the league's financial situation seemed to be getting even worse. Mark Cuban, who had loaned the league $5 million in seed money (roughly the price of a solid backup quarterback in the NFL), was now suing to get that money back. (Cuban and Hambrecht would eventually work out a settlement, and Cuban says he still has a "debt and not an equity interest in the league.")

The league still had no national media rights deal and looked like it would forgo it completely. Six million dollars left over in bills from 2010—most notably, for worker's compensation—had not yet been paid. The Virginia Destroyers' players had no pads or helmets. (One media pundit in Virginia took to calling the UFL the "Unreliable Football League.") Most troubling, the league had built its season schedule with the expectation that the NFL would have some sort of work stoppage because of the lock-out, either for part or all of its season. The UFL had bet it all on black.

All of these issues would come to a head in July, just when camps were scheduled to begin. That was when Huyghue and the UFL owners would decide to delay the start of the season by thirty days, giving themselves some time to plan and to try to come up with the funding they needed to save the season. And that was when they turned to Joe for help. He was in on nearly every important conference call. In August he flew to Martha's Vineyard to meet Hambrecht and Huyghue and brainstorm. Joe never offered his own money. The league was the sort of unstable investment that he generally shied away from. But he did work hard on trying to solve the league's problems throughout the season. "I always wanted him on the calls, though I don't think he always wanted to do them," says Huyghue. "I think he thought, *Hey, Fassel is spending all day coaching his team, not on the phone*. But Joe's insight was invaluable. His take was fresh. He had no sacred cows."

But Joe actually volunteered to be on the calls because while he had no financial stake in the league, he did have another stake, one that meant much more to him than money: He desperately wanted the season to be played as much as or more than anyone else. He needed the experience for his résumé. If giving them his financial advice would help make sure the season happened, then he was eager to do so. But money wasn't the only problem the UFL had.

In the middle of August the league came up against another kind of trouble. Nevin Shapiro, a University of Miami booster who was in jail for coordinating a $930 million Ponzi scheme, told an interviewer that he had provided illegal benefits to seventy-two Miami athletes from 2002 to 2010. Shapiro had been a part owner of Huyghue's sports agency. And in the interview, he claimed that Huyghue had helped him provide these "benefits" to the college athletes. Huyghue denied the allegations, and Hambrecht stood behind him. "There's never been an ounce of evidence or proof that I did anything wrong," says Huyghue. Still, the UFL's image took yet another hit.

Huyghue says that during the thirty-day delay he actually suggested to the owners that they cancel the season and start fresh in 2012. But Hambrecht believed that losing the 2011 season would sound the death knell for the league. In the end, the owners found just enough money to start the 2011 season. They cut costs by killing the Hartford franchise (Jerry Glanville's team) and by shortening both training camp (to two weeks) and the season (now six games instead of eight) for the four remaining teams. Somehow, the UFL's 2011 season was on.

Hambrecht believed that playing the league's third season would help him secure future investors, a media deal, or maybe even a partnership with the NFL. It was a Hail Mary pass, except that instead of throwing the ball from the 50-yard line, Hambrecht and the other owners were backed up to their own 1.

CHAPTER SIX

Training Camp, Take Two

In late August the Nighthawks report to camp again. Energy crackles through the Kroc. The kids enrolled at the center's day camps stare, wide-eyed and open-mouthed, at the giant men lumbering around in their midst. The players and coaches are ecstatic—if still in something of a state of disbelief—to be here, to have this season brought back to life after it had seemingly flatlined. None of them know the significant role their coach played in saving it.

Some big challenges await the team. The Nighthawks have what amounts to only two weeks of training camp. There's been some serious roster turnover since last they were together—twenty-one of Omaha's players were signed to NFL training camps, the most of any team in the UFL. This is a testament to Mueller's skills as a talent evaluator, but it will make camp more complicated, especially on the offensive side, with new players having to learn the playbook. The team's final roster won't be settled until September 5, the day after the NFL's final cuts, when the Nighthawks may get back some of the players they'd wanted, or add some others.

The night before their first practice, when they will finally take the field for the first time, Joe addresses the full team. They have no idea what they are in for.

Joe stands in the Kroc's dining area. He's dressed in a black Nighthawks T-shirt and shorts, and has a whistle hanging from his neck. He starts out speaking in a low murmur, as if he wants to force the players and coaches to focus intently in order to hear him. He lays out what he calls his fundamental philosophies. Only a few of them have anything directly to do with the game of football itself.

The first philosophy, and the one he will mention at every game and nearly every practice and meeting, is the one that Joe believes to be the fundamental guiding principle of life itself: be a man.

"A man is someone who stands on his own two feet and accepts responsibility for his actions," he says. "We don't have a lot of rules here with the Nighthawks, but the foundation of our program is built on this concept. It carries over into everything you do in your life. It carries over to your families, to how you treat your parents, your wife, your girlfriend, your kids. It carries over into your careers. It carries over into how you handle yourself every day. There is nothing in life that this doesn't touch."

A couple of the players nod. But most sit in silence, perhaps waiting to see where this is going.

"Respect is a by-product of being a man," Joe continues. "You guys have been stars all your life. You've been treated differently than nearly everyone else because you have a gift: you are great football players. This treatment has given you—all of us—a feeling of entitlement that sometimes diverts our focus. We feel this sense of entitlement, but we shouldn't. We need to take responsibility for our own lives. We need to treat everyone with respect, to treat everyone like you would treat your own family. Treat the women you see here at the Kroc, in Omaha, just as you would your own mother."

As Joe says this, a woman who is hidden behind a curtain somewhere in the dining area suddenly calls out, in a world-weary voice: "Amen, brother!"

Then comes Joe's selling point. "We—the staff here on the Nighthawks—will do everything in our power to get you into the NFL," he says. But he tells them making it there will ultimately come down to their actions: their play on the field, their consistency on tape, their ability to rebound from a bad play and not make the same mistake twice. "The NFL will be halfway through its season by the time we're done. You will have played six games. You will be ready."

Then, the business pitch, words perhaps never uttered before to these football players. "I've found throughout my career in business and football that if you are really going to be successful, you have to figure out how to differentiate yourself from others. This means leveraging your core competencies. Discover your strengths and talents and use them to get your competitive advantage."

Suddenly, the players are students in an MBA class.

"Again, this extends to more things than just football. This will help you in your life, as a husband, a boyfriend, a son, a father."

Then, unexpectedly, comes talk about the end of their careers. "The reality is that you absolutely know that your football career has a limit. Whether you end up playing another five days or another five years, it's time to start thinking about what you will do with the rest of your life." Every week during camp and the season, Joe tells them, he will be hosting something he calls "Life after Football," where he will talk about things like how to find a job and how to establish a personal budget. These sessions will be voluntary, he tells them, "but I would suggest you take advantage of them."

Joe stops for a moment, the dramatic pause of a seasoned speaker. He looks down and brings his fingers to his lips. "At the end of the day, this is what I see," he says, with just the slightest passing note of an Inwood accent. The players sit up straight in their chairs, wondering where this could possibly go next. "'Football is life,' goes the old mantra. It is the greatest game on earth. And yes, it does teach you about life. But it is not life. The bottom line is that it is a game. But it is a game we have all chosen to be part of. Enjoy it. Treasure it. And most of all, have some fun."

The last line seems to resonate with the players. These are guys who were once the best players on their teams, in their states, maybe even in the entire country, as Joe has reminded them. They were once highly recruited high schoolers, courted by the world's greatest football factory colleges. Then they were college players—great ones—with their own ESPN.com player pages and NFL draft rankings. They seemed to overflow, once, with potential greatness.

But for whatever reason, that potential was never fully realized when they got to the professional level. They got injured, overlooked, cut. Some had had a taste of the NFL only to have it taken away. Some had never had a seat at the table. They were now professional athletes at the very margins of their sport, scrambling for their last shot to capture the glory that was now fading like daylight at the bottom of a deep, cold canyon. Their big dreams, which had once seemed very achievable if not inevitable, had been dashed along the way, in a sometimes brutal fashion. It had been a while for many of these players since the game of football had been all about fun.

⊢┼┼┼┤

After that first meeting, the players knew that this season would be different from any they'd experienced before. It was a good bet that no other professional football coach in the country was talking about core competencies and life after football.

Joe had gone out on a limb and opened himself to possible

ridicule. He was an unproven commodity, out of football for decades. His players and most of his coaches had never even heard of him until just a few months beforehand. And here he was, talking mostly about things that, on the surface, seemed to have little to do with their game. In this cynical, snarky age, his words could have been seen as exceedingly corny and easily mockable. They seemed like something a college coach—or even a high school coach—would say. And indeed they were, for they were the same words Joe himself had once used. The game might have changed and the level at which he was coaching certainly had. But Joe had not. That stuff about being a man and treating women with respect? It was literally right out of the playbook of his first head-coaching job at Archmere Academy, back in 1971.

Except now he was dealing with players who, for the most part, and for better or for worse, had already been molded into men by the ups and downs and various hardships of the game and their lives. They were professionals. They still loved the game, but they played it for money. They would be naturally harder to reach. It was a risky approach on Joe's part. His players could feel pandered to, could feel like they were being treated like boys. But this was Joe. This was how he did things, as a coach, as a businessman. This is what he believed was right. He was not afraid to put himself on the line.

Some players bought in right away. Others held back, slightly skeptical.

During training camp in football, there is no sense of individual days of the week, save for Sundays, when players report to the facility at noon, allowing them to sleep in or attend religious services. Camp is a blur of meetings, practices, weight lifting, treatment, and eating. As part of the NFL's new collective bargaining agreement, their teams can no longer practice in pads twice in a given day (known as "two-a-days"). The UFL doesn't have that rule. And for the first week of camp, Joe drives his team hard, making them do two-a-days for five straight days in temperatures that reach as high as ninety-eight degrees. With time so short, he feels like he has to push them. But there is a delicate balance between going too hard and not hard enough.

The practices all start with "individual" drills. The offensive linemen gather in the corner of one end zone with Don Lawrence, and endlessly work on the transition from a three-point stance (one hand on the ground) to the standing position, where they shuffle backward on their feet as they "punch" the onrushing defender. At the other end of the field, coaches Brandon Noble and Mike Gallagher bounce huge exercise balls at their defensive linemen, who sprint toward the balls, then bend down and thrust their arms skyward to catch them. The drill is meant to help them focus on gaining leverage at the line of scrimmage. Brock Olivo uses a broomstick with a red boxing glove taped to one end to try to punch the ball loose from his running backs, who all seem to be made up only of thick legs, big butts, and rounded trapezius muscles. Kevin Daft's comparatively lithe receivers run through agility ladders splayed on the ground and catch balls fired at them with serious velocity from a JUGS machine.

Eventually, practice moves into its "team" phase, where the coaches run the offense against the defense, first in seven-on-seven plays, then with the full eleven-on-eleven.

The offense, as might be expected because of the unfamiliar scheme, looks off-kilter. The linemen are having trouble maintaining the wide splits, which are completely foreign to them. Joe goes so far as to bring an actual yardstick to the field, and he frequently stops practice to measure the distance between the linemen, to make sure they are spread far enough apart. Later, Don Lawrence will pore over the practice film of his guys, using a remote control device known as a Cowboy clicker to maniacally rewind and fast-forward individual plays. What he'll see is linemen who are slow to react, who are still learning, and who are routinely being run through by the defense. Lawrence will just shake his old, bald head. "That's a tough deal," he'll say, over and over again.

Crouch and Masoli are particularly off, missing open receivers on short routes and demonstrating little ability to throw effective deep balls. Andrus's offense is designed to make big plays, but right now even the small ones seem unachievable. It doesn't help that Maurice Purify, perhaps the Nighthawks' best receiver, who once had a cup of coffee with the Cincinnati Bengals, tears a medial collateral ligament in his knee during the first practice and is done for the year.

The defense, however, looks solid, particularly in the secondary, which is loaded with NFL veterans like Reynaldo Hill (Titans), Ricardo Colclough (Steelers), DeMarcus Faggins (Texans), Clinton Hart (Chargers), Stuart Schweigert (Raiders), and Eric Green (Cardinals). It is not unusual for the defense to be ahead of the offense in camp: with fewer plays to install, that side of the ball is more instinctive early on. But with the Nighthawks offense playing so poorly, Olivadotti says he has no read on the quality of his defense.

The problem of player evaluations is particularly challenging in the UFL for several reasons. "The cart is before the horse here. Usually, you look at a guy on tape then bring him in. Here we bring a guy in to see if we want to look at him on tape," says Olivadotti. "And usually there are three phases to the evaluation period of the players you've got. The coaches install the plays. Then the players put on pads and forget everything they've learned. Then there are the preseason games, where the real competition for spots and the real evaluation takes place." Since the UFL has no preseason games, Olivadotti says he won't know what he really has until after the first game.

Nonetheless, Joe finds his rhythm right away. He situates himself into his coaching pose on the slanted Kroc field: legs akimbo, arms across his chest, thumb and forefinger on his chin, the brim of his Nighthawks hat pulled over his eyes. During the first week of camp, he stops practice occasionally to chastise the players for being sloppy, or for not paying attention to the action when they are on the sidelines (what he calls taking "mental reps"). He seems relaxed and very much in his element. Joe often stands deep in the secondary during team drills, scanning the field, intently watching the entirety of the action. "You need not see what someone is doing/to know if it is his vocation/you have only to watch his eyes," as Auden wrote.

Still, he feels the pressure and knows the stakes. "The bottom line is that if I don't win any games this season, I'm pretty sure my career in football is over," he says.

In the evenings, Joe makes the last half hour of dinner mandatory for everyone on the team. The reason: each night, for the duration of training camp, he will be asking the players and coaches, one by one, to stand up at dinner and introduce themselves. He wants them to talk not only about their careers in football but also about their lives. A few of the more bashful players will end up talking for only thirty seconds or so. But most of the folks jump at the opportunity to share their stories.

A few of the coaches go first. Olivadotti is short and to the point, briefly glossing over his impressive résumé to tell the players that they "all have God-given talent and it would be a sin for us not to get it out of you." Robert Hunt, who assists Don Lawrence with the offensive line, talks about his own short NFL career, with the Tampa Bay Buccaneers. "I still have my signing bonus. I'm driving it right now. I've been driving it for twelve years." (It's a big black Suburban with dinged-up bumpers and balding tires.) Richard Kent, the jittery special teams coach, stands and speaks in his "hoarse farmer's voice," as Joe calls it, and admits that he's "a little weird sometimes."

Then it's the players' turn. Some of them talk about their jobs outside of football. Crouch sells medical devices that help women deal with vaginal prolapse. ("You don't want to know what that is," he tells the team.) Linebacker Angelo Crowell, once the captain of the Buffalo Bills defense, is a Jersey Mike's Subs franchisee. Hulking defensive end Curtis Johnson is a professional bass fisherman. Linebacker Morlon Greenwood, who sports a black tattoo that encircles his bald head like a Roman wreath, is a rapper known as Ultimate 56.

Safety Stuart Schweigert talks about his four-year stint as a starter for the Raiders, and says he has a young daughter. "If anyone has any advice for having a boy, I'm all ears," he says. Someone from the crowd yells: "Keep your socks on!" Schweigert also mentions his collection of more than 150 throwback sports uniforms, including a 1987 Central Michigan University Dan Majerle basketball jersey ("He's a bad-ass white boy from Michigan, just like me," says Schweigert) and a 1978 New England Whalers Gordie Howe hockey sweater. The only one he doesn't seem to have is a Greg Louganis throwback diving Speedo. "I don't think I'll be getting that one," he says.

The introductions go on every night. Walter Curry Jr., a gentle-looking bearded giant, tells the room that he's a member of the PEFL: "Played in Every Football League." And indeed many of these players and coaches have been, for most of their professional football lives, in the here-today-gone-tomorrow subculture of alternative football leagues.

One common thread among the guys who have had careers in the NFL is that injuries are the reason many of those careers were derailed. Nose tackle Dusty Dvoracek was All-Big 12 in both academics and football at the University of Oklahoma. He was drafted by the Bears but was injured in his first two seasons. In the fourteenth game of his third season—a stellar one to that point—he tore his biceps while tackling the Vikings running back Adrian Peterson. "No NFL team wants a guy with an injury history like mine," he tells the room. "I want to show that I can stay healthy, and make it back to the NFL. I love the violence of this game. I love the locker room."

Fellow defensive lineman Jay Moore, a big, brooding blond-haired man, was drafted out of Nebraska in 2007 by the 49ers, but was hurt almost immediately and had to sit out a year. Then he, too, tore his biceps the following year. He is now back living with his parents in Omaha, which has a few perks, like the free taxi service they provided him to and from social gatherings.

Chad Jackson, whose eyes have the luster of black onyx, was taken by the Patriots in the second round of the 2006 NFL Draft, but he tore his ACL in the AFC Championship game that year against the Indianapolis Colts. Christian Anthony, a defensive end, had a heart attack in 2010. Dan Gay, an offensive lineman, has a cyst on his heart. "No NFL team wants to touch me," he says. Cornerback Dovonte Edwards intercepted a Brett Favre pass on *Monday Night Football* in 2005 and returned it for a touchdown. The next year his NFL career came to a halt because of an arm injury.

Many of the players are professed Christians, especially Schweigert, the receivers, Andrew Brewer and Roy Hall, and the long snapper, Matt Overton.

One of the players went to Yale (the punter, Tom Mante).

Another common theme for many of the players is that they came from broken—sometimes badly broken—homes. Clinton Hart's father was in jail during most of his childhood, and the safety still has a visible dent in his head from where his aunt dropped him when he was six months old while she was fighting with her boyfriend. Reynaldo Hill stands one night, his bushel of cornrows held behind his head with an elastic band, and talks about his drug-dealing father, and how he turned to other members of his family and outdoor play for succor as a child. The sugarcane company next door to his house used to burn its fields every year, and Hill would chase down the fleeing rabbits for food. (That's how he found out he was quick.) Both of running back Noel Devine's parents were dead of AIDS by the time he was eleven years old. Devine had two children of his own by the time he was in junior high.

Football has been the centerpiece of these players' lives. It is the reason they were injured. It is the reason that they fight back from these injuries. Football is what saved them from their fractured home lives, from futures that might have been irretrievably lost, from the fate of others—both family and friends—who weren't lucky enough to be big, strong, fast, and agile.

On the seventh night of training camp, Maurice Clarett, the troubled former Ohio State star, stands to speak at dinner. This is the introduction that many have been waiting for. The dining room goes utterly silent; there are no forks scraping plates, no ice tinkling in water glasses.

Clarett speaks in a raspy, barely audible whisper. His voice, like Mike Tyson's lisp, doesn't seem to fit his body—five-eleven and 230 muscled pounds—nor does its softness jibe with what the public knows about his past. His gentle, thoughtful demeanor does, however, seem in sync with his current path, which is taking him on a long, slow walk toward redemption.

Clarett begins by telling the room that football was his first true love. He played the sport nearly every afternoon in his Youngstown, Ohio, neighborhood. When it rained he played carpet football with his brothers inside the house. He would pretend to be Emmitt Smith or Thurman Thomas.

But trouble happened to be his other passion. He was arrested multiple times before he was fourteen years old, mainly, he says, because he was trying to impress the older kids in the neighborhood. In the eighth grade he was arrested for breaking and entering a house. While attempting to flee the scene, he jumped out of a second-story window and hit his head. He got thirteen stitches for the wound. That's why, since high school, he has always worn the number 13 on the football field.

He was sent to a juvenile detention center. There he met a high school football coach who took him under his wing, and who intervened on his behalf with the judge and negotiated a house arrest. Clarett worked out with the coach every day after school.

In high school, Clarett was a dynamo on the field. He rushed for 248 yards in one of his first games as a freshman. He says he never really went to class, and he was allowed to slip through the academic cracks because of his football ability. In his senior year he was named the best prep player in the state of Ohio. He was heavily recruited, but decided to stay near home and attend Ohio State. He loved the coach there, Jim Tressel.

Clarett made the team as a freshman as a backup running back. Tressel told him that in the team's first game—at home against Texas Tech—Clarett would get three series of work. "I did nothing in my first two series," says Clarett. But on the third one, he broke a long run. The home crowd went crazy. "The fans put you in games, at least at Ohio State," he says. He finished that game with 175 rushing yards and three touchdowns.

He was a hard worker in practice and in games. But off the field, he was living a completely different life. "I took golf, fishing, and softball as classes," Clarett says. "Away from class, anything you can think of I did in my thirteen months at Ohio State." Drugs and women were two of the things. Cars were another—he owned three of them at a time, including a brand-new Cadillac and Lexus. "I was living the NFL life in college," he says. "I got paid more in college than I do now in the UFL."

In the 2003 national championship game against Miami, Clarett made the two crucial plays that led to Ohio State's win: He stripped the ball from Sean Taylor's hands after the Miami safety had intercepted a pass in his own end zone, which led to three important points for the Buckeyes. Then he scored the championship-winning touchdown in overtime. The sky seemed like the only limit for Clarett.

Instead the sky fell on him. Clarett was suspended from the team for receiving what were deemed "improper benefits." He also falsely alleged that $10,000 worth of goods had been stolen from him. (He later pled guilty to the lesser charge of failure to aid a law enforcement official.) Clarett tried to enter the NFL Draft. But by NFL rules, a player had to be at least three years out of high school to become eligible. He sued. His case eventually went to the Supreme Court. He lost.

The next two years were lost in a fog of drug and alcohol use. "I would ride around in my car carrying life sentences, with pounds of weed and bricks of cocaine," he says. In 2005 he worked out at the NFL's Draft Combine and performed woefully, mainly because he was high on marijuana most of the time. Surprisingly, he was drafted by the Denver Broncos in the third round that year. In Denver's training camp, he says, he was partying hard at nights and clashing with his coaches during the day. He was cut before the end of camp.

And that was when the real trouble began. "I was popping pills and getting paranoid. I was robbing everyone I knew," he says. In January 2006 he was arrested in Columbus for allegedly robbing two people at gunpoint and taking $150 and a cell phone. His trial was postponed until September.

Clarett says he didn't want to go to jail. So he attempted to pay off the man whom he had robbed. He wanted him to drop the charges. The man refused to be bought. On a night one month before the trail, Clarett's life literally came to its crossroads.

Clarett jumped into his car wearing Kevlar body armor and carrying a loaded assault rifle and three handguns. He drank half a bottle of Grey Goose vodka as he drove. He missed his intended exit off the freeway. He got off at the next exit and made an illegal U-turn. A cop car happened to be there. The cops pulled him over and used Mace to subdue him.

That U-turn may have saved his life and the lives of several others. He'd been on his way to that man's house.

He was sentenced to seven and a half years in prison. "Contrary to popular belief, prison does not give you street cred. Anyone who glorifies it is an idiot," he says. "It only lets your dumb ass know that you got caught doing something wrong."

But prison turned out to be a good thing for Clarett. It was where the fog finally started to lift. "I cleared my head, away from the drugs and drinking," he says. "Suffering causes you to mature." He became a voracious reader, knocking out 150 books in prison, including the works of Tolstoy, Twain, and Confucius. He became particularly interested in finance and subscribed to *Forbes*, *Fortune*, and the *Wall Street Journal*, teaching himself about the stock market. He read everything he could about his new hero, Warren Buffett. He started a blog, *The Mind of Maurice Clarett*, filled with aphorisms that he read over the prison phone to his girlfriend, who posted them. He was released from prison early for good behavior, to a halfway house. He tried out for the Nighthawks in 2010 and made the team, playing sparingly while struggling mightily to get back into shape.

Clarett ends his introduction by talking about his long road to redemption, the joy he finds in simple freedoms like watching his five-year-old daughter run around the house. He talks about the positive example he wants to set for people, to help them avoid the trouble he'd found in his life.

"I don't want people to say 'Don't be like Maurice Clarett,'" he says. "In fact, I want the opposite. I want people to see me now and say they want to be like me. And I'm working every day to earn that."

As Clarett wraps up, there are audible gasps and a few whispered "holy shit"s in the room. Some of the coaches stare at Clarett with stunned, almost fearful looks on their faces. There is a brief silent pause as Clarett sits down. Then the players and coaches slowly disperse.

When Joe gets up to speak, the last to do so after two weeks of introductions, he tells the team about his coaching and business background. But he mainly focuses on his childhood. It was by no stretch of the imagination as rough as what some of his players went through. But Joe's childhood was no piece of cake. He can relate to their experience. He had the same toughness, the same powerful motivation to get out. And just as football saved many of these players from wasted lives, to a large degree it had done the same for Joe. "Here's the bottom line," he says. "If you came from a privileged background, then you owe it to yourself to do well in life. If you came from a background that was bad and you made it out, that's a competitive advantage." Around the room, there are more nods now. The business-speak is starting to make more sense.

Joe's idea for doing these introductions was to allow the team members to get to know each other better, to help them find people with similar interests, even to encourage them to network for future jobs. But what these introductions end up doing is creating a strong emotional bond, something approaching love.

CHAPTER SEVEN

Game On

Since there are no preseason games in the UFL, the Nighthawks are forced to hold two intrasquad scrimmages. They are announced via the team's website and Twitter account, and through the *Omaha World-Herald*, which is the only press outlet that's covering the team. (The beat writer is a bearded man named Steven Pivovar, who, deep in Cornhusker territory, wears a University of Texas hat. "I like to swim upstream," he says.)

Joe is sure that Virginia, the first opponent the Nighthawks will be facing once the season begins, will have scouts at both scrimmages, even though it's technically against league rules. But Joe sees this circumstance as a chance for a bit of subterfuge. In the press and on blogs and websites, the Nighthawks' new offense has mostly been characterized—wrongly—as a true option offense, akin to the old Wishbone attack, where the quarterback runs and either keeps the ball or pitches it to a back running parallel to him. Joe wants to play up that perception so that Virginia might use up valuable practice time preparing for it. He draws up two plays for the scrimmages, "UFL Option Pitch," in which the quarterback will pitch the ball to the running back, and "UFL Option Keep," in which he will keep it and run. "Let the defense know when either play is called," says Joe. "We want the runners to gain some serious yards before they are tackled."

Olivadotti, who wants to remain the alpha dog of his defense and not call a soft play, says, with a serious laugh: "*You* tell the defense and *you* make that call for them, Joe."

On the day of the first scrimmage, which is held at the Kroc, it's ninety-five degrees outside. The blustery prairie wind offers no relief and instead feels like the breath of a dragon. A smattering of fans gathers, draping their arms over the fence that encloses the field, like railbirds watching the racehorses. Four of them are wearing overalls, looking like they just stepped off the tractor. Joe calls the first play, "UFL Option Keep."

Masoli, who has just returned to the team after being cut by the 49ers, receives the ball in the shotgun formation and rolls to his right. He fakes a pitch to the running back, Shaud Williams, then turns upfield, no doubt expecting to gain an easy fifteen yards before being gently taken to the ground.

But there's a problem. A new guy had come in late the night before, a rookie safety named Mike O'Connell. He's a bit undersized for the position, but he is known for his ferocious hits and total lack of regard for his own body (he had once perforated his bowel while blocking a kick in high school). Someone forgot to tell O'Connell about the special plays.

So instead of a leisurely run through the defense, Masoli is met at the line of scrimmage and violently popped into his back by 200 pounds of eager white safety.

O'Connell jumps to his feet and pumps his fist, turning to what he believes are the welcoming arms of his new defensive mates. But his teammates are actually throwing their arms up in the air. "*What the hell is wrong with you, kid?*"

Later on in the scrimmage, during a kickoff, O'Connell—on the coverage team—makes a classic tackle on the returner, wrapping him in his arms, picking him up off his feet, and driving him into the turf. This time his teammates return his backslaps. Joe turns to Olivadotti and raises his eyebrows. "I like that kid," he says.

Otherwise, the scrimmage is putrid. The special teams are completely disorganized. The offense is worse, committing four turnovers that the defense returns for touchdowns. And the stifling heat turns what Joe envisioned as a crisp, energetic scrimmage into more of a slow-walking death march. Joe gathers the team at midfield after the final whistle. "This does not cut it!"

Later, at the coaches' meeting, Joe first addresses Andrus and his offensive staff. "We are focusing on too much stuff that doesn't matter. I'm starting to get worried about time. We have one more week of camp, then it's game week. There really is no time. I would rather run one play, and run it really well, than run fifteen crappy plays."

Then he turns his gaze on Kent, the special teams coach. But before he can get a word out, Kent speaks. "I'm sorry, Coach. That was chaotic out there. I'm really embarrassed."

Joe's message to him is similar to the one he had for Andrus. "Don't be embarrassed, but let's fix this. Don't do too much yourself, or you'll just keep spinning your wheels. Be phenomenal at the things you have to do, cut back, or ask for help."

In the week leading up to the second and final scrimmage, Mueller springs some surprising news on the coaching staff. He has signed Troy Smith, the 2006 Heisman Trophy–winning quarterback who started six games for the 49ers in 2010, and was named the NFL's offensive player of the week after one of those starts. The 49ers had not re-signed Smith. He had nowhere else to go. Joe tells the coaches that Smith will be the third-string quarterback, at least until he learns the offense. Some coaches and players express concerns that Smith, who is known for being willful and vocal in the locker room, will not accept that diminished a role on the team. But Joe has spoken to him at length on the phone. "I told him if he's trouble, we'll cut him," says Joe. With Smith the Nighthawks now have two former Heisman-winning quarterbacks. He will be making the UFL-mandated salary for a third-string quarterback: $2,000 a game.

The three Nighthawks quarterbacks are a study in contrasts. Crouch is clean-shaven with a boyish shock of brown hair, the All-American kid. He wears a white towel around his neck at nearly all times, giving the impression of a boxer who has just finished a training session. Masoli has big, curly, unkempt hair and a perpetual five o'clock shadow. He has a body more like a running back's: short and squat, with calves shaped like bowling pins. He's nearly a dead ringer for the Vincent Chase character on the former HBO show *Entourage*. (To perfect the resemblance, Vince would need to stand in front of one of those funhouse mirrors that make you look shorter and wider.) Smith, the only one with NFL experience, has a neatly trimmed Afro and Fu Manchu, and he wears diamond studs in his ears. The other two may run a bit better, but Smith throws the best deep ball of the trio, by far. But he has weeks to go before he will completely grasp the playbook. And anyway, despite his credentials, he'd have a tough time cracking the starting lineup right away. Joe has a virtue that can sometimes become a fault: he is intensely loyal. Crouch and Masoli have been with the team for most of the season, starting in minicamp. They have proven their loyalty to Joe and the team. Joe, in return, will reciprocate. If Joe and the team lose because of that loyalty, then so be it.

The second scrimmage, to be played in the Nighthawks' home stadium, TD Ameritrade Park, will be a true dress rehearsal. (The park got its naming rights in 2009, after Joe left TD Ameritrade, and before he joined the Nighthawks.) Joe wants the team to do exactly what they will do on game day, from wearing their actual jerseys, to performing the pregame warm-ups, to going into the locker room at halftime. The day before the scrimmage, he even has the team practice standing for the National Anthem. These details may seem trivial, inessential. But they do matter. John Wooden, the great UCLA basketball coach, used to have his players practice putting on their socks. "Details create success," Wooden once said.

The details matter for Joe personally, too. As much as he wants his team to go through the motions, he also wants to simulate the experience for himself so that *he* will be more comfortable on game day, so it will all be less of an unknown. After all, he hasn't actually been responsible for leading a team on the field for nearly thirty years.

The scrimmage will also be the last act before final cuts. The roster of 70 will need to be trimmed to 51 (the NFL has rosters of 53; the UFL slices off two from that total, presumably to save some money).

Joe is still worried about the offense. He does a spreadsheet. By his count, a redshirt freshman college quarterback will have taken 6,440 snaps in a particular system before he starts in his junior year. Crouch and Masoli will each have taken 659 snaps by the end of camp. And Andrus still hasn't fully installed the powerball portion of the offensive scheme. "I think I've put an unfair burden on the offense," says Joe. "It's haunting me."

He's not terribly worried about the defense even though, with the offense's struggles, it's hard to know just how good the unit is. Olivadotti will miss the second scrimmage. His mother has died and her funeral is on the same day. Her death caps off a very tough year for Olivadotti, who has also lost his father and stepfather (the latter to a suicide) and learned that his four year-old granddaughter has leukemia. (On the night of the scrimmage, Olivadotti will go to a beach in New Jersey to fulfill his mother's last wish to have her remains spread in the surf. But when he tosses the ashes, his Super Bowl ring comes loose and is flung into the ocean. It has escaped the "safe" that is his finger. The next morning, knowing that it was a long shot, he went back to the beach to look for it. He didn't find it, but he did meet a rotund, mustachioed man with a metal detector who was walking the beach. He offered the man $1,000 if he found and returned the ring, which is about $9,000 less than it takes to replace it. The guy actually did find it. He sent it back to Olivadotti along with a few pictures of him and his friends—Giants fans, it turned out—posing with the ring on.)

Marvin Sanders, the secondary coach, and Pete Kuharchek, the linebackers coach, will fill in for Olivadotti. Football teams essentially become large, overnight families, where wins and losses—personal and on the field—are shared, and responsibility is picked up when needed.

Just before the scrimmage the Nighthawks get a few more players back from NFL camps, most important among them George Foster, a Brinks-truck-bodied left tackle who was with the Saints until their final cuts; and Greg Orton, a wide receiver who'd been in camp with the Broncos and whom Joe calls "cross-country" because of his spindly lower legs. Greg Ryan, an offensive lineman from Western Kentucky, is signed on the day of his wedding. He and his new bride leave their reception and drive overnight to camp. "Let's give them the honeymoon suite at the hotel," says personnel man Matt Boockmeier.

In the second scrimmage, the offense finally shows some signs of life. Crouch and Masoli take the majority of the snaps, and they each toss a touchdown pass. Smith gets in for the last ten minutes, and looks confident at the line of scrimmage. Maybe 1,000 fans show up for the free intrasquad game. Joe gets a microphone at the end of the scrimmage and thanks them for coming. He has his players sign autographs in the stands for half an hour after the game.

ⱶⱶⱶⱶ

Then it's cut day, which is always brutal, but perhaps more so in the UFL. This is pretty much the end of the line (the CFL and the indoor leagues being alternatives that few of these men would accept). The UFL is a cruel twist on the Liza Minnelli/ Frank Sinatra song: If you can't make it here, you can't make it anywhere. The former NFL players all have horrible stories from cut days, of players openly weeping or falling to their knees and begging to stay. One cut player was found at a pawnshop attempting to purchase a gun. There really is no right way to go about telling players that they didn't make the team. But there are some wrong ways to do it—namely, out in public, in front of everyone else. Noble, the defensive line coach and former NFL player, remembers one cut day with the Dallas Cowboys when the personnel guys walked around practice as the players were stretching and tapped guys on the shoulder for the ride to the airport. The person who delivers the news to a cut player goes by a few different names. One is "the reaper." The other is "the Turk," a name derived from the Ottoman Empire, which at one time apparently led the world league in beheadings.

The unspoken truth in professional football is that the players are, ultimately, commodities. Once vigorously pursued and wooed, if they don't deliver on expectations they are dumped. This is the part of the pro game that Joe hates. It's something he wouldn't have had to face in the college game. But he has to play the part now.

Shockley and Clark are let go to make room for Smith. Shockley is a tough cut because he is very well liked and respected by his teammates. Clark takes to Twitter to voice his displeasure, charging the Nighthawks front office with leading him on. Linebacker proves to be a difficult position to trim down. In the end, Matt Wenger, a solid rookie—but still a rookie—goes while Steve Octavien, who has the name of a Roman Caesar and the body of a gladiator, stays. O'Connell makes the team, pretty much based on his two hits in the first scrimmage. Punter Tom Mante from Yale—the only Ivy Leaguer in the UFL—is kept.

The only real conflict comes with Clarett. The offensive coaches believe he's had a terrible camp. He hasn't run with any burst, and he's had trouble catching the ball out of the backfield, an essential skill for a running back in Andrus's offense. There is also a sense that he's been a bit of a malcontent.

But there is something else in the coaches' voices as they talk about Clarett, something that sounds a bit like fear, as if they are wary of him, the way one would be around a stray pit bull. That he could snap at any moment. They tell Joe they want to cut him.

Joe dances around the issue for a few minutes, asking if they are sure, if there's really no room for a power back (the team has no other running back as big as Clarett). But they say they don't want him.

But Joe knows something they don't. What Clarett had left out of his introduction speech was his relationship with his new coach. After the 2010 season with the Nighthawks, Clarett wasn't sure he wanted to keep playing football. But when Joe was hired to coach the team in early 2011, they talked on the phone multiple times. Clarett told him his story. "I told him I wanted to turn my life around," he says. Something about Clarett hit Joe right where it counted. He saw a man looking for help, something he thought he could provide. He asked Clarett to try out for the 2011 team, promising to help him during and after the season.

Late that spring, before minicamp, Joe remembered Clarett's interest in finance and his reading about a certain famous Omahan. He got an idea.

"Want to meet Warren Buffett?" Joe asked Clarett.

On a Saturday afternoon, Clarett walked in the doors of Berkshire Hathaway and there stood Buffett, paper come to life, and a man whose circumstances could not have been more different from his own. "It was overwhelming at first. I had no idea what we were going to talk about," Clarett says, looking back on that day. "I'm young and black. I don't get many opportunities to get access to a man like that." But the two men got along splendidly. Buffett says they talked about "life and chasing your dreams."

Joe had tried to help Clarett even further, calling Father Steven Boes at Omaha's Boys Town, hoping to secure a job or internship or anything for Clarett after the season. "I'm really sorry, Joe, but we can't take convicted felons," Father Boes had told him.

Joe listens to his coaches talk about Clarett for a while, then suddenly stops them. "Look, I have confidence in your decisions as coordinators and coaches. That's why I hired you. But Maurice is different," he tells them. His face, which reddens easily, is doing so now. "This guy's been in friggin' jail. I visited his mother. He moved his family here. I had to talk to his probation officer. He wants to do better. We are not turning our back on this guy. This is not an excuse, however. He still has to live up to his commitment to us.

"When I hired you, I asked you if you bought into this program. You all said you did. This goes right back to our core values. We're in the business of motivating and inspiring people. People continually remind me that this game—pro football—is a business. I gotta say, I'm sick of hearing that. I know this game is a business. I think I know a thing or two about business. And the most important thing to know about business is that it's about people. That was true at TD Ameritrade. That's true in football. This *is* a people business. We will never turn our backs on that." This is the lesson he learned from his mother.

Joe has taken responsibility for Clarett. He intends to live up to it. Clarett is on the team. He will get only a handful of carries in actual games, and will primarily be used as a cover man in special teams and as a scout team running back in practice. He will accept this role on the team with the eagerness and gratitude of a drowning man who has been thrown a lifeline.

And at precisely the moment when Joe needs him the most, Clarett will richly reward his loyalty.

⊢┼┼┼⊣

The team of fifty-one is set for its first game, against Schottenheimer's Virginia Destroyers. Leading up to the game, there are reports that Hurricane Irene has damaged some of Virginia's practice facilities. Some coaches believe that's a good thing. Joe's not so sure. "If we're going to beat someone, I don't want it to be because God interfered with something like a hurricane," he says. "Now, if He wants them to lose an untimely fumble, that's a whole other thing."

⊢┼┼┼⊣

On a chilly and wet night in Omaha, the Nighthawks win the coin toss and decide to kick the ball. The kickoff coverage team takes the field, wearing the team's imposing all-black uniforms and helmet adorned on each side with a stencil of a flying F-115 fight plane (known as the "Nighthawk," of course). On the back of the helmet, just above the player's number, is the acronym "B.A.M," the same three letters found all over the walls of the team's practice facility, the locker room, and at the bottom of every piece of paper printed for the organization. It stands, of course, for Joe's daily reminder to each member of the team to "Be A Man." Two of tonight's referees would have a difficult time doing that: they are female. Just before the opening whistle, the scoreboard reads "VD vs. ONH" momentarily, until someone wisely changes it to "VA vs. OH." Then the ball is kicked off.

Omaha forces a punt on Virginia's first drive and takes over possession at its own 18-yard line. The offense, the primary source of concern in the Nighthawks two-week camp, takes the field.

But Crouch, in his first live game since 2006 (then with the CFL's Toronto Argonauts), eases that anxiety somewhat on the team's first drive, quickly moving the offense into Virginia territory with four pinpoint passes. But the drive stalls, and the Nighthawks punt.

The first quarter goes back and forth like this, with Olivadotti's defense holding against his former boss's offense, and the Virginia defense doing just enough to keep Omaha's offense—which is moving well behind both Crouch and Masoli—from scoring. Omaha's biggest problem is itself: on offense, there are dropped passes and numerous penalties for false starts, holding, and illegal formations. The special teams are having penalty problems of their own, flagged for being offside and for having twelve men on the field.

Schottenheimer spends the game expertly working the refs—jawing, cajoling, smiling—particularly one of the women, who is on his sideline. Joe is calm on the sidelines. He talks into his headset and occasionally huddles with Andrus and Kent. (Olivadotti coaches from a box high above the field from which he feels he can see the action better.) Joe spends a few minutes early on standing away from the players and coaches, near the 20-yard line, observing his team from a distance, striving, it seems, for some perspective. The light rain continues to fall, turning the stadium's grass a luminous green. The crowd of sixteen thousand is very attentive and very loud.

The first quarter ends in a scoreless draw.

Early in the second quarter, Omaha's offense reveals its potential weakness, the reason that coaches in the pro game have shied away from it. Crouch throws a short incompletion, then his receivers drop two passes. The offense is on the field for less than a minute, in real time. The problem with these short possessions is that they result in the opposite of the offense's intended effect: they tire out their own defense.

After the punt, Omaha has its first lapse on defense. Chris Greisen, Virginia's veteran quarterback, completes a 73-yard pass. Two plays later, Dominic Rhodes—who gained 113 yards and scored a touchdown in the 2007 Super Bowl for the victorious Indianapolis Colts—rumbles in for a 3-yard touchdown. (In 2011 Rhodes was suspended by the NFL for his third violation of the league's substance abuse policy. He was free to play in the UFL, though, and would end up the league's offensive MVP.)

But Masoli responds, leading the team on a 70-yard drive, using both his arm and his legs. The drive ends with his beautifully rainbowed, 20-yard touchdown pass to Chad Jackson.

The ballgame is tied at seven.

But another special teams penalty gives the ball to the Destroyers at their own 40-yard line with eight minutes left in the half. Joe purses his lips into a scowl on the sidelines, the first sign of his mounting frustration with his team's mistakes. Behind short, effective passing from Greisen and punishing runs from Rhodes, Virginia drives for another touchdown, leaving 1:30 on the clock before halftime. Omaha has the ball. Crouch is under center. Many NFL coaches would have taken to the ground and bled the clock, content to go into halftime down by only seven. But the Nighthawks offense has no other gear. In theory, time on the clock is nearly irrelevant because they essentially run a hurry-up drill for the entire game.

Crouch begins the drive with a twenty-yard pass down the sideline, which moves the ball to near midfield. An Omaha field goal attempt, at the very least, looks plausible. A dropped pass on the next play leaves one minute on the clock. Crouch takes the snap from the shotgun. On the left sidelines, Jackson has sprung free from his defender, and begins to veer toward the middle of the field, near the Virginia 20. Crouch sees him just as a Virginia linebacker, who has shed his blocker, trucks right at him. Crouch fails to set his feet before he lets the pass fly. The ball slips a bit in his hand. The pass is high and wobbly. All heads on both sidelines gaze up into the lights and raindrops, watching the ball reach the apex of its ascent, then come falling back to earth. The ball is well behind Jackson, who tries desperately to stop his forward momentum to get back into the play. But he can't. Jerome Carter, the Virginia free safety, places his body under the ball and lets it nestle into his hands and chest, the catching motion of a punt returner. He runs the interception back to near the original Omaha line of scrimmage at the 50.

After one long completion, Virginia kicks a field goal as the first half ends. The Destroyers have a ten-point lead, but it somehow feels much larger than that.

Early in the third quarter, Joe's emphasis on aggressive special teams pays off. Ricardo Colclough blocks a Virginia field goal attempt. But on the ensuing drive, Masoli throws an interception. In the second half, Omaha's offense stalls. There are several quick three-and-outs, a Crouch fumble, and another Masoli interception, this one giving Virginia the ball at the Omaha 8-yard line. Olivadotti's weary defense holds Virginia to a field goal. But the Destroyers now lead 23–7 with three minutes left on the clock.

The Nighthawks have one more burst in them. Masoli leads the team on a ninety-two-yard drive that culminates in his two-yard touchdown run, to pull them within ten points with a minute to play. But, after a botched two-point conversion and a failed onside kick attempt, the game is over.

Joe and Schottenheimer meet at midfield for the postgame

handshake. Schottenheimer's face appears even more relaxed than it did before the game, perhaps from the relief of not losing a professional football game to a former Wall Streeter. His team had perfectly executed his preferred style of play, known in football circles as "Martyball"—polished and conservative play calling that lulls the other team into mistakes, then takes advantage of them. Schottenheimer will admit after the game that preparing for Omaha's offense "gave me some nightmares."

This is just what Joe intended, but the words offer little solace. Though the Nighthawks outgained the Destroyers both on the ground and through the air, and had six more first downs, they lost both the critical turnover (3-0) and penalty (11-2) battles. With few exceptions, the offense had been herky-jerky all night. The special teams had been plagued by mental gaffes. And even the defense had given up a backbreaking big play. Joe had lived his life based on the mantra that mistakes happen, but they should only happen once. In the short time they had all been together, Joe had drilled this into his team. But the Nighthawks lost the game because, ultimately, they failed to live by this creed. "That's my fault," Joe would say later.

After the game, in the funereal Nighthawks locker room, Joe addresses the team. "I feel bad that in our first game together as a team we played badly and made mistakes," he says in a low rasp. His voice then rises, the words becoming more distinct. "I feel good, though, that we never let up. We have a good team. Let's correct our mistakes. Let's have a great season, men."

Joe leaves the locker room and retreats into the silence of his coach's office, out of sight from his players and staff. There, the pain of losing begins to manifest itself physically. His eyes are bloodshot. His red hair shoots out from his head at odd angles. He looks totally spent as he sits down in his chair, stares into middle space, and, with a deep sigh, seems to sink into himself.

At this moment, he seems to forget his admonition to Bo Pelini about this just being a game, about being able to handle defeats. This loss hurts.

⊢+++⊣

The Nighthawks suffer two big injuries in the game. One of the team's best linebackers, Pat Thomas, tore both a knee ligament and a hamstring on the opening kickoff. Somehow he managed to play the rest of the game. But he is done for the season.

And Crouch tore the meniscus in his knee on a routine running play on which there was no contact. Though he, too, played for the game's duration, he will also be out for the remainder of the season. His football career is very likely over. He had set out to play this season to prove that he could be a professional quarterback. His stat line wasn't pretty: while sharing snaps with Masoli, he completed 9 of his 24 passes for 124 yards and one interception, and ran for 32 yards on six carries. But he had moved the team well. And he had been a leader since day one.

Because of scheduling quirks created by the new UFL schedule, the Nighthawks now have a bye week immediately after the Virginia game. "Nothing like having a whole extra week to stew over a bad loss this early in the season," grumbles Olivadotti. Joe gives the team the entire week off because, well, he has to. The UFL does not pay its players a cent during a bye. Though most of the coaches stick around to prepare for the next game, against the Sacramento Mountain Lions, most of the players go home for the week.

Bye weeks are generally fairly mellow by design, a chance to catch up on sleep and heal the body and mind. Not for Joe, however. He intends to use the week not to sleep, but to try to figure out ways to avoid another disastrous loss. The pressure is building on him. The season—his trial run, and perhaps his dream—has only five more games left.

CHAPTER EIGHT

Young Father, Young Coach

Joe started his coaching career at age nineteen, the same year he married Kathe and became the father of a green-eyed little girl named Kelly. He was a sophomore at Fordham University. Joe was only a few years older than some of the players he coached on Fordham Prep's JV squad.

After a season with the JV, Prep's head coach, Bruce Bott, elevated Joe to the varsity to coach the offensive line and linebackers. "He just had this intensity about him," says Bott. "He would go *through* things instead of around them." Bott was also impressed with how well he related to his players. "He could be street-wise with the tougher kids, but he was also smart enough to reach the valedictorian."

Joe could yell with the best of them, and he had no problem grabbing a face mask to get a player's attention. But he connected with the kids because he was first and foremost a teacher. He immersed his defense in the proper techniques, training his cornerbacks to swivel their hips at just the right time as they ran with a receiver, and showing his linebackers how to hold their lanes on running plays. But, more than anything, he taught his players to love football, the game that had helped saved him from the fate of those in his neighborhood who weren't fortunate enough to have something like football to love.

Joe had one fairly serious problem to overcome in his early coaching days. The single most important trait a good coach must have is the ability to communicate—directly, succinctly, and quickly—during both games and practices. But just as Joe started to coach, his stuttering problem, which he'd for the most part managed to hide, resurfaced, in a bad way. "He would drive me nuts on the sideline," says Bott. "He'd start to tell me something was happening and it would be the end of the first quarter before I understood him."

But Joe worked on it. He practiced play calls at night in front of the mirror. He wrote down all of the words that he had particular trouble getting out and, beside them, wrote down easier-to-pronounce synonyms. He even changed the pronunciation of his last name—dropping the proper silent "G" in "Moglia" in favor of a hard one—to make it easier on himself and his players. At the end of the 1970 season, Joe told Bott that he wanted to be the keynote speaker at the team banquet. Bott was wary, but he agreed to let him do it. Joe spent twenty hours rehearsing his five-minute speech. "To his credit, he went right through it," says Bott. "Knocked it right out of the park."

By the time Joe graduated from Fordham, he knew exactly what he wanted to do with his life: he wanted to be a college football head coach. But he knew he had to start at a lower level. He was audacious enough to believe that he could jump from being a twenty-one-year-old high school position coach to a twenty-two-year-old high school head coach. He sent out 180 applications to schools around the country. Only one of the schools responded. And that one hired him.

That place was Archmere Academy, a private Catholic school of four hundred kids in Claymont, Delaware, a suburb of Wilmington. In 1971 Joe was hired by Archmere to coach the football, wrestling, and freshman baseball teams, and to teach economics, political science, and European history. At age twenty-two, he became the youngest head coach in Delaware high school history. He had a Herculean task ahead. The school had a terrible football program, and it was populated by fairly well-off kids who were, to put it in blunt football terms, soft. They'd had a decade of losing seasons. "The program had been adrift for a while," says Paul Pomeroy, who was working at Archmere when Joe arrived and who eventually became his assistant coach. Joe had to break it down completely and build it back up from scratch.

Joe arrived in the summer, in his mustard-yellow Plymouth Belvedere, with Kathe and Kelly in tow. He called a team meeting the day before training camp, and as he was doing the roll call, "kids were just sort of trickling in late the entire time," says Pomeroy. Whenever a kid came in late, Joe would simply stop what he was doing and say "that's ten." No one had any idea what he meant.

At the end of the meeting, Joe told the team that thirteen kids had been late, which meant that the next day—during their first practice—the team would do 130 wind sprints, ten for each late arrival. His message was clear: this is a team, not a group of individuals. "In previous years, we seemed to have an annual rash of flat tires, traffic jams, and broken alarm clocks," says Pomeroy. "But strangely, all of that cleared up when Joe showed up."

Joe issued each member of the team a thick playbook. Half of it was taken up with things unrelated to football plays. There was a section on "being a man." There was another on how the players should carry themselves off the field that included the proper ways to address young women in the school hallways. "When Joe showed up, it was like someone had just stepped off a spaceship," says Larry Cylc, an offensive and defensive lineman on the team. (Cylc, now a high school football coach himself, still uses Joe's playbook.)

Practice started eleven days before school opened. Joe made everyone—players and coaches—sleep in the gym. The first of sometimes *four* daily practices started at 6:00 a.m. Every day the players ran thirty-yard sprints up a steep hill by the football field. "If some kid was having trouble, others would grab him and drag him up the hill," says Pomeroy. "Everyone had to finish, or they'd all do additional sprints."

During one particularly long day in camp, a player came up to Joe and told him he was quitting the team. "You can't quit in the middle of my practice!" Joe replied. "Get back out there!" The kid finished the day.

The players nicknamed the summer practices "the death camp." Some thrived. Others wilted. "There were people there who deified him and would have followed him to the gates of hell," says Pomeroy. "There were others who wouldn't have followed him out of hell." Says Cylc: "He really challenged your inner workings as a man."

Joe admits that he probably went overboard in his earliest days as a coach, almost as if he was trying to compensate for his young age. "I was a bit like my father," he says. "I yelled a lot." But as his four years at Archmere progressed, Joe became less of a screamer and more of a nurturer. He learned from the styles of the older, more established coaches in the state whom he met at coaching conferences, particularly Tom Olivadotti, who was then the head coach at the one of the state's best programs at the Salesianum School. "He got better as a coach, in his tactics and in the way he handled the kids," says Pomeroy. "He was always tough, but he added other essential elements as he went on."

Archmere went through two more losing seasons before turning the corner. It was pretty clear to his players and coaches that Joe had bigger things awaiting him in the future. "I knew he was going to be a college head coach some day," says Cylc.

Joe and Kathe were living on the tightest of budgets in Delaware. By Joe's third year at Archmere, they had three children. Joe was coaching and teaching and getting his master's degree in education from the University of Delaware. He was making only $10,000 a year. Their house was in the low-income area of Claymont known locally as "Fort Apache." (It has since been torn down.) Joe wore clothes he picked out of the school's lost and found. "We would go scouting in his yellow car and we'd empty our pockets for change to buy some ice cream," says Pomeroy. "We'd have enough for the ice cream, but not for sprinkles."

When Joe's brother Johnny first visited him in Delaware, he says he brought bottles of booze and wine from his bar, "because I wanted to drink them." But he quickly realized that money was so tight for his brother's family that they were eating pasta every night. "I started bringing steaks when I came," says Johnny. "It was cheap meat, but I figured the kids needed some protein."

At the end of the 1974 season (in which the team posted an 8-1 record), Joe took the head job at Penncrest High School in Media, Pennsylvania. He left the Archmere program in excellent shape, having completely turned around a formerly moribund football team. The year after Joe departed, the team went 9-1. They would go to the state finals for the next eight straight years. He left an impression on his players, too. "There aren't too many other men who have made a bigger positive effect on my life," says Cylc.

Penncrest was a bigger school than Archmere, and they played in Pennsylvania's prestigious Central League. But like Archmere before Joe showed up, Penncrest had a downtrodden football program and had been getting routinely crushed in the league. In fact, it was in even worse shape than Archmere had been. Taking a job there was the high school equivalent of taking the Vanderbilt job in the Southeastern Conference. But it was another rung on the ladder Joe was trying to climb.

"The school had an absolutely terrible football legacy," says Dennis Roccia, who was an assistant offensive coach there under Joe. For the Penncrest players, who were mostly from an affluent suburb of Philadelphia, losing had become a habit. Joe set out to change that.

As he had at Archmere, Joe first focused on the players' off-the-field lives. "Be a man" and "treat others with respect" became daily mantras. He wanted to reshape and mold the kids. "He instilled in them these fundamental beliefs that football was more than a game. It was this manifestation, really, of a way of life," says Roccia.

He adds: "It's funny. I've since seen Joe on CNBC twenty times. He gives the exact same speech now, almost forty years later, as he did then."

Joe taught the Penncrest players a sense of aggression, coupled with a care and concern for their teammates. He made them greet each other with Roman Centurion handshakes. "He just changed everything we did, our entire outlook on life. And he was fired up about it," says Pete Alyanakian, a slotback and linebacker on the team. Joe didn't put on any airs. "He was what he was. He was a coach," says John Thomas, a lineman and kicker. "I remember him on the practice field, wearing baggy shorts, his hair uncombed, the elastic in his socks all shot."

Penncrest is where Joe first employed his somewhat radical ideas on offense. He came to them out of necessity. His team had smaller kids than the other teams in the Central League. His offensive linemen averaged around 150 pounds. So Joe figured, on offense at least, he needed to emphasize speed and quickness as opposed to bulk and brute force.

Joe installed a quick-read, spread option offense at Penncrest, similar to the one he would later run with the Nighthawks. His offensive linemen set up on the line of scrimmage one yard apart from each other. The quarterbacks made their reads at the line, deciding whether to run or pass. They threw a lot of short, safe passes in lieu of running plays that would have required bigger and stronger offensive linemen to be successful. The scheme was similar to what Bill Walsh—at the time an assistant coach with the Cincinnati Bengals—was running, which would later become known as the West Coast offense. "No one in the league had ever seen anything like it before. It completely baffled them," says Roccia.

But Penncrest had a ways to go before it would become a winning program. In Joe's first two years, the team went a combined 4-15-1. But things began to jell in Joe's last year, when the team went 6-4-1, its first winning season in a decade.

As much as Joe loved high school football and cherished his time at both Archmere and Penncrest, he had his sights set on the next level: college. The problem was that Joe had no idea how to get there. His coaching career had been basically self-made. He had no real coaching mentors, no one to show him the ropes and to give him advice. Bott had helped a bit initially. Olivadotti provided some guidance in Delaware. But, otherwise, Joe had figured things out pretty much on his own.

In the spring of 1977 Joe befriended Walt Buechele and John Furlow, the defensive coordinator and head coach, respectively, at West Chester University, a Pennsylvania school fifteen miles from Penncrest. They both told Joe that he needed to start networking if he wanted to crack the college game. "I thought I could just get there by proving myself as a high school coach," says Joe. But he found out that in the college ranks, a lot of it was whom you knew.

So Joe decided to take their advice about making and cultivating contacts—starting with them. That spring, he helped out with West Chester's practices, coaching the secondary. While there he made an impression. Buechele and Furlow recommended Joe for the secondary coach position at Lafayette College that same spring. Joe got the job and packed up Kathe and their now four kids (Kelly, Kim, Kara, and a new baby—their son, Kevin) and moved to Easton, Pennsylvania.

A Catholic priest who was a friend of the family had married Joe and Kathe in a quiet ceremony on a Wednesday night. The only people in attendance were their immediate families. "In those days it wasn't the thing to do to get pregnant before you were married," says Kathe. "So everything was hush-hush." To save money, the two nineteen-year-olds decided to move into the basement of Kathe's parents' house in Yonkers. Kathe was very attached to her own family, but she immediately loved Joe's mother, too ("She was a very special lady") and at least understood his father ("I always felt sorry for him because in my eyes he was never able to show his family any love"). Kathe would have preferred to stay in Yonkers (or move to Inwood) to raise their children, because roots and family were more important to her than anything else.

But roots were hard to establish when married to an ambitious football coach like Joe, who was constantly on the lookout for new opportunities to advance his career. That, of course, meant lots of moves. Kathe always supported Joe's coaching career. "I was so proud of him. He was an amazing coach and had such great influence on his players," she says. But the constant uprooting took a toll on her. "She would be just settling in to a new place, then, *poof*, Joe would get a job somewhere else," says Paul Pomeroy, who remained friends with the Moglias after they left Archmere. "I think she would have preferred that Joe stay in one place, that he would sort of install himself somewhere like Archmere and coach there for the rest of his life. But that wasn't Joe."

That said, the first few years in Easton turned out to be the time the kids look back on as their favorite part of their childhood. The family was together, a unit. The Moglias lived in a small house on the Lafayette campus, right next to the president's mansion. "It was a really nice neighborhood that had kids all over the place," remembers Kelly. "Mom had a good support group. We were happy there."

Kathe was naturally shy, the opposite of her outgoing husband. "She was never comfortable at big parties," says Kelly. "She preferred hosting small dinners." Her tight-knit group of friends in Easton allowed for plenty of that.

In Easton, the Moglia children roller-skated, swam in the college pool, and played on the nearby statue of a leopard, the Lafayette mascot. At home, Joe settled disputes among his girls by making them wrestle each other (Kevin was a toddler at the time). "If we had a disagreement, it was *ding-ding-ding*," says Kim. They also put on dancing parties, where Joe and his girls would sing. "Proud Mary" was a particular favorite. "Dad was always Tina Turner and we were the backup singers," says Kara. "We were a big singing family even though Grandma [Joe's mother] was the only one who could actually sing. But Dad had no problem trying."

Their lives revolved mostly around football. "We felt like we were part of the team there," says Kim, who would sometimes curl up in her father's lap and watch game films at home. The family went to nearly every game, home and away. "For the first twelve years of my life, I never knew Saturday cartoons existed," says Kelly. "Mom would just put us in the car and we'd go to football games. It was so cool to see our dad down there on the sidelines."

"If we won, we would all run down on the field," says Kim. "But if we lost, everything was somber. Mom would say, 'Dad needs some time.'"

Financially, things were still very tight. Johnny remembers visiting his brother in Easton one winter. "Their house was really drafty. Jim [Joe] had the heat set at fifty-five degrees. It was freezing. I asked him to turn it up and told him I'd pay for it. He said no, that it would set a bad example if they only turned up the heat when I was there."

Still, the Moglias did find the time and money to go on one-week vacations during the summer. Unlike his father, Joe would actually stick the week out. They usually went to visit Joe's childhood friend, John O'Leary, at his beach house on the New Jersey shore. "Dad was never really relaxed on vacations, but he was a lot of fun. He rode bikes with us and told us tons of stories," says Kelly.

Joe coached the secondary and the special teams at Lafayette, which turned out to be the Leopards' only strengths. "Our offense was pretty miserable," says Joe. In the 1978 season the team went 5-3-2 despite having serious trouble scoring points. The defense and special teams carried the squad. In the team's two ties that year, the scores were 0–0 and 7–7. They won one game by the score of 9–7. Joe's special teams set an NCAA record with thirteen blocked kicks that year. (One of Lafayette's kick-blocking specialists was an All-American linebacker named Joe Skladany, who later became an assistant coach for the linebackers and special teams for the Nighthawks.)

At the beginning of what would be Joe's last year at Lafayette, things between him and Kathe began to sour. Fights became more frequent, though they were careful not to argue in front of the kids. The fights mostly centered on the amount of time Joe spent on his work. Part of his job at Lafayette was to coordinate recruiting, which, combined with his coaching duties, meant he was totally focused on football for all but a month or two during the year. He was also busy writing a football book. "I wanted some family time, but Joe was too busy making his career," says Kathe.

They tried counseling but it didn't work. In the winter of 1980 Kathe filed for divorce and took the kids to live with her parents back in New York. But with Christmas around the corner, she and Joe decided to reconcile for the kids' sake. She returned to Easton after two weeks.

At the end of the 1980 season, when Lafayette went 3-7, head coach Neil Putnam was fired. A new coach named Bill Russo was brought in. Russo asked Joe to stay on the staff as the offensive coordinator. But Joe had been offered a job at Dartmouth to lead the defense. Though the talent difference between the players at Lafayette and Dartmouth was negligible, Joe believed the Dartmouth job carried greater prestige.

Joe was now thirty-one years old. He had already been coaching for thirteen years. It was his obsession. He loved the game planning, the repetition of the practices, the molding of dozens of eager-eyed boys into one unified whole. He loved recruiting, the identification of talent, the sales pitch to the player and his family, and the sealing of the deal with the commitment letter. Since age nineteen, he'd had his sights set on one thing: running his own college program. And the Dartmouth job, he believed, was exactly the right step in that direction. Head-coaching aspirants took their licks as assistants for years. If he found success as the defensive coordinator at Dartmouth, he was sure that doors would open in a big way.

But Kathe put her foot down. The move to Hanover would have been the family's fourth uprooting in a decade. She liked Easton. She told Joe that she and the kids were staying put.

Joe went anyway, believing—*hoping*—that she would follow. He signed a contract to become Dartmouth's new defensive coordinator for a starting salary of $30,000 a year. He found a place to live on his own, a little green house on Prospect Street in Lebanon, a neighboring—and cheaper—town.

Kathe and the kids did eventually move up in the summer.

But Joe and Kathe's relationship continued to deteriorate. Dick Maloney, then the offensive line coach at Dartmouth and now the head coach at the University of Chicago, says one night in October of that year, just a few games into Joe's first season, all of the coaches were in a meeting, going over the game plan for their next opponent, when Hanover's sheriff walked in and asked to see Coach Moglia.

"We thought there was a death in the family," says Maloney.

Instead, the sheriff served Joe his divorce papers. "Joe just took them, then quietly returned to the table and put them under his seat and we continued the meeting," says Maloney. Joe was deeply embarrassed but he tried not to show it. "He was very private and he never talked about any trouble at home, but we all knew what was going on," says Maloney. "But he never brought it to the field."

Indeed, on the field, Joe was working near miracles. Joe Yukica, Dartmouth's head coach, gave Joe freedom on his side of the ball. Joe ran a base 3-4 defense, meaning he usually started with three linemen at the line of scrimmage. But his defense was based on flexibility. They could easily jump into a 4-3 (with four down linemen). They had as many as fifteen different coverages. "What he did so well was adapt the defense to the skills of the players he had," says Ed Simpson, a linebacker on the team. "We weren't big at all, but we were fairly smart and coachable. He taught us discipline and responsibility."

Although Joe had toned down his yelling, he worked everyone very hard. "He had this uncanny ability to grind the kids and, at the same time, convince them that he had their best interests at heart," says Don Brown, a graduate assistant on that Dartmouth staff and the current defensive coordinator at the University of Connecticut. And "he had great positive energy. If we lost, he never dragged his tail, and that rubbed off on the players. He made them feel good about themselves." This was a critical part of his coaching strategy, because he knew he had to get his defensive players to believe that they were good, to believe that if they played together as a true unit, they would succeed, despite their lack of size and speed.

And it worked. Led by Joe's defense, which was the top-ranked one in the East, the Big Green tied for the Ivy League Championship in 1981. That same year, Joe published his first book, *The Perimeter Attack Offense*. The book was based on the thesis that the key to a great offensive attack is the ability to create an exploitable moment of doubt, a hesitation, in the minds of the linebackers, cornerbacks, and safeties—those players responsible for stopping both the run and the pass. Basically, it was the type of offense that had given his defenses trouble over the years.

In December 1981 Joe and Kathe decided to separate. Kathe hadn't pushed the divorce proceedings along, but they both realized that they could no longer live under the same roof. Joe made plans to move into the unheated storage room at the Davis Varsity House, over his team's locker room, when he returned from his Christmas break recruiting trip. They decided Kathe would tell the kids while he was away.

Joe says the day he left for that trip—knowing that he wasn't coming back to his family—was "the hardest single day of my life." He kissed his kids good-bye, walked out into the freezing New Hampshire winter day, and got into his car. "I remember looking back at the house as I pulled out of the driveway," he says. "And there was my little girl, Kara, with her face pressed up to the window, watching her daddy leave."

"We had no idea he wasn't coming back," says Kelly.

A day after he left, Kathe gathered the children together in the kitchen. Kara and Kevin were too young to recall much about that day. But the older two children remember it well.

"We were all in the kitchen," says Kim. "I was sitting in a chair. I remember how my feet barely touched the ground as I swung them under the chair." Kathe told them that she and Joe were separating because they didn't want to fight so much anymore, and that Joe would no longer be living with them. "I had this sense of panic," says Kim. "The room went white. I thought then that he was never coming back."

Kelly remembers walking upstairs and seeing her mother packing up her father's clothes. When she asked her mother what she was doing, Kathe replied, "I told you he's not coming back."

Joe moved into the cold and dusty loft, his only company a flight of noisy, fidgety pigeons that occupied the windowsill. He still saw his children regularly. They came to the games. He spent holidays with them. But the life they had shared as a family was over.

In Joe's second year at Dartmouth, the team traveled to Williamsburg, Virginia, for an out-of-conference game against William & Mary. The night before the game, after meetings had wrapped up, Joe and some of his fellow assistant coaches went to the hotel lounge for a beer. Yukica, a coach firmly out of the old school, never mixed with his assistants in casual situations. "He wouldn't have liked that we were getting a beer, but he was probably already asleep by then," says Joe.

It happened that the lounge was holding a dance contest that night. Joe, like his father before him, fancied himself as quite the dancer. He decided, on a whim, to enter the contest. He suddenly leapt up from his chair and grabbed a young woman who was sitting next to him and his fellow coaches. The songs in the contest were right in Joe's sweet spot—classics like "Mustang Sally" and "Wipeout." Joe swiveled his hips and worked himself into a great sweat. His coaching companions robustly cheered him on. "Joe always put a lot of energy into whatever he did," says George Landis, Dartmouth's defensive backs coach. "And he always wanted to win."

And he did. The MC of the contest called Joe and the woman back up to the stage. He asked their names. The woman said, "Sally."

Then he turned to Joe. "It hit me right then that it might not be a great idea to give him my real name," says Joe. So he came up with a new one on the spot: Sandy McFadden. The MC assumed they were married. Sally and "Sandy" won a free weekend at a hotel in the Florida. Joe gave the trip to Sally.

The next morning, the entire team, led by Yukica, walked out of the hotel together to get on the buses for the game. They walked right by the lounge. A huge sign hanging over the door screamed: "Congratulations to Sandy and Sally McFadden, our dance contest winners!"

"You couldn't miss it," says Joe. The other coaches snickered as they walked by. "Yukica would have blown his lid if my name had been on there."

"We called him 'Disco Joe' from that point on," says Landis.

That year, Dartmouth tied for another Ivy League title, propelled again by Joe's defensive unit, which once again was one of the best in the East. But after that season, Joe started to have uneasy thoughts about his future. By then he had been living in the storage room for close to a year. "You could just tell that he wasn't happy," says Maloney. "In quiet moments, this miserable look would spread across his face." He still dreamed of becoming a head coach one day. And why not? With two Ivy League championships to his credit and a top-notch defense, he was well on his way. But the closer he got to achieving his dream, the more it seemed like an impossibility because of what was going on with his family life.

Joe's main desires no longer matched up: He wanted to be a head coach. And he wanted to provide for his family and live close enough to them that he could see them often. Becoming the head coach at Dartmouth was perhaps the one college job that would reconcile the two wishes. But Yukica was happy in the job and successful. He wasn't going anywhere.

The other problem was that Kathe and the kids weren't going anywhere, either. If Joe applied for head coaching jobs, he was at the mercy of the inherent geographic uncertainty of the job. He could literally land anywhere—California, Montana, Florida, maybe even Massachusetts if he was lucky. But he didn't want to leave it up to chance, then find himself a thousand miles away from his kids.

In Joe's third season, Dartmouth came within a season-ending loss to Penn of winning a third-straight Ivy League championship. But Joe was stuck in a bind. Even after a raise, he was still making only $33,000. He and his family were still living on a shoestring budget. When Kim fell off her bike and got some gravel stuck in her knee, Joe took her to the football trainer because he couldn't afford to go to a doctor. When Kathe called and told Joe that the food money was getting low, Joe started shuttling over doggy bags full of leftovers from the team's training meals. In effect, Joe had the worst of two worlds: he couldn't be with this family and he could no longer support them. He gradually realized that he had to make a choice about his career.

And on that ice-cold early morning in the storage room, Joe made the decision to leave the job that he felt born to do. "It absolutely killed me because I would have chewed my own leg off to keep coaching," he says. Like his father before him, he had determined that providing for his family was his primary responsibility in life. He needed to be a man.

He was done with football for what looked like forever.

+++++

When Joe told Yukica that he was leaving the team to try to get a job on Wall Street, the older man peered at him over his bifocals that were perched on the tip of his nose and scoffed: "You're not going to get one of those jobs."

As implausible as it seemed to others, getting a job on Wall Street made total sense to Joe. He had an interest in economics. And the jobs on Wall Street sounded similar in many ways to coaching: The trading floor was an adrenaline-packed place; success was predicated on preparation; making sales resembled the pitches involved in recruiting; and you made your hay on wins. One other thing appealed to him about the street: "I decided that if I was going to leave coaching, I was going to make a lot of money."

In retrospect, Joe admits he had no earthly idea what he was doing at the time. But the lack of knowledge didn't matter. Force of will and desperation would carry him.

+++++

Joe would eventually find remarkable success in the business world. But it would come at a high cost, starting when he left New Hampshire for New York in early 1984.

Joe and Kathe were officially divorced that year. As in all divorces, the main narrative is filled with various subplots that ultimately all end up in cul-de-sacs. But the overriding reason for their divorce was that they just grew to become incompatible.

They had married at a very young age. As they grew older, they became unable to fulfill each other's needs. "My parents were exact opposites," says Kim. "Every strength my mother has is his weakness, and vice versa."

Joe and Kathe still maintain an amicable relationship. "He is the father of my children, so I've always wished him the best," says Kathe. She has kept up with his career and even listened to all of the Nighthawks games through a website. "I believe coaching is what he was meant to do and I am very proud that he is getting back to where his heart belongs," she says. Joe still supports her financially, for which she says she is "eternally grateful."

For the first few years after Joe left coaching, money was still an issue. He wasn't making much more when he started out at Merrill Lynch than he had as a coach. The lack of funds was hard on his family. Kathe took on three jobs: She was a receptionist at a local inn, a bank teller, and a cashier at Dunkin' Donuts, from which she often brought home leftovers. "To this day, when I see a Dunkin' Donuts, I feel sick," says Kevin. "We used to chow down on those doughnuts."

The kids paid an emotional price, too. In focusing all his energy on making a new career in finance, Joe sacrificed key time with his children. And as lonely as Joe was and as much as he missed seeing his kids during his first few years at Merrill, the children felt those longings even more intensely. His kids missed having him around when they were growing up.

Says Kelly: "He is so driven. If he hadn't been, he never would have accomplished what he has. I can respect that now, at age forty-two. But that wasn't so fantastic at age fifteen. He gets so focused. But when that focus is elsewhere, it's not on you. But that never meant he didn't love us. It just took a while for us to realize that."

"I think he chose to lead by example instead of being the dad who was always around, driving his kids to games and the prom," says Kara. "I don't think he was being selfish. It's just a trade-off."

The subject is a sensitive one for Joe, but he offers no excuses. "The beginning of my career at Merrill was pretty perilous. It could have all been over just like that. Guys were getting fired left and right. I had to get my career right. Otherwise, I would have been back in that fruit store."

No excuses does not mean no regrets. "I regret the hell out of it. It pains me. It saddens me. We all paid a price, and that's my fault. I really started to become aware of it as my career went on. But I never loved my career more than my children," he says. "I just did what I believed I had to do."

During his childhood, Joe had witnessed firsthand what it's like to be stuck doing work that makes you miserable, the negative effects it can have on both the person and his family, how it can twist a man and harden him beyond recognition, to himself and others. So part of him was always running away from his father's fruit store, even as another part of him was reenacting what he always believed to be his father's most honorable trait—the ironclad commitment to providing for his family. "My father took that responsibility very seriously, and I always respected that," says Joe.

Like Joe, his father paid a price for his choice—a higher price, to be sure; but also like Joe he managed in later life to recoup part of what he paid.

At Dartmouth, Joe was in charge of recruiting the New York/New Jersey area. On one trip, he decided to drop by Yonkers to say hello to his father. John wasn't at home, so Joe went to the Bronx, to Plato's Cave, the topless bar that his brother Johnny owned at the time, to see if Johnny knew where their father was. It was the middle of the afternoon. Johnny wasn't there. The only person in the entire place besides the bartender was an old man, slumped over in a booth.

Joe left. But he turned around almost as soon as he walked out of the door. There had been something familiar about that old guy. Joe walked back into the bar. He gently lifted the old man's head up. It was his father, passed out drunk.

John, always a drinker, had developed into a full-fledged alcoholic by the 1980s. He basically drank his fruit store away and eventually fell into bankruptcy. He was too proud to ask any of his children for money. To his credit, though, after a little over a year in the abyss, John pulled his life together and found another job. He worked for an hourly wage in the produce department of a grocery store called Turco's, stacking boxes and helping to bag groceries in the checkout lines. He was in his seventies. He joined a gym and began to work out. He ran the one and a half miles from his house to church every day, in his suit. He became very generous with gifts at Christmas and birthdays, signing cards, for the first time, "Love, Daddy." He worked and was active and fit until his mideighties, when the onset of Alzheimer's disease forced him to retire and remain homebound. The coda to John Moglia's life was surprisingly warm and pleasant, like an Indian summer day. He died in 2005 at age eighty-nine.

Joe learned much from his father's virtues as well as his failings, and the choices he made in life reflected that legacy.

CHAPTER NINE

California Dreamin'

Joe starts the Nighthawks' bye week reviewing his own performance in the game against the Virginia Destroyers. He knows he has to do a better job managing his coaches to help cut down on mistakes. But he also has to be more assertive on the field. Schottenheimer had outfoxed him when it came to the referees. He had worked them over the entire game, using his leverage as a coaching legend. Joe decides he will make it a point to meet with the officials before the upcoming game against the Sacramento Mountain Lions, and stay on top of them throughout it. He might not have Schottenheimer's football gravitas, "but I can be a pretty persuasive guy," he says.

He also spends time analyzing what he will be up against next.

Dennis Green's Mountain Lions had lost their first game, too, against Fassel's Las Vegas Locomotives. But it had been a tight contest (23–17), and Sacramento's quarterback—rookie Ryan Colburn from Fresno State—had looked good, throwing for two touchdowns in the game. He was sort of a Ben Roethlisberger lite: tall (six foot three) and big (235 pounds), yet nimble on his feet and able to extend passing plays by shedding would-be tacklers or sidestepping his way out of trouble. He was the type of quarterback who drove defensive coordinators like Olivadotti crazy. You could play nearly perfect pass defense against him, but if he made a tackler or two miss in the backfield and gained just a little more time, the defense would break down and the receivers were almost sure to get open. On film, Sacramento looked better than Virginia.

Then Joe turns his attention to his two major areas of concern on his own team: the offense and the special teams. He trusts that Olivadotti has the defense on the right track. His task is to get the other two coordinators headed the same way.

First he meets with Kent and his special teams staff. Kent is a stickler for the small stuff, but Joe believes he may be going overboard, still taking on too much. "We should have dynamite special teams. We have a great scheme and we practice the hell out of it," Joe tells them. "This should be our differentiator. We can do something really special."

But what about Colclough's field goal block in the first game, Kent wants to know, trying to put a positive spin on things. Good, but not good enough. The special teams had been a cauldron of mistakes, all of them mental. Those outweighed the positive of the block. "Let's get the mental part right," he tells Kent.

Offense is a bit of a different story. Joe meets with Andrus and his coaches in the Nighthawks' main classroom. A new banner has been put up on the wall. It reads: "All things are possible to him that believeth." It's a quote from the Bible, from the Gospel of Mark. Though Joe is not necessarily a religious man, the quote is fitting because he believes the problem with the offense might be a lack of belief... in him.

Because he's been out of the game for so long, Joe worries about his credibility. He's not worried about Olivadotti believing in him. Their long friendship and their shared philosophy of coaching outweigh anything else. Besides, Olivadotti would just tell Joe if he thought he was doing something wrong. Joe doesn't have that comfort level with Andrus. And, anyway, offensive and defensive coordinators are entirely different beasts, who need to be handled accordingly.

Generally speaking, defensive coordinators are similar to engineers. They must figure out the problem (in simple terms, how to keep the offense out of the end zone). They draw up plans and stick with those plans until something goes awry. And when something (inevitably) goes awry, they adapt, adjust, tweak. While a defensive scheme can be creative, that side of the ball, by its very nature, is inherently reactive.

Offensive coordinators, on the other hand, tend to be more proactive, even artistic. They have to create every play and think a few steps ahead. They attack a defense. They are the protagonists in the narrative of each game, initiating the action. Hence coordinators on this side of the ball are generally stubborn, accustomed to thinking for themselves and not always very open to hearing other points of view. This is usually a good thing. You don't want a shrinking violet for an offensive coordinator.

Joe realizes this with Andrus. Joe loves the offense Andrus has designed on paper and he believes it can work if executed properly, if everything is actually put in that's supposed to be in, and if the skills of the players are taken into account. But already, just one game into the season, Joe is worried that Andrus may be too stubborn about his scheme and a bit unwilling to make—and really embrace—what Joe sees as some obviously needed changes. First and foremost, Joe wants powerball fully installed. It's not. Joe sees powerball as the absolutely necessary changeup to the Nighthawks fastball offense.

And this is where the credibility issue comes to a head. "Schottenheimer has been coaching for thirty-plus years straight," says Joe, reflecting on how different his own position is. "He's one of the winningest coaches of all time. If he asks his offensive coordinator to do something, the guy will just do it. I don't necessarily have that credibility, and I didn't have time to establish it. My challenge is to get Bart to embrace what I want on offense. He has to internalize it, has to buy it, and actually want to do it. And

I have to get him do that without making him feel scolded or penalized."

A patient approach is what Joe needs now. But with almost no training camp, an abridged season, and the instability of the league, he is currently running short on that virtue. "My patience is gonzo right now," he says. "I have to get it back." And over the ten-day break, he does. He meets with the offensive staff every day, never yelling, always nudging.

Bye week is also a time when the Nighthawks make some personnel moves. Injuries from the last game prompt two of the changes. The promising rookie linebacker, Matt Wenger, is brought back in to replace Pat Thomas. D. J. Shockley takes Crouch's roster spot; he will be the third-string quarterback. Garrett Wolfe, a former Bears running back, is signed. So is Kyle Nelson, an original draftee of the Nighthawks who had been on the Chiefs practice squad. But this last move creates a tough cut.

Matt Overton, the Nighthawks long snapper, is one of the more vocal leaders on the team. He stayed in Omaha during the league's thirty-day delay. He promotes the team relentlessly through social media, and has always been available for the voluntary, team-related activities in the Omaha community. "He is the face of our team," running back Shaud Williams had declared during training camp. "Which is pretty weird, because he's a long snapper. I bet we're the only football team in America that can say that."

But now, with the addition of Nelson, Overton is gone. The Nelson signing makes perfect football sense: He is a long snapper who also happens to be a very good tight end, a true two-for-one player. But the cut is difficult on the personal side. "I was shocked," says Overton. "But I know how it goes."

Joe just shakes his head. "I can't stand this part of this game," he says. Three days later, Joe hires Overton to work in the Nighthawks public relations department.

⊢+++⊣

When the team reassembles, Joe can see that Troy Smith, still the team's best pure passer, has yet to master the offense. On the field, he is thinking too much. Andrus likens it to someone learning how to drive a stick-shift car. "You can see the pauses, the lurches, the hesitations," he says.

Joe is also eager to watch Jeff Wolfert, the placekicker, who had not had much action in the first game, with just one extra point kick. Wolfert had taken to his position a bit late in life. He was a star diver and soccer player in high school in Kansas. But he always wanted to try kicking in a football game. His senior year, he made the football team. In his first and only high school game, Wolfert broke his hip while kicking the ball off.

Wolfert received a diving scholarship to the University of Missouri. His sophomore year, he walked onto the football team. He walked off a few years later as Missouri's all-time point-scoring leader. He was especially known for his uncanny accuracy. During his collegiate career, Wolfert was a perfect 185 for 185 on point-after attempts, and he hit an impressive 75 percent of his field goal attempts. The only knock on him coming out of college was his leg strength. When he missed, it was usually from beyond 50 yards. After school, he had tryouts with the Bears, Chiefs, Falcons, and Jets. All of the teams loved his accuracy, but ended up signing kickers who could boom the ball.

The UFL was a perfect place for a player like Wolfert. The league gave him a chance to show what he could do in a live game. After being turned down by the NFL, Wolfert signed with the Nighthawks in 2010. That season, he went 9 for 10 in field goal attempts and was, by far, the best kicker in the league. In 2011, after the NFL lockout, Wolfert was signed by the Browns.

But making the team was a long shot: Cleveland already had Phil Dawson, one of the best kickers in the NFL.

Joe and Mueller had desperately wanted Wolfert back. And a few days before the first game, they got their wish when he was cut by the Browns.

Wolfert is what is known on a football team as a "specialist." These players—kickers, long snappers, and holders—occupy a strange niche in the game. They are simultaneously a part of the team—they, too, wear helmets and pads—but they are also very much apart from it, especially during practice. While the offense and defense run team drills under the watchful eyes of the coaches, the specialists stand far away from the action, on the other side of the field, either jawing with each other, or endlessly working on snaps and holds, or stretching, or scuffing up slick new balls to their very particular likings. (The only differences between NFL and UFL balls is that the latter have black laces and the signature of Michael Huyghue instead of Roger Goodell.) The specialists get in for just a handful of plays during practice.

To keep himself occupied during the practices, Wolfert challenges himself with a kicking game. When the team is on one side of the Kroc's practice field, he sends the punter, Tom Mante, to stand behind the goal posts in the opposite end zone. Wolfert then sets himself up thirty yards away on the sideline, angled rather extremely—forty-five degrees and sometimes more—from the goalposts. Then he kicks three balls from the position, trying to split the uprights. He moves his position up and down the sideline to get different angles. He is amazingly good at these games. The idea behind doing them is to make a straight-on shot during a game "look" easier to his eye. Wolfert, switchblade thin with short, thick sandy-blond hair, is an avid golfer. The angled kicks make him feel like he is on the links. "I like to think of my leg as an eight-iron," he says.

Wolfert is not the only Nighthawk who appears sharp in practice. Masoli looks more comfortable, no longer sharing snaps with Crouch. This is his offense now, and though he is quiet, he's become the leader. His receivers are finally making the catches they're supposed to make. The offensive line is getting more accustomed to the wide splits.

One reason that practice is sharper is the presence of Denny Marcin, a legendary football scout who now plies his trade for the New York Jets. Marcin, round and bald and wearing a thick gold chain around his neck, stalks the sidelines carrying a little black bag adorned with a Jets helmet. He watches every snap in practice and occasionally takes an assistant coach aside to talk to him in private, all the while scribbling notes on a legal pad. After practice, Marcin joins Olivadotti for lunch. Marcin is a former college defensive coordinator. The football-coaching fraternity is a relatively small one, so he and Olivadotti have known each other for thirty years. Marcin tells Olivadotti that he's most interested in the Nighthawks' rookies, like former UMass running back John Griffin ("How did thirty-two teams miss on that guy?" he asks).

The reason Marcin likes rookies: they're a lot cheaper than the veterans who are hoping to get back into the NFL. Minimum rookie pay in the NFL for 2011 is $375,000. Add just two years of NFL service, and that shoots up to $525,000. NFL vets on the Nighthawks like Schweigert, Dvoracek, and Colclough, with their many years in the league, would have to be paid close to $700,000 were they to sign with an NFL team. NFL vets in the UFL have a much tougher road to the big league than do the rookies. The brutal truth in the NFL is that teams will sign rookies with slightly less skill to fill out the bottoms of their rosters in order to create more room for the bigger paychecks commanded by their marquee starters.

Getting back to the NFL, most of the players know, is doable, but it's a long shot. Perhaps that's why thirty of the fifty-one Nighthawks players come to Joe's first installment of "Life after Football." Many of the vets are in attendance—Schweigert, Dvoracek, Shockley, Hill, and Clarett—but so are some of the rookies, whose NFL dreams may be more realistic. The safety Mike O'Connell is here. So is Mante, the Yalie who spurned an internship offer from a consulting firm to play in the UFL.

Joe talks to them about the first step in finding a career outside of football: figuring out what you want to do. To do that, he stresses the Platonic maxim: "Know thyself."

"You have to know your own strengths and weaknesses. It will help you find a career. It will help you better handle yourself under pressure," Joe says. He leans back in his chair. He is very comfortable in this setting, with the pressures of football momentarily in the background.

Some players furiously scribble notes. Others use their iPhones to record Joe. George Foster, the left tackle, asks Joe what he thinks about getting graduate degrees. Foster wants to go into broadcasting someday. Joe's view, perhaps unsurprising given his own background, is that real-life experience almost always trumps education. "You've gotta get your ass in there and do it," he says. The meeting goes on for two hours.

Walking out, offensive guard Damion Cook turns to a teammate and says: "I've never actually had a coach who gave a crap about that stuff."

Though Interstate 80, one of the nation's great east-west rivers of asphalt, connects Sacramento to Omaha, the Nighthawks take to the air for travel. After consulting with the players, Joe decides that the only rule on travel attire is that everyone must wear a collared shirt. The players' styles vary wildly. Rookies like Masoli wear untucked short-sleeved polos and baggy pants. NFL vets, with more experience on professional team road trips and, presumably, more money, get spruced up. Smith wears a silk shirt. Eric Green, a cornerback who played with the Cardinals for four years, wears a three-piece gray suit. Nearly all of the players have oversized headphones, either on their ears or hanging around their necks. One player's assertive cologne wafts through the cabin of the plane.

Many of the players sleep through the entire flight. Some of them play a card game called Bourré (pronounced "booray"), which is somewhat similar to spades, and is very popular among American professional athletes. Because the losing player has to match whatever money is in the pot, it's also an easy and fast way to part with a lot of money. "I've seen people lose their entire game check on one flight," says Robert Hunt, the assistant offensive line coach who played in the NFL. A Bourré dispute is supposedly the reason that NBA star Gilbert Arenas brought two guns to his team's locker room in a 2009 incident.

But on this flight to Sacramento, no serious blood is drawn. Maybe the small paycheck in the UFL has made players more cautious.

An hour before kickoff, it's still sunny and hot, eighty degrees in the early California evening. Joe huddles with the officials, trying to gently exert some influence, then passes the time before the game reading *Crash of the Titans*, a book about the precipitous fall of his old firm, Merrill Lynch.

Bill Hambrecht, the UFL's primary owner, is in attendance. Carrying a clear plastic cup of ice water that drips with condensation, he works the VIP tent that's set up behind one end zone in

ıe Moglia family—Joe, Mom, Dad,
ıd baby Johnny—in 1951.
he Moglia Family)

Eight-year-old Joe with his extended family in 1957 (clockwise): John Moglia, Frances Moglia, Joe, Johnny, Bernadette, Paul, cousin Mark, Aunt Felicita, and "Uncle" Al, his godfather.
(The Moglia Family)

hn Moglia (middle) at his fruit stand in
ı64, with Johnny (left) and Tony.
'he Moglia Family)

Joe in his playing days at Fordham Prep, 1966. (The Moglia Family)

Graduating from Fordham Prep, 1967. (The Moglia Family)

Joe in 1983, his last year coaching at Dartmouth. (The Moglia Family)

Joe (middle) coaching Fordham Prep, with Norm Muro (left) and Bruce Bott. (Courtesy of Bruce Bott)

Joe during his tenure at Merrill Lynch. (The Moglia Family)

Joe (left), with his brothers Paul and Johnny in 1990.
(The Moglia Family)

Jake Albright and Joe finishing the 1986 NYC Marathon.
(The Moglia Family)

With his father, John, and son Kevin, at Joe's 1995 wedding to Amy.
(The Moglia Family)

Amy and Joe's wedding, 1995 (from left): Kelly, Kim, John, Joe, Amy, Kara, Jeff, and Kevin. (The Moglia Family)

Christmas 1995 at Amy and Joe's: Li'l Johnny, Mary, Paul, Bernadette, Joe, and (seated) Joe's father, John.
(The Moglia Family)

Joe cradling his first love in the lobby of Ameritrade, 2004.

: Kelly's graduation (from left): Kevin, Kathe,
im, Kelly, Kara, and Joe. (The Moglia Family)

The kids: Kelly, Kim, Kara, and Kevin.
(The Moglia Family)

e Moglia and Warren Buffett playing
exas hold 'em in 2006.
Courtesy of the Omaha World-Herald.)

The CEO of TD Ameritrade.

Joe and Amy Moglia in 2009, at the American Institute for Stuttering. (Courtesy of Guest of a Guest)

Joe and Bo Pelini, at the 2009 Holiday Bowl, during Joe's tenure with the Nebraska football team. (Courtesy of Scott Bruhn-Univ of Nebraska Media Relations Dept.)

Joe and offensive coordinator Bart Andrus, at the Las Vegas game. (Courtesy of Brooke Andrus)

With Jim Fassel, coach of the rival Las Vegas Locomotives, before a game. (Courtesy of Josselyn Timko)

Maurice Clarett at a Nighthawks practice. (Courtesy of Denman Freeman)

e and Richard Kent, his special teams coach, efore a home game against Las Vegas.
ourtesy of Monte Burke)

Eric Crouch at practice session.
(Courtesy of Denman Freeman)

Joe at a Nighthawks practice.
(The Moglia Family)

Joe and defensive lin
man Stuart Schweige
before a home gan
against Sacrament
(Courtesy of Jim McQuilla

Last-second prep with Coach Andrus in Las Vegas. (Courtesy of Brooke Andrus)

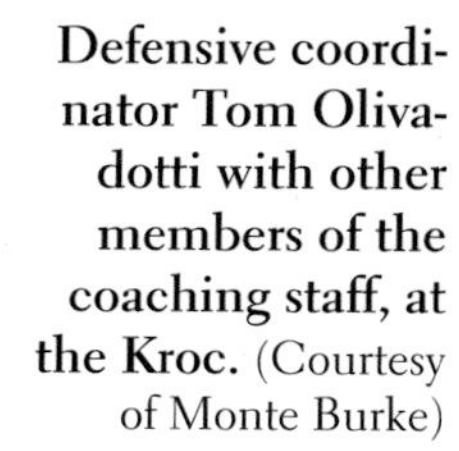

Defensive coordinator Tom Olivadotti with other members of the coaching staff, at the Kroc. (Courtesy of Monte Burke)

the stadium, which is normally home to Sacramento State. He's a tall man, casually dressed in a short-sleeved oxford shirt and, despite the heat, a pair of corduroy pants. He greets everyone he sees with a congenial, grandfatherly smile.

Paul Pelosi, owner of the Sacramento franchise, is nowhere to be seen.

Jerry Glanville, the erstwhile coach of the erstwhile UFL Hartford franchise, is on the field. He's doing color commentary for the local broadcast of the game. He's in his signature all-black outfit, and at his waist he's wearing a belt buckle the size of a flounder. As Glanville works the field—shaking hands, smiling, offering various opinions—a five-foot-tall Filipino man who's dressed in a smart gray suit follows him. The man is described as Glanville's "helper."

"This is 'Dynamite,'" says Glanville upon introducing the Filipino man. Dynamite smiles.

Denzel Washington, father of the Sacramento running back John David Washington, settles into his folding chair on the Mountain Lions' sideline. He keeps autograph and photo seekers at bay by constantly talking into a phone pressed to his ear.

On the first play from scrimmage, John David Washington squirts through a hole on the right side of Omaha's defensive line. A few steps later, he jukes a linebacker with a head-fake. Then it's nothing but an open field of artificial turf.

As John David scampers down the field, Denzel, who had been sitting in the VIP area looking like the essence of nonchalant cool—long legs crossed in front of him, arms splayed across the backs of the two chairs adjoining his own, low-effort smile on his lips—leaps to his feet and maniacally pumps his fists, looking every bit like the Herman Boone character he portrayed in the movie *Remember the Titans*. His son, a short and stocky back who had played at Morehouse College and who had once signed with the St. Louis Rams, is here for another shot at the NFL. More runs like this one will help his cause. He's finally tackled forty-five yards later, on Omaha's 22-yard line.

The Nighthawks, unfortunately, have picked up right where they left off in the first game against Virginia. They started the game with a mental mistake on special teams—a fifteen-yard "unsportsmanlike conduct" penalty on the opening kickoff when Curtis Johnson got into a fight with a Mountain Lions player. This occurs after Joe had just warned his team that Sacramento was known for dirty play, and that two men fighting each other while wearing helmets and pads was flat-out silly. ("The only way to hurt someone wearing pads is to kick him in the shins, and how's that gonna look?" he had asked the team.)

Then came the defensive lapse that resulted in Washington's huge run and fired up the Sacramento crowd of close to twenty thousand.

But Olivadotti's defense, as it will all season, clamps down when backed up against its own end zone. They force three straight incomplete passes. Dennis Green brings on his kicking team for a thirty-nine-yard field goal attempt. The kick sails wide. The Nighthawks players jump up off their bench and pump their fists in the air. Denzel calmly sits back down.

After the missed field goal, the game doesn't settle down like it seems it should. It gets more manic. On Sacramento's second possession, Colburn throws a deep wobbly pass down the sideline that's intercepted by Colclough, who returns the ball to the Mountain Lions 44-yard line. Three plays later, Masoli overthrows his receiver and gives the ball right back. Three plays after that, Colburn is sacked and fumbles. Schweigert recovers the ball right where the whole deal started—the Sacramento 44.

But on this drive, the Nighthawks cash in. Masoli moves the team down to the Mountain Lions 6-yard line. Then it's fourth and one. "Let's go for it," Joe says into his headset. It's a bold call this early in the game. Shaud Williams gets the carry, and makes the first down, but then fumbles the ball. A Nighthawks player recovers it at the 1. Then Williams punches it in.

After a successful Sacramento field goal, Omaha running back John Griffin—the player that Marcin the scout had liked above all others—fumbles the ball deep in Nighthawks territory. Colburn cashes in with a touchdown throw and suddenly the Nighthawks are in a hole.

As the first half winds down, Omaha drives to the Sacramento 36. The offense gets stuck there, and soon it's fourth down. A field goal from here would be a very long fifty-four-yarder. Joe turns to Wolfert on the sideline. "Can you make it, Jeff?"

Wolfert, the man who has been shunned by five NFL teams because of his supposedly weak leg, never hesitates. He runs out onto the field and kicks the ball through the goalposts. It's a new UFL record.

The Omaha locker room is buzzing at halftime. Though it's 10–10, the Nighthawks seem very much in charge of the game. Turnovers are the only reason Sacramento is hanging around in this game.

One of Olivadotti's favorite coaching maxims is that there really is no such thing as the "halftime adjustments" that the TV talking heads love to prattle on about. Ten minutes is simply not enough time to overhaul a game plan. But there occasionally is a halftime adjustment that goes beyond the X's and O's.

Joe gathers the team just before they retake the field. The room goes silent. "Guys, let's keep this thing going. Let's keep up the tempo." He is yelling now, his red face in a scowl. "And let's just jam the ball down their goddamn throats!"

The players erupt. Their coach, so measured and cool throughout their entire time together, has let loose.

The Nighthawks get the ball and quickly drive down the field. Wolfert is now called on to attempt a fifty-six-yarder. He nails it, breaking his own record, which had been set in the first half. The Mountain Lions eventually respond with a long drive that begins the fourth quarter and ends in a touchdown run by Washington. Wolfert responds with another "no problem" field goal from forty-two yards. Omaha is down by one, 17–16.

But Sacramento keeps coming. Colburn hits his tight end for a touchdown, making it 23–16 in favor of the Mountain Lions. An extra point will put them up eight points, meaning the Nighthawks would need a touchdown and a two-point conversion to tie. But Colclough blocks the extra point attempt. Omaha is down by just seven points.

Then Masoli throws another interception. But Colburn gives it right back, a replay of the first quarter's give-and-take between the quarterbacks. It takes Masoli one minute to drive the team forty yards for the tying score. Omaha's offense, despite the turnovers, seems to be finally working as originally planned. They are fast. And they are exhausting Dennis Green's defense.

The game is tied at 23. But it is far from over.

On the next possession, Colburn avoids three would-be Omaha tacklers, then heaves the ball fifty yards downfield. The ball nestles over the shoulder and into the hands of his receiver, who runs to the end zone. It's exactly the type of broken play that had worried Olivadotti, who will say later that this game "took years off of my life. Years I can't afford to give."

It's 30–23, Sacramento.

But the Nighthawks strike quickly again, taking all of two minutes to drive sixty-five yards for the tying touchdown. This seems to be one of those games in which the team that has the ball last will win.

⊢+++⊣

When people think of American football, they think about bodies—running, jumping, hitting. It is quite obviously one of the most physically demanding games on the planet. But it is also, contrary to conventional wisdom, one of the most mentally challenging. Each week, football players spend hours in classrooms—and additional hours in their spare time—learning plays. Basketball, ice hockey, and soccer players have, at most, just a handful of plays to digest. Baseball players must memorize their managers' and coaches' quirky hand signals. But no major American sport approaches football when it comes to use of the mind.

Football is much more than just a physical and mental test, however. Perhaps above all, the game is governed by emotion. "It's such an emotional game because it's so combative," says Olivadotti. "No one wants to look like a coward out there." Every play at the line of scrimmage is a battle of willpower, which is, at its essence, the ability to control one's emotions—and to exert that control over someone else.

These emotions are felt individually. But they can become collective. A touchdown can spark a euphoric, team-wide high. A turnover can sink everyone into a depressive low. And sometimes a perceived bad call from a referee can stir the emotions into a volatile mass that bursts forth in an explosion.

⊢+++⊣

With five minutes left in the game, Sacramento has the ball on their own 26. Two Washington runs net eight yards. On third and two, Colburn drops back to pass. Omaha defensive lineman

Kevin Basped bull-rushes his opposing offensive lineman, winning the battle of wills. He reaches Colburn, then wraps him into a bear hug. The duo is face mask to face mask, locked in an embrace. Basped falls on Colburn. The sack seems almost gentle. It's a loss of eight yards, and the Mountain Lions will be forced to punt and give the ball back to the Nighthawks humming offense.

But there is a flag. The referee has determined that Basped's sack has resulted in a helmet-to-helmet "roughing the passer" penalty. Joe goes apoplectic on the sideline, ripping off his headset. The players jump up and down, heaping slurs and curses on the ref. The ball is placed on the 50-yard line with 2:15 to play, giving Sacramento new life. But the call, instead of devastating the Nighthawks, has suddenly bonded them together.

Colburn drops back to pass again. Dennis Green is looking for the dagger, the one play that will put his team in range of a game-winning field goal. But Claude Herriott, a native Jamaican who has been signed and cut by four NFL teams, brushes by a lineman and sacks Colburn again. This time there is no flag.

Omaha gets the ball back at its own 35 with two minutes to play. The dark blue California sky is streaked with ribbons of pink clouds. Masoli does his best Colburn impersonation, stepping out of trouble and finding Chad Jackson for a thirty-five-yard pass play. Three consecutive runs position the Nighthawks at the Sacramento 21. The clock winds down.

Wolfert is on the sideline, warming up his eight-iron with kicks into a net. He jogs out onto the field, then coolly hits the game-winning thirty-nine-yard field goal as time expires. Nighthawks players jump on Wolfert's shoulders and slap the back of his helmet. It is the best game he's ever had, with four field goals converted, two of which were well over fifty yards. Tonight he is accurate *and* long. Tonight, he looks like an NFL All-Pro.

Denzel sits over on the sideline, his arms now crossed over his chest. His son has played a hell of a game, rushing for 114 yards. But his team has lost. The players dump a bucket of Gatorade on Joe's head. It's his first win as a head coach of a football team in thirty-four years.

Even better, the former CEO has beaten an NFL lifer.

CHAPTER TEN

Who the %#*! Is This Guy?

To an outsider lacking any context, the fixed-income trading floor at Merrill Lynch on any given day in the spring of 1984 would have seemed like an insane asylum.

The scene:

A few adults, trying to get someone's—anyone's—attention, bounced up and down like school kids, frantically waving their arms above their heads while somehow managing to keep phone receivers pinched between their necks and shoulders.

Others sat, still as statues, staring fixedly at one of the hundreds of computers on the floor, trying to decipher the meanings of the constantly blinking, ever-updating numbers and symbols on their screens, the 32,000-year update of Paleolithic cave paintings.

Traders yelled into "hoot-n-hollers," open lines connected with unseen faces on the other side of town or, perhaps, the world.

Phones pealed ceaselessly for attention.

And over the hive hum, distinct fragments of dialogue occasionally surfaced:

Salesman, with client on the phone, yelling to his trader: "Offer me $20 million long bonds."

Trader shouting back to salesman: "At 17!"

Salesman to client on phone: "How's 17?" Pause. "No? Sixteen, you say?"

Salesman, now with hand over phone receiver, back to trader: "He wants 16."

Trader to salesman: "Tell him to go screw himself!"

Salesman to client on phone, hand now off receiver: "We're staying at 17."

This entire exchange would have taken maybe fifteen seconds. The floor was not a place for the timid, the weak, or anyone susceptible to seizures.

Mike Quinn, the head of the New York fixed-income desk, loved being on the floor. It provided a peek under the hood at the engine that made Wall Street purr, the high-rolling casino where both the house and the players won the majority of the time. Its manic energy was infectious.

One of Quinn's favorite rituals was taking a new hire on a tour of the floor. The point of this "perp walk" was, ostensibly, to introduce the new hire to his or her future colleagues. But Quinn's real intent was to give these raw recruits a taste of what, in a matter of months, lay in store for them.

After all, the floor would be very different from anything these new hires had ever experienced in their working lives. In fact, most of them had very little experience actually "working." They'd gone to the country's best undergraduate institutions, then continued their education in MBA programs at prestigious schools like Harvard, Stanford, Northwestern, Virginia, and Dartmouth. They were the best and the brightest.

In the early 1980s Wall Street firms like Merrill Lynch, Salomon Brothers, Goldman Sachs, and Morgan Stanley had begun to funnel their young new hires into training programs. These three- to seven-month finishing schools were the Wall Street equivalent of basic training in the military. There the recruits honed their skills and zeroed in on their expected specialties (equities, fixed income, etc.), after which, upon graduation, they joined a desk and a team.

Most of the recruiting for Merrill's young hires was done by the firm's human resources department. HR had all of the proper contacts within the top universities' MBA programs, and had developed a tried-and-true formula for hiring, using metrics like class rank and grades, as well as less scientific measurables like pedigree.

On occasion, however, Mike Quinn, as the head of his division, used his clout to circumvent the HR department and would hire someone who didn't necessarily fit the mold. "Sometimes you just had a gut feeling about a person," says Quinn.

And sometimes that gut feeling was dead-on.

On a sunny day in the spring of 1984, Quinn walked on to Merrill's fixed-income trading floor. At his hip was his latest hire. The perp walk was on.

The traders and salesmen on the floor paid as little attention as they could to these walks. After all, in just a few short months these newbies would be the competition, and they didn't want to be bothered worrying about what was to come. When Quinn approached with a new hire, the traders and salesmen were generally cold, croaking out a hello, then quickly turning back to the flow of the floor and forgetting the encounter ever took place, like river water quickly repairing itself after the splash of a tossed pebble.

But on that day in 1984, something about this particular new guy made the normally remote folks on the floor pause for just a bit longer than usual, giving the new hire the once-over, nodding their heads in head-to-toe glances. When Quinn and the new guy moved on, they left a sea of sardonic smiles and smirks in their wake. This recruit was different. And not in a good way as far as anyone could tell.

Joe Petri was a trader who had been on the floor for three years. He'd seen Quinn's dog-and-pony show countless times, and like the others, he generally ignored it. All of the recruits looked pretty much the same anyway—midtwenties, precise haircuts, gray Brooks Brothers suits (for men) and conservative white blouses (for women) that their parents had bought for them. The ripest fruit plucked from the nation's best business schools.

But this guy... this guy made Petri lose his train of thought. He looked up from his computer screen, standing to get a better view as Quinn and the man came closer.

The new guy was nothing like the other recruits. First off, he appeared to be at least a decade older than the others. He was big. He held his chest out and walked in a slow swagger. He smiled, but with a look of utter confidence and not a trace of nervousness. He shook hands with force, like he was trying to pull elbows out of sockets.

But it was his clothes that really made him stick out. That wasn't a Brooks Brothers suit he was wearing. That wasn't even a suit.

That was a plaid jacket. And, yes, those were black pants with loud white stripes.

Petri said—out loud but only to himself—the very first words that popped into his head:

"Who the *fuck* is this guy?"

That guy was a football coach who had just given up on his dream, who had failed in his marriage, who had moved back into his parents' house at the age of thirty-four, who no longer lived with his four children, who was now financially supporting six people. He was a man more desperate and more determined to succeed than anyone on the floor.

Quinn and the man walked over.

"Petri, this is Joe Moglia. He starts today."

In 1984 the United States was running at full sprint. After the malaise of the 1970s and the misery of the recession that started the decade, there was an almost hyperactive optimism and eagerness in the country, a general feeling that Ronald Reagan captured brilliantly with his "Morning in America" campaign re-election slogan.

That optimism was felt with special force at Merrill Lynch, which was in the throes of a swift and dramatic transformation. In the 1950s and '60s, the firm became the one of the biggest and best brokerage houses in the world, powered by its legions of stockbrokers, who signed up and shepherded the investment accounts of individuals (what's known as "retail investing"). Those stockbrokers were known, collectively, as "the thundering herd." They didn't necessarily outsmart the rest of Wall Street, but by damn, they did overwhelm it through the sheer force of numbers.

But sometime in the mid-1970s, Merrill Lynch realized that in order to keep up with its competitors on the Street (Goldman Sachs, Salomon Brothers), it had to change its tactics. Investment banking—in which a financial institution could originate stock offerings and sell and distribute them through its own bank—was the best way to do that. The big money wasn't with the individual stock investor. It was with the institutional investors—the massive companies—and the pension funds that had billions of dollars in assets.

Merrill began its transformation by acquiring White Weld, a Boston investment bank, in 1978. But the firm couldn't just buy its way into the game; it also had to grow its investment bank from within. One of the primary architects of that strategy was a man named Roger Vasey. Under his guidance, the firm began to focus on the highly lucrative world of fixed income—that is, gathering interest on government, municipal, and corporate debt that was paid to the lender on a fixed, or regular, schedule. By 1984, that year of optimism, Merrill was rising fast, well on its way to catching up to Goldman and Salomon.

Oddly enough, the unlikely hiring of a thirty-four-year-old former football coach would help them get there.

But the journey to Wall Street was in no way easy for Joe, even though the move made perfect sense to him on a number of counts. It gave him the possibility of making big money, which would allow him to provide handsomely for his kids, and perhaps assuage some of the pain that leaving football would cause him. New York was close enough to his family that he would still be able to visit them fairly often. And while he was getting started on his new career, he could move back in with his parents in Yonkers, which would solve the problem of not having enough money for rent. (His mother was ecstatic to have him home; his father was proud of his attempt to get a "real" job.) It helped, too, that the financial world did actually interest him. He'd been an economics major at Fordham. So what little he knew about the Street seemed to jibe with his needs, his personality—and even his professional background.

Contrary to what others might have thought, Joe really did believe that being a football coach was actually a pretty good way to prepare for life on Wall Street. The problem, he knew, would be convincing others that that was the case. He realized that he wasn't the typical candidate for a Wall Street job. His only degrees were a bachelor's from Fordham and a master's in education from Delaware. He didn't have an MBA and had neither the time nor the money to get one. At thirty-four he was nearly a decade older than the typical recruit. Plus he lacked the pedigree: He was a poor kid from the inner city. He didn't always speak the King's English. He had a family of six. He didn't know a soul on the Street.

But none of that would matter.

Joe had gone after a Wall Street job with everything he had. After studying up on it, he decided that he would focus on the institutional side rather than the retail one. The retail guys were part of the old-boy network that had been entrenched in their jobs forever. They had the family summer homes in the Hamptons. But the real money was now on the institutional side, in the selling and trading of bonds to corporations and governments. The institutional guys got dirt under their fingernails. Sure, they were still predominantly Ivy Leaguers, but Joe believed he had his best shot at breaking in there.

He started with a simple but typically well-thought-out game plan. He got all of the alumni books from the four colleges he'd been associated with, as either a student or a coach: Fordham, Delaware, Lafayette, and Dartmouth. He circled the names of anyone who worked on Wall Street who'd had anything to do with the individual school's football program. Then he called every one of them.

He gave them all what he called his "one-minute pitch," which he rehearsed endlessly in front of his bathroom mirror. The pitch went something like this:

"I grew up in a rough neighborhood in New York City. I got out. A lot of my peers didn't. I've been coaching football for sixteen years. I started when I was nineteen years old. I won two Ivy League championships as the defensive coordinator at Dartmouth. I've written a book about coaching. I am now looking to change careers. I believe that the skill sets needed for coaching football are the same ones needed for Wall Street: You need to be intensely competitive, mentally tough, and exhaustively prepared. You need to perform well under pressure. You need to be able to sell yourself and your program. And the end goal is to win. Period."

Joe was relentless. If a person took his call, he wouldn't let him off the phone until he coughed up a contact. Joe believed that if could just get a face-to-face meeting with a decision maker, he could sell himself and his story. He told no one about his divorce, at least not on the phone. "That seemed like a weak card to play," he says.

But, a few months in, his strategy just wasn't working. Though he turned up a few Wall Street contacts on the phone, he couldn't manage to land any crucial meetings.

And so, in the spring of 1984, Joe decided to take the matter into his own hands. One morning he took the train into the city from his parents' house in Yonkers. He walked through the doors of Merrill Lynch at One Liberty Plaza unannounced (this was back in the day before corporate buildings had much in the way of strict security procedures). He was looking for Brian Barefoot, who was a bigwig in the fixed-income division.

Joe rode the elevator to the seventh floor and, after twenty minutes of searching and sweating, he finally found a door with Barefoot's name on it. He walked in and was greeted by a secretary in the anteroom.

"I'm here to see Mr. Barefoot," he told her.

"Your name?"

"Joe Moglia."

"I'm sorry, sir. He's in a meeting."

Joe looked past her and saw Barefoot sitting at his desk.

"Isn't that him right there?" Joe asked, pointing.

"I'm sorry, sir. He's in a meeting."

Joe didn't want to make a scene. He took out his résumé and put it on her desk. "Please do me a favor and make sure he sees this. Please."

She promised she would. As he was leaving, Joe glanced once more into Barefoot's office. He hadn't budged.

Joe followed up the next week with three phone calls to Barefoot's office. They were never returned.

A month later, Joe finally caught a break. A Dartmouth alum put him in touch with a Merrill Lynch branch manager in Florida who happened to be friends with a man named Bill O'Connor, who ran the national sales desk in New York. Joe called O'Connor, but never got past his secretary. But she, out of pity it seemed, passed Joe on to the head of New York fixed income: Mike Quinn.

Quinn showed up for work one morning and saw Joe's résumé on his desk. "It certainly stood out," says Quinn. There was no MBA and no experience in finance. There really wasn't much at all. Quinn agreed to see him anyway. "He walks in wearing this wine-colored shirt that has a white collar and these white striped pants. It was not the usual outfit. But I could tell immediately that he was very comfortable in his own skin, that he didn't care a whit what he dressed like. To be honest, I was just impressed that he'd gotten himself in the door." (For the record, Joe says he would never wear pants with white stripes. "They were yellow," he says.)

Joe told Quinn his life story, this time including the divorce. Quinn was fascinated. "He was really a rough stone. It wasn't just the way he dressed. He was from the streets. He had this street accent," says Quinn. "And he really had no understanding of how the fixed-income business worked. At all."

Joe wrapped up his story with one last thing:

"I am going to be the number one salesman at Merrill Lynch," he said.

"That's good," replied Quinn. "We want people to aspire to that."

"I don't think you understand me," said Joe. "I'm not going to *try* to do it. I *am* going to do it."

Quinn smiled. "There was a point during the interview when I thought to myself, *This guy is a complete lunatic*. But his intensity was incredible. He wanted it so badly. And he couldn't really afford to fail. I'm a big believer in appetite. He'd been through a lot. Sales was a business where you got beat up every day. You had to be a Weeble Wobble. And it was pretty clear that this guy could take a punch."

Quinn hired him. He wanted to put Joe in the MBA training program to get him up to speed. The problem was that Merrill's human resources department was in charge of filling those spots, and Joe didn't have the MBA usually required for the program. But Quinn, as a division head, went around HR and placed Joe in the program. "They were like, 'Are you sure?' Those folks wanted to show well. They wanted people who looked good on paper, the well scrubbed, well-polished, well-schooled Stanford, Harvard, and Columbia guys. Then they got this thirty-four-year-old father of four with an inner-city accent and a Men's Wearhouse closet.

"Joe had a lot of things to overcome here. Internal resistance was a serious one. But I had a lot of confidence in him," says Quinn.

The human resources folks, however, did not. They resented the move from the get-go. And they let Joe know it.

Joe started in the Merrill Lynch MBA training program in the late spring of 1984. There were twenty-six people in the program at the time, most of them in their midtwenties. Twenty-five of those people had MBAs. Joe's classmates, for the most part, embraced him, impressed by his story and his dogged work ethic. They called him "Coach Joe."

But none of that seemed to matter much to the head of the program, a woman from HR. She had recruited and chosen the other twenty-five members of the class and seemed to resent the fact that Joe had been shoehorned into her class and that upon graduation, he would be in direct competition with her handpicked trainees for the best jobs.

During the first week of the program, she announced that there was to be a cocktail reception for the trainees with Jerome Kenney, who ran all of Merrill's institutional businesses. These get-togethers with big shots were a regular part of the training program, meant to inspire the trainees and give them a little schmoozing time.

As she stood in front of the entire program and announced the party, she added: "Only the regular class is invited." Joe, of course, was the only trainee who was not considered part of the "regular class." He went to the reception anyway. But the program head never strayed from her message. From that point on, any time there was a trainee gathering, she made a distinction between the regular class and Joe.

Joe took it all in stride (and continued to go to the parties). "I got a kick out of it. I was a man by then. I'd gone through a lot of stuff and learned how to handle stress and read people."

Still, Joe had to cram twelve to fourteen hours a day in an attempt to catch up to his better-educated peers. Everything he was being taught—from the math to the terminology—was entirely new to him. "I was so far behind the learning curve," he says.

But Quinn's assessment of Joe's appetite had been spot on. "I knew I had to make this work," says Joe. "I had so much on the line, I couldn't fail." Failure, he believed, meant going back to the fruit store.

In the fall of 1984 Joe went back to Dartmouth for a football game. The Big Green were playing the Quakers of the University of Pennsylvania. Joe wanted to check in on his old players, whom he'd coached and recruited. It was a perfect fall day in New Hampshire, sunny and brisk, the trees ablaze in a patchwork of yellows and reds. After saying hello to his former players on the field before the game, Joe took a seat in the stands by himself, soaking in the familiar sights and sounds. Shortly after the singing of the national anthem, the emotion hit him. "I just started weeping," Joe says. He tried to hide his face in his hands.

That year—his first away from coaching in sixteen years—Joe had somehow made the transition from football to finance by talking his way into one of the most competitive industries on the planet. He was succeeding there already. And though he wasn't yet making much money, it wasn't hard to envision a time—maybe soon—when he would be making more money in a year than his father had made in his entire career.

But none of that mattered on that beautiful fall day as Joe sat in the stands and self-consciously wiped the tears from his cheeks with his sleeves. As he watched the nose tackle that he'd coached skip over a chop block and smother a running back; as he watched his old linebacker screw up his gap responsibility on a draw play; as he watched his slow cornerback take a perfect angle to knock down a pass; as the crowd rose in throaty roars after a good play and hunched over in disappointed moans after a bad one...

At that moment, none of that success at Merrill, none of the promising future mattered.

"I was put on this earth to be a football coach."

When Joe got back to New York City, he decided he wouldn't go to any more football games. He didn't want to put himself through the torture.

In 1985 Joe became a junior fixed-income salesman. His job was basically to analyze the portfolios of large insurance companies and pension funds, figure out what their investment needs were, then cold-call them and try to interest them in doing business through Merrill. Graduates of the trainee program were always given the toughest accounts. "The new guys got the absolute crap—the companies that said they didn't want to do business with Merrill or the ones who hadn't returned a phone call in years," says Quinn. "But you had to earn your stripes."

And Joe still faced some prejudice. Despite the fact that he had successfully graduated from the training program, there was still a feeling among some senior salesmen that this football guy couldn't hack it. They made jokes about his background. "Some senior guys would say things like 'We should give that guy the pensions from the steamfitters and welders unions,'" says Jake Albright, a fellow trainee who became very close to Joe during their years together at Merrill. "I used to tell Joe, 'They won't be saying that when they report to you.'"

Joe kept up the fourteen-hour days, studying the portfolios of both his clients and potential clients, trying to figure out how he could help them—and thereby himself—make money. He honed a one-minute pitch for phone calls. He always believed—as he did during his job search—that if he could meet someone face-to-face, he could close the deal. "Sales back then was a people business," says Quinn. "Joe used his charm." Cathleen Ellsworth was a marketer for what was then known as Chemical Bank, which was one of Joe's clients. "He always laid out his reasoning for a trade in such detail. He was earnest. It was like you could actually see him walking himself though it as well."

Joe took nothing for granted. "Basically, the guy outworked everybody else," says Seth Waugh, who was head of Merrill's global debt market back then. "He wasn't the most intellectual guy, but he was always so prepared. Other guys would be going out and having ten beers, then showing up late in the morning. Joe would work at night, then show up early."

Joe spent hours rehearsing what he was going to say to his clients, partially because of his stutter, but more so because he wanted to deliver his pitch perfectly. "I remember going to the floor one Sunday because I had forgotten something," says Thomas Hughes, another of Joe's fellow trainees. "No one was around, just a few guards. I walk up to my desk and I hear someone talking. I look out and it's Moags. He's practicing his presentation."

Joe thrived on the floor. With its constant thrum of activity and its vast physical dimensions—the ceilings were thirty feet up—it even felt a bit like a sporting arena. The traders sat in the center of the room, surrounded by salesmen. Adrenaline crackled through the floor. Big decisions were made in seconds under intense pressure. Back in those days before the Internet, the floor was a very loud place. "The only way to communicate was verbally, on the phone or through hoot-n-hollers or just by yelling," says Walter Donovan, a trader who sat back-to-back with Joe. "People were crammed in together. You couldn't hear yourself think. I just remember that Joe was always leaning forward in his chair, always ready."

In sports parlance, Joe was back on the field, on this mental gridiron. He was no longer a coach. He was a player, a producer. Though he still believed his skills were best suited for management, for motivating and directing other people, he knew he would have to prove himself on the field first.

He got off to a helluva start. In his first year, Joe cracked some of those seemingly impossible accounts, raking in money for the firm. He became the most successful rookie salesman in Merrill Lynch's history.

The next year, 1986, Joe got even better. In just his second year on the floor, Joe was inducted into Merrill's "Circle of 30," an intrafirm club composed of its top producers. "He got there because he was an animal," says Albright. Members of the club received extra company stock, a trip to a sunny locale, and a significant boost to their stature within Merrill.

But that same year Joe suffered the biggest loss of his life. His mother had been diagnosed with colon cancer the year before. Though her smile never left her face, by 1986, she started to go downhill, fast. In June of that year, Frances McLarnon Moglia died. She was sixty-two.

Joe delivered the eulogy. He talked about the Rye Beach school trip, and the harsh disappointment his mother felt in her oldest child after he was caught with the bottles of liquor. He had vowed then never to let her down again, to make her proud one day.

Establishing and maintaining that pride was perhaps the single most motivating factor in Joe's very driven life. It remains so to this day. Joe may have learned his work ethic from his father, but from his mother he learned something much more valuable: that life is about people, about respect, about love. Joe's mother had sacrificed everything for her family. She had been his cornerstone, the shelter from his father's frequent storms, the warm, gentle heart in a neighborhood and family life that was often cold, harsh, and hard.

"I think Jim [Joe] was heartbroken that our mother never got to see him as a really big financial success," says Johnny. "But she was very proud of what he had done with his life. Very proud."

The long working hours, the lack of exercise, and the stress of his mother's death eventually took a physical toll on Joe. By the summer of 1986, two years into what was looking like a surefire starry career at Merrill, he'd fallen out of shape. "I saw him on the beach and said, 'Joe, you're gonna die, man,'" says Albright, a sinewy marathoner. "He got really mad and said, 'Damn it, I'm going to do something about it.'"

Joe told Albright that he'd run the New York City Marathon if Albright would train him. Albright agreed. The two started to run every day after work. "I beat the living hell out of him," says Albright. "But he never complained."

The running was good for Joe. He lost weight. His colleagues at work all noticed that change. Still, they had no faith in his ability to run a 26.2-mile marathon. The over/under at the office on his predicted finish time was four hours. Everybody but Joe and Albright put their money on the over.

The two ran the marathon in early November. Joe was doing great for the first twenty miles. Then he hit a wall. For the last six miles, "he was friggin' finished," says Albright. "But he just kept going and never said a word." They beat the four-hour mark by a few minutes. "We made a ton of money that day," says Albright. Joe has a picture at home in Omaha of the two of them at the finish line that year. Their hands are raised together, a victory gesture. Albright looks like he's holding up a dead man.

Joe later joined an over-forty baseball league. One day while fielding pregame grounders hit by Albright, a bad-hop ball popped over his glove and caught him in the mouth, knocking the top row of his teeth back into his gums. "Blood was everywhere," says Albright. Joe wiped off the blood and proceeded to play the game before finally going to a dentist.

"Nothing is recreation for Joe," says Albright.

In 1988 Joe became the number one producer in all of Merrill Lynch. In just four years on the floor he had fulfilled the promise he'd made to Quinn during their first meeting.

That year, Joe also helped change Wall Street.

Bob Bertoni, then a senior institutional salesman at Merrill, remembers the first time he heard about Joe, in 1985. Quinn called Bertoni into his office and told him that a trainee would be joining his sales team as the junior member. "He's kind of a goofy guy," Quinn told Bertoni. "He doesn't make the best first impression, and he doesn't know much. But if we let him hang around for a bit, he's going to be running the place."

Joe joined Bertoni and another senior salesman named Ed Sheridan on a fixed-income sales team. The two senior members of the team had both played football back in their school days. They took a shine to the coach immediately. And together, the trio came up with a radical new way to sell debt on Wall Street.

The sales teams on Wall Street were "teams" in name only. The Street at the time worked on a commission model, rewarding individuals for sales. That model was particularly ingrained at Merrill Lynch, which in the mid-1980s was still heavily influenced by its past as a brokerage firm, where individual commissions on sales made sense.

But there were a few big problems with the commission model on the institutional side. One was that it promoted individual glory and not teamwork. It was also an imperfect way of measuring the productivity and capability of a salesman. "We would have, say, the twelfth-best account on the Street with Prudential," says Bertoni. "That would bring in some decent cash because Prudential was so big, and the salesman with that account would make a pretty good commission. The problem was that Merrill was still number twelve at Prudential, which was horrible. Commissions were a terrible way of judging how an individual was doing his job."

But perhaps the biggest problem with commissions was that by the mid- to late 1980s, institutional products were becoming so numerous and so complicated that they were very hard to understand and sell. New derivatives of existing products were popping up overnight. A company like Prudential had billions of dollars in assets, and those assets were spread over many dozens of products, far too complex and too great in number for any one salesman to understand. The solution, Joe, Bertoni, and Sheridan believed, was to create a true team that would divvy up responsibility for mastering the key information they needed to know. The team concept fit the coach's worldview perfectly.

The trio decided to tackle the market together and split their pooled commissions. They broke the market down into three distinct sections: mortgages, corporate bonds, and government bonds. They produced exhaustive reports on all three and shared them with each other. Then they went out and sold.

By the end of 1988 they were producing huge money for Merrill. "On the institutional side, if you started putting up big numbers, you started getting attention and earned some leverage within the firm and the industry," says Bertoni. "Suddenly companies were actually coming to us."

Senior management within Merrill began to take notice, too. In early 1990 the firm hosted a three-day conference in Chicago. All of the institutional traders and salesmen were required to attend. Joe's team was asked to do a presentation on their new concept.

"You have to understand what we were walking into there," says Bertoni. "This idea of individual commissions was firmly entrenched at Merrill, and on the Street for that matter. There were hundreds of salesmen at Merrill who had only known the commission model and, by damn, that's the way they liked it. We were these punks who were threatening their entire way of life."

They knew they'd face pushback. So Joe took the lead in getting them prepared for their moment in the spotlight. (The team now included Albright and a man named Dave McCarthy; Sheridan had been promoted.) In the month leading up to the conference, they enrolled in public-speaking classes and hired a speech coach. The men practiced their talks for hours after work.

When the big day came, four hundred restless traders and salesmen sat in the audience in a convention hall in Chicago. Bertoni, Albright, and McCarthy did the first presentations. "We did okay," says Bertoni. "But we were nothing like what was coming next."

When Joe took the stage, he had no notes and no slides. "He basically delivered a halftime speech," says Bertoni. "His face was red, he was yelling, spit was flying all over the place."

Joe told his four hundred colleagues in that room that the way they did business was going extinct, and that if they wanted to survive, they had to adapt and adjust to a new way. The traders and salesmen did not like what they were hearing. They felt threatened. They crossed their arms over their chests and shook their heads. Condescending smiles spread across their faces. "They were sitting there thinking, *Who the* fuck *is this guy?*" says Bertoni.

Some of them openly laughed at him. Others snickered behind his back. "Joe didn't care at all," says Bertoni. "The number one thing about Joe is that he is never afraid."

Seth Waugh was in the audience that night. "Joe really put himself out there to be ridiculed. But you couldn't walk away from that and not think, *Wow, this guy is gutsy as hell.*"

Joe was also right. Within a few years, Wall Street moved away from the commission model. Salesmen and traders began being paid a salary and a bonus that was based on how well their teams did. That model is still in place today.

By 1990, Merrill, basically starting from scratch, had surpassed Salomon Brothers and caught up to Goldman Sachs on the institutional side. No retail firm in history had ever so successfully transformed itself. "I give all the credit to the group we had there on the institutional side," says Roger Vasey, who was head of the division. "And Joe was a huge part of that."

In 1991 Vasey promoted Joe to the head of New York fixed-income sales, a position that Brian Barefoot—who by then had become friends with Joe—had once held, and that Mike Quinn was in when he hired Joe. The only thing Vasey asked of Joe was whether or not he had a plan in mind for taking over. Joe handed him a book of detailed documents three inches thick. His game plan. "I'd never seen anything like it," says Vasey.

Yet there was still some skepticism about the move. "Everyone thought Joe was a great salesman, but no one thought he could be a manager," says Thomas Hughes. But the doubters overlooked one crucial element: In becoming a manager of people, Joe was moving back into the role in which he was most comfortable. He was now in charge of hundreds of people. In essence he had been taken off the field of play, given the headset, and moved to the sidelines. He was a coach again.

Within a year, Joe was promoted to the head of global fixed-income sales.

⊢┼┼┼┼┤

Joe managed to keep the promise he'd made to himself on that fall day in 1984, after attending that Dartmouth game. Joe never went to a college football game during his tenure at Merrill. (It would be 2001 before he went back to one, and his attendance at that game would be more or less forced on him.) Plenty of his colleagues at Merrill had season tickets and box seats for New York Giants and Jets games. Super Bowl ticket offers made the rounds in the office every year. But Joe never went to a pro game, either. He didn't even watch football on television during the weekends. "I just blocked it out," says Joe. He was completely focused on his Merrill job. Thinking about football was looking backward and only produced heartache. And Joe is not one for wallowing in misery, or nostalgia.

But he did see *some* football during those years. His son, Kevin, the youngest of his brood, played football at Lebanon High School in New Hampshire. He was a fullback and a linebacker. Joe attended a handful of Kevin's games each year. And it was apparent to Kevin that his father clearly missed football. "Dad would sit all by himself in the stands. He had a Dictaphone and he would chronicle every one of my plays. 'Second and ten, you made the tackle. Third and three, you shot the wrong gap.' Things like that."

After every game he attended, Joe would take Kevin back to his hotel room. "We would sit there and go over every single play I had in the game," says Kevin. "Sometimes, this would take longer than the game itself."

Kevin was a good athlete. He was going to attend Bentley University, outside of Boston, where he'd decided to play ice hockey—his best sport—instead of football. Joe went to Kevin's final football game as a senior in high school, the last one Kevin would ever play. "I came out of the locker room after the game and I thanked Dad for coming and then told him that I was going to hang out with my boys," says Kevin. "I'll never forget the look that came over his face when I said it. It was like I had ruined the family name or something. I said, 'Are you all right?'"

Then Kevin noticed that Joe had the Dictaphone in his hand. "We're going to the hotel room, right? To listen to the tape?" Joe asked.

Kevin told his father that his football career was officially over, and that what he really wanted to do was go out and celebrate with his teammates instead.

"He just looked so sad and disappointed," says Kevin.

At around this time, it began to sink in on Joe just how tough it had been on his kids since he'd left New Hampshire. He had of course made trips to see them over the years, but they were sporadic, and there never seemed to be enough time for him to really focus on each one of the children. So he decided he would change the way they spent time together. Rather than taking the whole gang out when he visited them in New Hampshire, he would concentrate on one kid at a time. He would schedule one visit around, say, Kim, and take her out for pizza. "This was great and a lot of fun when it was your turn," says Kelly. "But it wasn't when you had to wait a month or two before you saw him again."

As they got older, his children started to demand more of his time and attention. He'd missed a huge chunk of their childhood, and they had little sense of what he had done with his life since leaving them. That changed when Joe decided he needed to find a way to make up for his absence from their lives, and began flying his kids down for weekends in New York. "We really had no idea what he was doing or how successful he'd been until we started going to New York," says Kim. "He didn't talk much about things like money." Kathe knew, of course, because he still supported them, but she didn't talk much about it, either. When the kids visited him, they started to understand. This had nothing to do with his apartment. By then Joe had long since moved out of his parents' house, but he lived in a studio apartment in Battery Park—quite a modest dwelling for a man now worth millions. It was the things they did together in the city—Yankees games, good restaurants, private cars—and the respect he commanded at his office that hinted at how changed his circumstances were. Although Joe was never extravagant, he was certainly different from the penny-pinching coach they'd known in New Hampshire.

He was also different from the man who had been so focused on his career that he didn't have time for his children. "Once he started to realize that we needed more, he was there for us," says Kim. Indeed, he happened to be out of the office—making a rare weekday visit to one of his children, who had called out to him in a moment of need—on the day that he suffered the biggest disaster of his business career.

Joe was put in charge of all municipal lending in 1993. It was by far the toughest assignment he'd faced as a manager at Merrill. He had to rebuild a division that had been absolutely devastated.

Earlier that year Merrill Lynch had gone through an episode that, until its complete meltdown in the 2008 financial crisis, was the most embarrassing in the firm's history. A trader in the munis division convinced the government of California's prosperous Orange County to place risky, highly leveraged bets with its municipal fund. When interest rates unexpectedly rose, Orange County went bankrupt, then eventually sued Merrill for getting them into the mess to begin with. (Merrill ultimately paid the county a settlement of $400 million.)

The disgrace left Merrill's municipal division in shambles—disheartened, embarrassed, unmotivated, and unproductive. Dave Komansky, who led the institutional side of Merrill at the time, thought he had exactly the right guy to turn it around.

"Joe didn't know a thing about muni bonds, but he knew how to manage people," says Komansky. "The division needed a charge of get-up-and-go."

When Joe looked at the municipals division he saw a risk-averse group of people stuck in a rut of doing things the way they'd always done them, not unlike those fixed-income salesmen he'd roiled a few years earlier. At the time the munis division made bids for trades in partnerships with other Wall Street firms. Doing the trades in this manner helped spread the risk. But it also pinched the gains. Joe decided he needed to change that approach and push them to become bolder. He brought in the muni managers and coached them up: "These other firms aren't your friends. Gimme a break. What, you don't have the brains to do these trades on your own? You either know what the hell you're doing or you don't."

Dave Andersen, a senior munis manager, remembers making the calls to his peers at Salomon, Goldman, and JP Morgan and telling them that he would no longer be making bids with them, but against them. "It was painful. I felt like they'd been partners. We'd all been doing this the same way for years. They were livid."

The heads of the municipal divisions at the rival firms called Joe and told him that if Andersen followed through on his intentions, what he was doing was going to take down Merrill. Joe used their threats to his advantage. He called Andersen into his office. "Dave, I just got a call from your buddies at Salomon and Goldman," he said. "They told me I should fire you."

"That pissed me off," says Andersen. "It also got me very fired up."

Still, Joe believed he had to make an even bigger splash to get the rest of the team on board. He wanted them to think bigger, to take more risks. He decided he would show the way.

Municipals at the time were trading at historically cheap levels. Joe thought they had to rise in price sometime, so he placed a $1 billion bet that they would (called "going long"). But with that much money at risk, he needed to make a hedge. So he decided to make a bet that Treasuries would go down ("shorting"). Joe had to clear the trade with the risk management desk, which took a week or so, but one gray winter day, the trade went through.

It so happened that Joe was leaving the office early that day. His youngest daughter, Kara, who was at Taft, a boarding school in Connecticut, had called to tell him that she was terribly homesick. "I don't know why I called him and not my mom," says Kara. "I just needed my dad." She was the captain of the basketball team. She had a game at Choate. Could he possibly come?

Hearing his daughter in pain on the phone crushed him. Despite the big trade he had just put through, Joe knew that he had to go see Kara.

When he left the office that afternoon, the trade was stable. All seemed well. Outside, the first few flakes of a gathering snowstorm had begun to fall. Joe jumped into a rental car and started the two-hour drive to the game in Wallingford, Connecticut.

At this point in time losing $200,000 in a day in the munis division was considered horrible, possibly grounds for being fired.

The traffic on the road was slow because of the intermittent snow. Joe eventually made it to Choate, just in time for the last ten minutes of Kara's game. "I looked up in the stands and saw that he came," says Kara. "It was a very big deal. It was probably the first time that I felt my dad was there for me." After the game, Kara had to leave on the team bus. Joe kissed her good-bye.

When he got back in the car, there was a message on his phone. It was from one of his muni guys. The man sounded panicked. "Um, Joe, we've got a problem." The hedge had blown up. Munis had gotten crushed and plummeted. Treasuries had had a phenomenal day and shot up. It was the exact opposite of Joe's supposedly hedged bet. "I was a wishbone," says Joe. "And I just got ripped apart."

Meanwhile, the few flakes of snow from a few hours ago had become a full-blown blizzard. The wipers on the car couldn't go fast enough to clear the windshield of the snow. Joe's headlights were useless, serving only to blind him further by illuminating the white flakes. He crawled down I-95 at twenty-five miles an hour.

After a sleepless night, Joe was the first one in the office the next morning. He checked the damage on the trade. It was staggering. Joe had lost the company $14 million. It was, by far, the biggest loss on a single trade in the municipal division's history. "It was unheard of, virtually considered impossible," says Joe. And what made it even worse: There was no way to get out of it immediately. There was still more serious blood to be shed.

Joe leaned back in his chair. He was devastated.

A few hours later, Joe saw Dave Komansky lumber into his office. Komansky is a big man with a Marlon Brando-in-*The Godfather* growl. As the person in charge of the entire institutional side, and the one who had put Joe into his current position, he was Joe's immediate boss. Joe knocked on his door.

Komansky was well aware of the disaster. He sat behind his desk and smiled at Joe. Komansky himself had grown up in a tenement building in the Bronx. He was a sympathetic ear. That probably saved Joe's job. "I liked Joe a lot," says Komansky. "He was different. He was loud and bellicose and very rough around the edges, not like a lot of guys walking around Merrill in those days, the Ivy Leaguers. The big difference between Joe and the other guys in similar jobs was that Joe was getting things done.

A lot of those guys who seemed like the perfect package couldn't find their ass with a road map."

Komansky asked Joe what had happened. Joe laid out the logic behind the trade, then admitted that "we got our balls ripped off." Then he explained that selling out now would make it even more catastrophic.

Komansky admired the fact that Joe was courageous enough to take risks. It was why he'd put him in charge of municipals in the first place. And he trusted that Joe was smart enough to learn from his mistakes. "In the trading business, if you have guys who never lose money, they aren't doing their jobs," says Komansky. "You just have to hope that they win more than they lose."

Joe would lose more—a lot more—before he could even begin to win again. Because of the aftershocks of the trade, Merrill lost another $8 million on the second day. But Joe learned a lesson that would come in very handy during the rest of his business career: "I never wanted to be in a position where you had to sit and hope the markets will take care of you."

Joe continued to tweak new and different hedges on the munis desk, eventually figuring out that hedging municipals and mortgages was a winner. And just as Komansky had hoped, Joe started to win more than he lost.

After Joe's very rocky beginning with the municipals division, Merrill ended 1993 as the largest bond underwriter in the world, a streak that has continued, unabated, to this day. Beginning in 1993 and at the end of every year from then on, Joe would have a large banner made up, proclaiming the wins of the previous twelve months. He had them hung from the tall ceilings on the trading floor, and as the banners proliferated over the years, their presence enhanced the sporting arena feel of the space. "It was like being in the Boston Garden," says Andersen.

When Merrill Lynch blew up during the 2008 financial crisis and lost $28 billion as a firm, the municipals division—still largely Joe's team, though he himself was no longer there—actually made $500 million. Bank of America bought Merrill on the cheap that same year. They laid off entire divisions and absorbed others. But one of the few they left wholly intact was munis.

By insisting that Merrill make its own bids against—and not with—the Street, Joe revolutionized the municipals business. He did it against some pretty strong headwinds. "Without him, we never would have changed the way we did things," says Andersen, who is still with the division now in its new home at Bank of America. "All these years later we still bid exactly the way he changed it, and now so do most of our competitors."

In just a decade, after starting basically from scratch, Joe had become unbelievably successful at Merrill. But football, as much as he tried to forget it, never seemed to let him go. In 1994—out of the blue—Joe received a call from the University of Buffalo. The athletic director wanted to know if Joe had any interest in the vacant head-coaching position.

Now in his forties, Joe had been out of football for eleven years. He had fast-tracked his way through Merrill. He had huge responsibilities as a corporate leader and was finally making serious money, with even more serious money on the near horizon. But the call from Buffalo awakened something within him that had been dormant for so long that he had been unaware that it was still alive. "All of a sudden I couldn't breathe," he says. "I didn't realize that I still had all of this desire to coach."

He did a four-hour interview with the athletic director. He started making calls to potential staff members, including Olivadotti and Chuck Johnson, the head coach at Ridgewood High School in New Jersey. He even let a few colleagues know that he was considering going after the job. "I was pretty shocked," says

Quinn. "He was on track to do anything he wanted at Merrill. He was doing great, making great money. And we didn't want to lose him."

Joe thought about it for a week. But as much as he wanted to entertain the thought of coaching again, Joe realized he would have to pass. Things were going too well at Merrill to quit then. And there happened to be another reason he wanted to stick around.

That reason was a woman, a pretty, petite, brown-eyed divorcee and mother of two boys named Amy Jardine.

In 1992 Amy was living with her young sons in the oceanfront town of Rumson, New Jersey, an hour south of Manhattan. Fresh off her divorce, she was slowly wading back into the dating pool, dipping in one toe at a time. Her friends Dave and Ginny Bauer believed she needed to dive in, head first. And they believed they had the perfect person to help with that in Joe, whom Dave knew from Merrill Lynch. "They asked me if I wanted to go on a date with this guy. Ginny said she had no idea if I would like him, but she said I'd have a blast at dinner," says Amy. She agreed to meet him only if the four of them double-dated.

But the foursome had a difficult time finding a time when they were all free. Joe eventually took the initiative and called Amy. He proceeded to call her weekly for the next three months before he finally convinced her to come to the city for a date. Joe wanted to take her to Cellar in the Sky, a fancy restaurant located on the top of the north tower of the World Trade Center. She agreed. He asked her what she'd be wearing so he'd know how to recognize her. A blue dress, she replied. "I'll be the short, fat, dumpy one," he told her.

On the evening of their date, Amy decided to take the ferryboat from Rumson to the city. She got to the dock and waited. And waited. She finally saw a man standing on an adjacent dock. She asked him when the next boat would be along. "Next year, ma'am," he replied. "The last ferry of the season was last week."

Amy was supposed to meet Joe for the restaurant's prix fixe dinner, which was served at 7:00 p.m. It was now 6:00 p.m.

She called Joe and told him that she couldn't make it. "That's not okay," he told her. Amy got in a cab headed for Manhattan. When they finally got to the city, Amy jumped from the cab and ran the last three blocks to the World Trade Center. Walking into the foyer, she was greeted by an elevator man who said: "Oh, you're the lady in the blue dress." When she handed her coat over to be checked, the man in the cloakroom said: "So you're the lady in the blue dress." The maitre'd said the same thing. "Finally, I ran smack into Joe," says Amy. "I must have downed a bottle of wine that night."

Her first impression: "Joe was really energetic, very strong and to the point. And he wasn't that short, fat, or dumpy."

They ended up dating for three years. "It was a long courtship, but it was very intense," she says. "That made it fun for me."

Joe and Amy were already engaged when Joe got the call from Buffalo. And Amy "would have rather plucked her eyes out than go live there," says Joe. He wanted desperately to coach again. But in his heart he knew the time wasn't right.

Amy and Joe were married in 1995 on a boat that cruised around the island of Manhattan. They—along with Amy's two boys, John and Jeff—moved to Chatham, New Jersey, thirty miles west of the city. Dave and Ginny remained their close friends for years. But Dave would be killed in the 2001 terrorist attacks. By then, he was working in the north tower of the World

Trade Center, the same place where Joe and Amy had had their first date.

⊢+++⊣

After getting married to Amy, Joe continued to scramble up the corporate ladder. By 2001, he had led two core parts of Merrill Lynch and was on the executive committee on both the retail and institutional sides. He also was the head of the firm's investment products, insurance, retirement and midsized companies (and two of his kids, Kara and Kevin, were working there). "Each step up he took was just more and more unlikely," says Quinn. He was perhaps just one layer removed from the very top.

Joe's era at Merrill—from the mid-1980s to the early 2000s—was its heyday, when the firm successfully transformed itself from a brokerage into one of the world's leading investment banks. Those glory years produced Merrill's "greatest generation," who would become big shots all over Wall Street and beyond. Joe's fellow trainee Thomas Hughes went on to become the CEO of the highly regarded boutique bank Gleacher & Company. Kelly Martin became the CEO of the biotech Elan. Seth Waugh has been the CEO of Deutsche Bank Americas since 2002. Roger Vasey retired from Merrill as a legend in institutional investing and founded his own private equity firm. Dave Andersen is in charge of risk management in Bank of America Merrill Lynch's municipals division, one of the last vestiges of the old Merrill. James Gorman, who ran Merrill's corporate sales when Joe was there, is the current CEO of Morgan Stanley.

And then there was Joe, who was right in the middle of Merrill's rise, which was propelled in part due to the way he transformed how the company—and Wall Street—conducted business.

"The guy just willed it all to happen," says Joe Petri, who became a good friend of Joe's. Much of his success, Joe still believes, was built on his previous career as a football coach. It made him mentally strong and prepared him to lead and, maybe most important, motivate. "People who worked for him at Merrill responded to his rah-rah stuff," says Dave Komansky, who became Merrill Lynch's CEO in 1997 until he retired in 2002. "They would never admit it, but they did. He could get at people's hearts."

As fortunate as Merrill was to have Joe, the reverse was true as well. During his run there, Merrill was as close to a true meritocracy as has ever been seen on Wall Street, thanks to people like Quinn, Vasey, and Komansky, who were able to look past easy labels and so-called pedigree and polish. Joe got his chance there because of his personality. He made the most of that chance because his skills and productivity were duly rewarded. But at most other Wall Street firms at the time, Joe would likely have run into roadblocks of ingrained prejudice that would have proven insurmountable.

Merrill's glory years ended in the mid-2000s, when the collegial team atmosphere that first made it great was fractured by the individual greed of some of its management. Though Joe had little shot at running Merrill, Vasey says given what he did later at TD Ameritrade, "There is no question that had Joe run Merrill for the last ten years, it would have been an entirely different outcome."

But he wouldn't get the chance. In 2008, the firm once known as the "thundering herd" would run right off a cliff.

By that time, Joe would be long gone.

CHAPTER ELEVEN

Know Your Limits

On the ride from Las Vegas's McCarran Airport to the Nighthawks' hotel, Joe stands up in front of the bus and repeats an admonition he'd delivered to his players the night before—one that might have come directly out of his Merrill playbook.

"Guys, if you're going to gamble, remember my one piece of advice: know your limit. Set that limit before you go out, and stick to it. Okay?"

Suddenly, there's a shout from the back of the bus. "What's your limit, coach?" It's Dusty Dvoracek, the scruffy nose tackle.

The players chuckle. Joe stops for a second, rumples his brow, and scratches his chin.

"Twenty-five million," he says, beaming. "And not a nickel more."

As the Nighthawks' bus threads its way through the dense Vegas traffic on the day before their third game of the season, the players stare, wide-eyed and mute, at the monuments to human excess that line the road—a miniature pyramid and Pharaoh, a Manhattan skyline, the gold sheen on the windows of the Mandalay Bay, a forty-foot-tall neon cowboy, and Steve Wynn's absurdly paradisiacal eighteen-hole golf course in the middle of it all. Vegas is a city built to distract humans from thoughts of anything other than pleasure. In other words, it's not an ideal place for a traveling team to fly into and keep their heads focused on a football game.

And despite the meetings and meals and the 11:00 p.m. bed check and the fact that the Nighthawks are staying at the Renaissance Hotel—owned by the Mormon Marriott family and thus absent any in-hotel slot machines—the players and coaches will still have some free time on their hands. There is always time in Vegas. Joe's players are adults. Telling them about limits can act only as a reminder—a plea, really—to stay focused. It's a tall task.

Bill Hambrecht, the owner of the UFL, also owns the Las Vegas Locomotives. He had handpicked Jim Fassel to be his coach, and his team has had basically the same staff and many of the same players for three straight seasons, making them pretty much the opposite of the Nighthawks. That continuity has been beneficial. Under Fassel, Las Vegas won the UFL's first two championships.

The Locos play in the thirty-seven-thousand-seat Sam Boyd Stadium, home to the UNLV Runnin' Rebels football team, and a solid twenty-minute drive (if there's no traffic) from the Strip. The stadium is named after an Okie who supposedly showed up in Vegas in 1941 with just $80 to his name, then somehow lived the Las Vegas dream, eventually turning that pocket change into one of the world's largest gaming companies.

Unfortunately for the UFL, the Locos—off the field, anyway—seem to be doing the opposite, which happens to be the more common experience for Vegas visitors: They're turning a large fortune into a small one.

⊢+++⊣

When it came to a limit, the owners of the UFL had decided that theirs was somewhere around $115 million. That's how much Hambrecht, Mayer, Pelosi, and a handful of smaller investors had already bet, and lost, on the league. The question now is whether they are willing to open their wallets any further.

Football is an expensive sport to put on, what with its large number of players, coaches, and supporting staff, its massive amount of equipment, and its insurance and stadium costs. Throw in a dash of mismanaged funds, no revenue-producing national broadcast contract, and a fan base that has become apprehensive about spending season-ticket money after the league's false start in July, and the cost of keeping the UFL afloat becomes potentially crippling.

In 2011, pretty much all league revenues will come through gate receipts. Omaha, Virginia, and even winless Sacramento have had attendance figures that average around fifteen thousand fans per game, down from 2010, thanks to the season's delay, but still solid. But this is Las Vegas's first home game, and the outlook for even a mediocre showing of fans looks very bleak. The game is being played on a Saturday night in a town with a lot of other options that don't require a twenty-minute cab ride to a stadium in the middle of the desert. It's also the first night of Yom Kippur, Judaism's holy day of fasting and praying (and of not attending football games). With the UFL so reliant on gate money, the expected poor attendance at this game is ominous.

The UFL players and fans don't know that at this point in the season—only two games in—the league has already come close to shutting down not just once, as happened quite publicly in July, but numerous times. Two days after Joe's first game, Joe and his fellow coaches had gotten a call from the league's owners.

The UFL's financial troubles, they had been assured in August, had been patched up for the 2011 season. It turned out that they weren't. Loans to the league owners had not come through as planned. Amazingly, there was talk about canceling the season after the first week of games.

Unbeknownst to the players, those calls had kept coming, on a nearly weekly basis. The league limped on.

⊢+++⊣

The Locos enter the game with the same 1-1 record as the Nighthawks. They, too, lost to Virginia and squeaked by Sacramento. The scouting report on the Las Vegas team is fairly straightforward. Their defense is very aggressive. Their safeties are large and hard-hitting, but prone to giving up big plays. Fassel calls the offensive plays and, like Schottenheimer, runs a conventional professional scheme—quarterback under center, lots of runs on first down, three-receiver sets on passing plays with his big tight ends acting as checkdown safety valves.

Olivadotti knows Fassel well from the four years they spent together with the Giants, where Olivadotti was the linebackers coach. One might think that Olivadotti's familiarity with Fassel—and the other two UFL coaches, for that matter—might help him better prepare his defense. But he doesn't think so. "It doesn't matter, really," he says. "These guys are all good coaches. They'll adjust to what they see of us on tape. Then we'll adjust right back."

Leading up to the Vegas game, Olivadotti's been in a bit of a mood, walking around the Kroc Center even more slowly than usual, occasionally stopping in midstride to shake his head. He's like a grumpy, white-haired bear who's been woken up early from his winter nap. His secondary is banged up. Two key members—Dovonte Edwards and DeMarcus Faggins—will miss the Vegas game due to injuries. And cornerback Reynaldo Hill, though he will play, is slowed considerably by turf toe. "We're running the JV team out there this week," Olivadotti growls.

Generally speaking, there are three types of football head coaches: The detail-oriented bureaucrats, like the Washington Redskins' Mike Shanahan, who obsess over every play in the game plans; the generals, like the Pittsburgh Steelers' Mike Tomlin, who rely on their offensive and defensive coordinators to put together the plans and merely manage these men, providing feedback and insight when needed; and those who fall somewhere between these two poles.

Joe is a general. For him, being a head coach is exactly like being a CEO. He hires people he trusts, then lets them do their jobs. His role, as he sees it, is to coach the coaches, and to inspire and motivate the players. Andrus draws up every offensive snap in practice, then crafts the entire game plan for the offense. Olivadotti does the same on his side of the ball. Joe leans on both men, and particularly Olivadotti, to run practices. What Joe excels at in coaching is what he excelled at in business. He provides perspective and an overview. Amy calls this talent of Joe's "the flyover."

"Joe sees the desert, the river, and the trees. Everyone down on the ground can get so worried and wrapped up in putting the fire out in the trees that they don't see the river of water running right nearby," she says. "When people get stressed and emotional, they get lower to the ground. But he stays up there. He does this survey thing when he can see it all and help people figure it all out."

What Joe sees in the week leading up to the Vegas game is something he doesn't like: mistakes. "We've been repeating the same ones over and over. Offsides on the kickoffs, false starts on the offensive line. These are all mental mistakes. And that's all on us, the coaches. I need to do a better job. We all need to do a better job," he tells his coaches.

The penalties are clearly driving him nuts. "In my coaching years—and yes, I know they were twenty-eight years ago, but this is still relevant—my teams always had the fewest penalties in the league. This was something I prided myself on. Now we are leading the UFL in penalties, by a lot. We need to fix that."

The shortened camp and season are big reasons for the mistakes, Joe concedes. But they are not excuses. He still believes that Andrus and Kent continue to try to do too much. In coaching and in business, Joe's forte has been getting people to simplify and to focus on the things that matter, to play to what he calls (in unadulterated business speak) their "core competencies."

"It's the beginning of our fifth week together. If you have twenty-five things that are your priorities, that tells me you have no priorities. Let's pare it down, do a few things and do them very, very well."

Five minutes before the start of the game, after warm-ups, Joe gathers the team together in the locker room at Sam Boyd Stadium. They've all heard the rumors about the paltry crowd that's expected, and they've seen for themselves that not many fans were in the seats for warm-ups. "Don't worry about that," Joe tells them. "There is nothing we can do about it. Just go out there and block it out just as you would block out a huge crowd."

Then he rolls into the pregame prayer, a common occurrence in football locker rooms around the country. During his prayer, Joe physically mimics some of the moves of a seasoned televangelist. He clenches his eyes shut. His voice rises and falls at key moments. Sweat beads on his brow. But the content of his prayers is different, in a big way. As offensive lineman Damion Cook puts it: "Man, sometimes it seems like Coach Joe is coaching God, too."

"Dear Father, we ask that you keep everyone on our team and theirs free from serious injury today. We've talked about respect, about having courage and dedication. We've talked most importantly about being a man, about standing on our own two feet and accepting responsibility for our own actions. Father, *help us to be men!* Help us with this concept of manhood. Help us not to quit on the field, to play every down as hard as we can."

Then everyone in the locker room holds hands, and Joe says: "Our Father, who art in heaven . . . ," kicking off the Lord's Prayer, which is recited communally—at warp speed—by the team. Not all of the players and coaches are Christians, but they all at least mouth the prayer. A football game is its own foxhole.

The Nighthawks take the field. Everyone in the stadium can see Bill Hambrecht, who is standing tall in a suite above the field. But the stands are virtually empty. Officially, the UFL will later announce a crowd of 6,500; in actuality, it looks more like 2,000. The lack of fans creates the sensation of a game being played in a canyon. Kicked balls echo up to the top row. Shouts from individual fans are heard with distinct clarity ("Omaha sucks!"). "There aren't even enough fans here to take down a goalpost," says defensive line coach Brandon Noble. The stadium may be the only lifeless place in Las Vegas. The eerie silence seems to affect the players, many of whom were accustomed to having more people than this attend their high school games. There is a distinct listlessness on the field, a lack of what Olivadotti says is the key to any game: *emotion.*

⊢+++⊣

The first two series for each team result in punts, the ball yo-yoing back and forth, with not much field position advantage gained by either team. Then Vegas gets a big play, a forty-seven-yard pass from scrambling quarterback Chase Clement to receiver Andrae Thurman. The ball ends up at the Omaha 6-yard line. And somehow, Olivadotti's defense holds the Locos to a field goal attempt, which is partially blocked. But the ball manages to tumble, end over end, above the bar of the goalpost.

On the next possession, Masoli overthrows his receiver and the Locos intercept and get the ball at the Omaha 17. And again, the defense stands tall. Another field goal makes it 6–0 Las Vegas. The Nighthawks have nothing going on offense, with their drives stalling after just a few plays. Late in the second quarter, behind the physical running of former Arizona Cardinal tailback Marcel Shipp, the Locos again get into the red zone, but have to settle for yet another field goal.

On the sideline, Joe is more animated than he has been in the first two games. He's becoming more assertive, especially with the players. "I'm proud of you guys!" he yells to the defense as they leave the field after a stop. He pats Masoli on a shoulder pad. "Let's go, Jeremiah. You can do this. Just calm down out there. Just concentrate. See the play. Play with your head."

Joe is trying to spark something in his team—anything. But it doesn't seem to be working. Everything about this game—the players, the fans—is lethargic.

At halftime, despite the fact that the Omaha offense has been completely impotent (they've held the ball for only eight minutes in the entire half), Omaha is down just 9–0 and is very much still in the game.

But in the second half, the Nighthawks' emotional apathy begins to take a physical toll. The Locos drive for a touchdown on their first possession, extending their lead to 16–0. Omaha loses key players on nearly every series. Shaud Williams, the team's best all-around running back, suffers a concussion. Dusty Dvoracek, the space-eating nose tackle, tears the posterior cruciate ligament in his knee. Chad Jackson, Omaha's best receiver, also tears a knee ligament.

But the most soul-crushing injury comes late in the third quarter. The Nighthawks finally string together a long drive, propelled by the running of John Griffin and Garrett Wolfe. They settle for a Wolfert field goal. On the ensuing kickoff, with the Nighthawks hustling down the field to cover the kick, there is what sounds like a shotgun blast that reverberates throughout the empty stadium. When the returner is finally tackled and the play is whistled dead, a Nighthawk player lies sprawled on the ground, arms and legs akimbo. It looks as if he has fallen asleep in the midst of making snow angels. Several Locos players are jumping up and down, screaming and beckoning to the Nighthawks bench to send in trainers. The player on the ground has not moved an inch.

The dual image of opposing players in a frenzied panic and a motionless body lying on the turf is terrifying. It's one of those sickening moments when even the most diehard football fans question their love of the game, wondering why they watch and patronize such a sport, and, perhaps, why anyone is willing to play it. The injured player is Mike O'Connell, the spirited rookie safety who made the Nighthawks team thanks in large part to a huge hit he delivered on a special teams play during the Omaha intrasquad scrimmage. Right now he is a large X lying on the field, out cold because of a huge hit made on *him* during this special teams play. Trainers rush to his side. Paramedics jump out of the field-side ambulance without being summoned, wheeling out a gurney and a backboard. The quiet crowd somehow grows even more silent. Five minutes pass as they work on him. It seems like an eternity.

O'Connell had been the first man down the field for the Nighthawks. He'd drawn a bead on the kick returner, but had failed to see the returner's lead blocker, the "up man," coming in from his right. The blocker had launched himself into O'Connell and delivered a vicious, but legal, helmet-to-helmet hit. The blow severely dented O'Connell's face mask.

As soon as the paramedics get to O'Connell they strap him to the backboard and cut off his jersey in the shape of a cross. He wakes up as his face mask is being screwed off (the paramedics leave his helmet on as a precautionary measure) and finally, to much relief on and off the field, he moves his arms and legs. He's rushed to the hospital. He has suffered a nasty concussion. His season, which once seemed likely to blossom into at least a shot with an NFL team, is now over.

Despite a late touchdown throw from Masoli, the game essentially ends when Clement runs for a six-yard touchdown in the fourth quarter. Shipp adds insult with a twenty-eight-yard touchdown run on a fourth-and-one play that puts the Locos up 30–10. Olivadotti leaves his perch in the box early to come down the field with a few minutes still left to play. His eyes are more bloodshot than usual. He apologizes profusely to Joe on the sidelines. He knows Joe counts on him to be his rock. "I'm embarrassed as hell. I let us all down tonight," he tells his friend and boss.

The loss is a total psychological and physical beat-down. Joe's team is outgained and thoroughly outplayed. The Nighthawks have lost four key players to injuries during the game, and perhaps for the season.

Hambrecht greets Joe on the field as he walks to the locker

room. There is a brief discussion about the lack of fans and what that means for the league. "Well, we'll see where we go from here," Hambrecht sighs. The season, Joe knows, is again in peril. He desperately doesn't want it to end like this.

In the locker room, Joe leads a prayer for O'Connell, who will, somehow, make the team flight home just three hours later. Joe prays more intently than usual.

If the season continues, the Nighthawks will play the Locos again in Omaha in just six days.

CHAPTER TWELVE

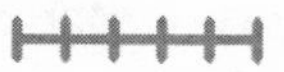

Baby, Vegas

Back in Omaha, rumors begin to swirl about the fate of the UFL. One has the league folding immediately, just three games into the season. Done. Kaput. Another has the season being shortened, and the Virginia Destroyers (who are 3-0) and the Las Vegas Locos (2-1) playing in a media-and-league-friendly championship game that would pit Schottenheimer's team against the two-time defending UFL champs. The third rumor—and the one most palatable to the Nighthawks—is that the winner of the Omaha–Las Vegas rematch will meet Virginia in the championship game.

Joe calls a coaches' meeting early Monday morning, normally a time when the staff would be preparing for the next game. He tells them what he knows. The Sacramento owner, Paul Pelosi, seems reluctant to pour any more money into his franchise, which is 0-3 for the season. And with bills remaining unpaid, the problems that faced the league back in July have not been resolved. Joe believes the season will indeed be shortened, and that the Nighthawks season may well be over. He says he'll have more information in a few hours, after a conference call with the owners. "This type of stuff has been going on all season, literally every week," Joe says. "I've tried to keep these issues away from you guys so you could focus on your work." That was no longer possible. The issues were now public.

The coaches shake their heads and look at each other across the room. The same jolt of sadness, of disappointment, that accompanied the delay in July is back. Marvin Sanders, the secondary coach, speaks up. His patience with the UFL's problems is blown.

"This is absolutely ridiculous. Again? Joe, I'm really worried," he says, speaking for everyone in the room. "The players are going to feel let down whether we play or not. Really, we are, too."

Joe nods his head. A flash of shared frustration crosses his face, then quickly passes. He narrows his eyes. "Marvin . . . All of you. Look, this is where we come into play. The bottom line is this is what we have. We can feel sorry for ourselves. We can feel sad. That's natural. But this is a test: Are we going to buckle? Or are we going to figure out how to make it work? Let's figure out how to make this work." The thought seems to buoy their spirits, if only for a moment.

With that, he dismisses the coaches. They file into their respective meeting rooms to watch film and prepare for a game that might not take place.

Later in the afternoon, Joe gathers the staff together again. He has news. Everyone nervously steals glances at Joe, trying to get a read on what he is about to say. Joe sits down at the head table in the meeting room, directly under the banner with the quote from the Gospel of Mark.

"Guys, I have some bad news," he says. "Later today, the UFL will issue a press release that says the league has folded."

Complete stunned silence. It's over.

"Just kidding," Joe says. He smiles.

The room explodes in relieved laughter.

All of the teams will be playing this weekend, he tells them. There's a chance that if the Nighthawks win, they'll play in the championship game. There's also a chance that even if they win, the season is over. Nothing is certain except for the fact that *this* game is on.

Minutes later, Joe addresses the players and repeats what he's told the coaches, minus the joke. "The bottom line is that whatever happens in the weeks to come, we absolutely have to win *this* game," he tells them. "That part of the equation stays the same."

In other words, now that the game is saved, all the Nighthawks have to do is go out and defeat a team that, just a few days before, had completely dominated them.

One afternoon after practice, Joe leads his third "Life after Football" seminar. This week's topic is personal finances. All but sixteen of the Nighthawks players show up for the meeting; eight coaches are on hand as well. (The league's probable demise has apparently jolted the men into thinking a bit more about a football afterlife.) Joe has brought in a group of managers from TD Ameritrade who will talk about credit card fees, retirement savings accounts, and stock portfolios, and answer what will turn out to be hundreds of individual questions from the players and staff, questions that range from mortgages and car payments to retirement plans.

But before the suits can take the floor, Joe stands up to address the room. He has a few things he wants to say first.

"Here's the one lesson I've learned over the years," he says. "No one, and I mean no one, cares about your money more than you do. It's an absolute must for you to know exactly how much money you have coming in and going out. You can't rely on other people to do that for you. I certainly don't."

Joe then hands out a sheet of paper that has thirty-six different categories listed on it, each with its own individual box. It's his own monthly and annual budget worksheet. "You'll see I've only included the categories and not the actual expenditures," he says with a grin.

The worksheet includes categories that one might expect to see. There are slots for maintenance on cars, cash given annually to his children, and dues for his golf clubs (Baltusrol and Omaha Country Club). But Joe also gets surprisingly granular on his sheet. There's a slot for the flowers he occasionally buys Amy and one for monthly cable TV. There's another labeled "fish food."

Joe, despite his millions, sits down with Amy every year and fills out this sheet by hand. Even though he has become a very wealthy man, he is as careful with his money now as he was back when he was a flat-broke high school football coach scrounging for change to buy sprinkles for an ice cream cone.

That the Nighthawks and Locos are playing each other twice within a six-day span is yet another challenging quirk in the UFL's reconstituted season. The Nighthawks will have limited time to regroup strategically and—more important—emotionally. A team defeated in the manner the Nighthawks were can suffer a loss even greater than the game itself—a loss of confidence, in themselves, their system, their coaches. Joe's task this week is to ensure that doesn't happen. And that starts with coaching his coaches.

He meets with his three coordinators and their respective staffs individually. Olivadotti is still deeply embarrassed by his defense's performance in the last game. "We screwed up and we will fix it," he tells Joe. All week long, Olivadotti subjects his players and coaches to repeated viewings of their disaster in Las Vegas. He wants them to really *feel* the same embarrassment that he does. During practice, with every glare at a player who has made a mistake, and every pat on the back of one who has done something well, Olivadotti is telling Joe *I won't let you down again*.

Kent, too, uses film as a motivator. He shows the special team units footage of all the kickoffs and punts. In every frame, the Locos physically dominate, making the bigger hits, tossing Nighthawks players to the turf. Kent refrains from showing the O'Connell hit again, but that play and injury serve as an implicit rallying cry.

Andrus says his side just has to put it together. The pieces are in place. But he wants more from Joe. In one meeting he asks Joe to more strongly demonstrate his faith in the offensive play calling. "I believe in you and this system," Joe responds. "Just do your thing and do it well."

The Nighthawks have more than a mental hurdle to overcome this week. There's a physical one, as well, in the form of the team members they have lost to injuries. During practice, the injured players are on the sidelines watching the action, all in something of a daze, like infirmary patients gathered in the TV room. The team's best receiver, Chad Jackson, stares at the turf below his tightly wrapped knee, perhaps in disbelief that he has suffered yet another injury in a career plagued by them. Dvoracek limps around in flip-flops. O'Connell wears a hoodie, peering out at the scene from the dark-circled eyes of a man who has suffered a serious head injury. Reynaldo Hill sits on a golf cart, foot on the dashboard, his injured big toe pointing skyward.

Although they're close to the action, it's as though the injured men have become invisible on the practice field (though they are well taken care of off the field). The coaches no longer talk to them much; their concentration is on the guys who will actually be playing. Even their teammates barely acknowledge them, an avoidance that seems almost purposeful. The injured players represent something unnerving to the healthy, a reminder of the sudden death blows that this game routinely and randomly doles out to men's dreams.

⊢+++⊣

The week wears Joe down. He can't sleep at night. He's on the phone every day with Hambrecht and Huyghue, trying to help sort out the league's finances (this time, they're joined by the other coaches). He is using every last reserve of energy to motivate his coaches and players for the battle against a team that just ran right over them. And, though he mentions this to no one, his own career is at stake here. He feels he must win this game. Going 1-3 in this league would pretty much verify the fears and doubts that all of those college athletic directors had about him. His team seems anxious as well. He decides they all need to loosen up.

At what might very well be the Nighthawks' last practice, on a sunny and brisk fall day, Joe makes a request of George Glenn, his chief of staff. He wants Glenn to start practice by playing the Surfaris song "Wipeout" on the big speakers that are wheeled onto the field daily and usually used to simulate crowd noise. Glenn complies.

Joe calls the team together in the middle of the field, and then signals to Glenn. At the song's manic opening words—"Ha, ha, ha, ha, ha, wipeout!"—which lead to the equally manic and annoyingly hard-to-forget guitar riff, Joe drops his clipboard and starts to swivel his hips, harkening back to his pseudonymous, prize-winning dance during his Dartmouth days. Walter Curry Jr., a big defensive lineman always up for a laugh, joins in. The players are into it. They gather around, hooting and hollering. Suddenly, seventy-four-year-old Don Lawrence jumps in, doing his own slow-but-very-determined twist. (He will check in with the trainer immediately afterward, complaining of pain in his back.) A Nighthawks media relations intern films the dance and posts it on YouTube, but without any sound. Joe will have it quickly taken down after a few ribbing phone calls from his friends. "It was so out of context," he says. "It was like seeing someone in his car singing his heart out when you can't hear the music. I looked like a dodo."

Still, Joe is never afraid to play the fool—in context, of course—*if* he thinks it will serve a purpose. And his performance is meant to set the tone for the practice, and for the game that is soon to follow: let's be intense, but let's stay loose and have fun.

It turns out to be one of the best practices of the year.

Realizing that this may be the last game of the Nighthawks season—maybe even the last of Joe's coaching career—Joe's family and friends rally to his side. Johnny, Mary, and Paul all fly in to Omaha with their spouses. His three oldest children, Kelly, Kim, and Kara, come with husbands and children in tow. (Kevin is stuck working back in New York.) Even Kathe briefly considers attending the game, but eventually decides to listen to it via a website radio feed (the only way for out-of-towners to follow the game thanks to the UFL's inability to secure a national TV contract). Joe's stepson Jeff, who has been an intern with the team (and was the "squirrely" guy who made Andrus so nervous during the tryouts) will of course be there. His other stepson, John, is flying in from Dallas. And a few members of the old Merrill Lynch crew—Roger Vasey, Bob Bertoni, Ed Sheridan, and Jim Smyth—make a surprise visit. Many of the TD Ameritrade gang are there as well, as they have been all season.

For Joe's two oldest children, being at the game has a certain cathartic effect. Seeing their father on a football field represents something bigger than the game, bigger and in some ways even better than Joe's attempt to recapture his dream. "It's so cool seeing him on the sidelines again," says Kelly. "I never really knew the Merrill Lynch and TD Ameritrade dad. Watching him coach again brings me back to a much better time, before anything bad happened, when he was just my dad."

Having all of these people present is actually beneficial to Joe, and helps take his mind off the worst part of game week for football players and coaches: having to endure the excruciating hours between waking up and going out on the field when the big day finally arrives. "I absolutely hate the day of games, especially with a late kickoff," says Olivadotti. (The Vegas game is at 7:00 p.m.) "The hay is in the barn. All you can do is wait."

On game days, there is an optional prayer gathering in the morning, then the offense, defense, and special teams each meet for a quick ten minutes just to mentally walk through assignments and plays one last time. Olivadotti and Andrus like to have their game plans set in stone by the day before the game, at the very latest. They are both thankful that Joe is not a last-minute tinkerer. "[Don] Shula used to come up to me an hour before the game and say, 'Hey, Tom, let's change this and this and this,'" Olivadotti says about his former boss. "I loved the man. Still do. But that used to drive me crazy."

In the midafternoon, everyone lumbers down to the dining hall for the pregame meal, exactly four hours before kickoff. The coaches always sit at the tables and let the players hit the buffet line first, like cowboys watching their cattle graze. The day of games is quiet, almost solemn. There is none of the usual laughing and horsing around, just the *tink-tink* of forks on plates and the gentle murmur of lowered voices. "Part of it I think is that they are concentrating on the game," says Olivadotti. "And another part of it is just zoning out, trying to forget the game so the anticipation doesn't drive you crazy."

Olivadotti gets some good—and very surprising—news a few hours before kickoff. Somehow, despite a badly torn knee ligament, Dusty Dvoracek has decided that he will play in the game. The trainers have advised him that doing so risks catastrophic injury to his knee. Dvoracek knows that. But it isn't stopping him. The coaches aren't, either: it's hard to deter a strong-willed, six-foot-three, three-hundred-pound nose tackle.

And, anyway, they need him. "Dusty is the most important player on our defense," says Brandon Noble. On the face of it this statement seems nonsensical, since Dvoracek's name rarely appears on the stat sheets (he averages only a few tackles a game). But what he does is perhaps the least selfish, least glamorous task in football. His job is to eat up space, to occupy at least two offensive linemen and hold them in place at the line of scrimmage. That allows the linebackers behind him, and his fellow defensive linemen beside him, to blast through lanes to attack the running back or the quarterback. Dvoracek does this at least as well now as he did during four injury-riddled seasons with the Bears.

This may very well be the last game that Dvoracek ever plays. He's suiting up for his own gratification—he loves the violence, the battle of wills, the chance to prove on every play that he can overcome pain and push himself beyond his own limitations. But he's also doing it for Joe. "I believe in him," says Dvoracek, who has a cherubic face on which he's raised a short but still scruffy, sandy-blond beard. "All of that 'being a man' stuff is true. It's what life is all about."

Dvoracek is a study in the contrasts that football seems to demand of its players. He is well spoken, philosophical and smart (he was Academic All Big-12 at Oklahoma). But he is also sometimes out of control. One drunken brawl during college led to his suspension from the Sooners football team. Another one after college resulted in an arrest.

He's paid a severe price for his love of football. Both of his knees are shredded. He can't lift his right arm over his head because of the 2007 tackle of Adrian Peterson, in which he tore his biceps. His hands are swollen to the size of oven mitts, and nearly all of his stubby fingers have been broken, sprained, or jammed at one point or another in his career.

In his unguarded and reflective moments, Dvoracek acknowledges the toll that the game has taken on his body, and what it might mean for his long-term health. Former NFL nose tackle Kris Jenkins once described his football job in gladiatorial terms: "You may not die now, like in an old Roman arena, but five, ten years down the road you could. You know that."

Dvoracek agrees. He sees the alarming number of former professional football players—and, in particular, linemen—who are dying at premature ages, wracked with injuries to their brains, hearts, and other key parts of their bodies. "I'd be surprised if I make it to fifty-five," the twenty-eight-year-old says quietly, with a calm, serious look on his face. "But I would do it all over again. I really would."

Herein lies the modern conundrum facing football players: Thanks to scientific advances, they are now fully aware of the physical and emotional toll that the game will exact upon them. But most of them choose to play anyway, for as long as they physically can.

The reason that Dvoracek would literally die for the game is that it provides him with something that he feels he can find nowhere else, something, paradoxically, that he feels is vital to living fully. In this battle of wills on every snap with another man (or in his case, often with two other men), he reaches something deep and profound within himself, some sort of absolute clarity. Every play on the field for Dvoracek is what T. S. Eliot once described as "the still point of the turning world." It's something he is not willing to give up just yet, no matter the cost.

In the locker room before the game Joe introduces Bo Pelini, the Nebraska head coach who has come up from Lincoln to watch his former intern in action. "If it wasn't for this guy, I wouldn't have had this opportunity," says Joe. Pelini waves a modest hello, then cedes the floor to Joe.

"Men, this is a gift we've been given here tonight. How many times in life do you get a real second chance?" Joe asks, before delivering a few succinct admonitions. The special teams units, he says, have to be more physical; they were blown away in the last game. The offense has to find its groove and score points. And the defense must redeem itself. Olivadotti nods, then stares grimly at the floor.

Angelo Crowell, the muscled linebacker and captain of the defense, walks to the middle of the room. "We all stood up individually before the season started and talked about where we were from, who we were, what our goals were. Tonight is the night we put all of those words into action, together."

Then the teams take the field. It's a beautiful, soft, Indian summer evening in Nebraska. The fans are out in full force, 17,600 strong, one of the biggest crowds in the UFL season. They are loud. They get louder when Joe and Pelini run out onto the field together. Then the sideline, in the VIP section, becomes a snapshot of Joe's life: His daughters and their husbands and his grandkids are standing next to his stepsons, who are standing next to his former Merrill and TD Ameritrade colleagues and Bo Pelini. Amy is in a skybox, as always, nervously watching over the proceedings.

On the opposing sideline, Fassel paces back and forth, his face already worked up into a game-day crimson. Hambrecht and Huyghue are in attendance. It's apparent that some decision on the league will be made here tonight.

Dvoracek runs out onto the field with a noticeable hitch in his gait, then takes a seat on the bench and starts violently vomiting. It's part of his pregame routine.

The Nighthawks kick the ball to the Locos. Omaha's defense sets the tone right away. Olivadotti has them ready. On the first play from scrimmage, four Omaha defenders run Locos quarterback Chase Clement out of bounds for no gain, their thudding feet sounding eerily like a troop of galloping horses. "C'mon, Clement, you got more than that, man!" seethes Crowell.

On the second play, defensive linemen Jay Moore and Kevin Basped plant Locos running back Marcell Shipp on his rear in the backfield for a loss.

On the third play, a slow-developing run, Dvoracek slaloms through a few offensive linemen. As the play unfolds, the Nighthawks players on the sidelines whoop and leap in the air, like a boxing crowd sensing an impending knockout. They get their wish. Dvoracek blasts into Shipp for another loss, this one of four yards.

The special teams match the defense's intensity. On fourth down, Matt Wenger—the rookie linebacker who'd been signed to take the place of the injured Pat Thomas—slices through the middle of the Locos line and blocks the punt. The Nighthawks recover the ball on the Las Vegas 8-yard line. The crowd works itself into a frenzy. Everything is going the Nighthawks' way.

But the offense doesn't get the memo. After a six-yard run by John Griffin to the 2-yard line, Shaud Williams is stuffed for a loss. On third down, Masoli rolls out to his left and throws the ball to Greg Orton, who, with Jackson out, is perhaps Omaha's best healthy receiver. Orton, in the end zone, is as open as a professional wide receiver could hope to be, which is to say that he has one small step on his defender, a narrow window that will close in a matter of seconds. The ball is thrown a bit low, but is catchable. Orton reaches his hands down to the tops of his shoelaces.

He seems to have the ball in his hands for a moment. But then he drops it. Wolfert hits a field goal the length of an extra point.

Early in the second quarter, Colclough almost returns a punt for a touchdown, but is tripped up by the last man standing between him and the end zone. After a few incomplete passes, Omaha's drive stops at the Locos' 14. On fourth and eight, Wolfert comes on for a thirty-two-yard field goal attempt.

During the week's special teams film sessions, Kent noticed that on field goal attempts, the Locos sometimes lined up only three men on the right side of the line of scrimmage, where he had four. Plays at the line of scrimmage come down to numbers. Whoever has more men usually wins. Kent thought if the situation arose, Omaha could run a surprise fake (they had not run one all season). The fake would entail Mante, the Yalie punter and kick holder, running the ball.

As the Nighthawks line up for the field goal attempt, Wolfert sees that there are indeed four Locos on the right side. He's supposed to kick. But he and Mante, through some confusion, make the wrong call.

The ball is snapped and Mante takes off with it. Mante, who is not a big man as professional football players go, six feet tall and maybe two hundred pounds, gains only two yards before the unblocked Locos player crushes him. With the unsuccessful fake, the Nighthawks fail to score a point from the 14-yard line. And the tackle results in a broken collarbone for Mante—something he will neglect to tell Kent about until after the game.

The Nighthawks defense, however, is still on fire. Led by Crowell, who has four tackles for losses in the first half alone, and Dvoracek, who's enabling Crowell and his linebacker brethren to have the space they need to disrupt plays, it's working exactly as Olivadotti had envisioned. With eight minutes left in the first half, Schweigert intercepts a Locos pass. Masoli leads the offense down to the Las Vegas 1-yard line. Garrett Wolfe gets a carry on third down, and runs parallel to the line, trying to gain the corner of the end zone. But he takes only one step before being taken down by a Locos defender who has blasted Omaha center Donovan Raiola three feet into the backfield.

Raiola jogs to the sideline with his head down. Joe runs over to him. Joe's face is flushed. Frustration with the offense is boiling over on the sideline.

"What happened?" Joe says.

"I wasn't ready, Coach," Raiola replies.

"What do you mean you weren't ready? The guy was right in front of you. Block his ass!" says Joe. Then, as if trying to move Raiola past the mistake, Joe adds: "Donovan, you're one of the leaders on this team. Now get your ass out there and show it."

Wolfert kicks another field goal. The Nighthawks go into the locker room leading 6–3. They've held the Locos to minus-one-yard rushing in the half. They've owned the line of scrimmage. They've dominated the game. Being up by only three points feels like a huge disappointment.

Because the average play in the football game, from snap to whistle, is only four seconds long, it may seem like folly to try to reduce a game to a single one. But sometimes the success or failure of one critical play ends up being the standard by which everyone and everything—the offensive scheme, the players, the front office, the coach—is judged. Games can change in four seconds. Seasons can, too.

Had Greg Orton caught that pass thrown at his shoelaces, the Nighthawks would have been ahead 7–0 and had all the momentum in the game. Holding the Nighthawks to merely a field goal after they had the ball at the 2-yard line was a huge lift for the Locos, a confidence-boosting victory in a key battle in the larger war.

On their opening drive in the second half, the Locos finally get something going on offense, using a mix of runs and play-action passes to keep Omaha's aggressive defense on its heels. But, deep in Nighthawks territory, a blitzing Crowell breaks through the line and pressures Locos quarterback Chase Clement into a forced throw. The ball sails directly at the chest of Omaha linebacker Steve Octavien, who seems surprised at his good fortune. So surprised that he turns his head just a second before the ball reaches his hands, already scouting out the lanes through which he'll run with the ball. But there will be no running because the football slips through his hands and bounces off his chest, falling harmlessly to the grass. On the Omaha sideline, professed Christians use their Lord's name in vain. A minute later, the Locos score a touchdown. And, astonishingly, they are now ahead by four points in a game in which they could have been down by at least fourteen.

The Nighthawks offense responds with an impressive drive, but one that ultimately stalls in the red zone. Wolfert, the UFL's best kicker and one of the most reliable kickers in NCAA history, comes on for a forty-yard field goal attempt. Mante, his holder, now hampered by his broken collarbone—which he still hasn't told anyone about—gets the snap and can't quite spin the laces away from the spot where Wolfert's foot is supposed to meet the ball. (Kicking the ball on its laces is thought to be a mortal sin; kickers believe it reduces their ability to control the flight of the ball.) The kick goes wide, and with it, Wolfert seems to lose the one thing he has relied on most throughout his successful athletic career, first as a diver, then as a placekicker: his confidence.

In the fourth quarter, on another Omaha foray into the red zone, he misses another kick, this one from thirty-seven yards. The Locos, buoyed by the misses, get one more drive going. They have a third-and-one at the Omaha 15. A touchdown will pretty much seal the game, given the state of the Nighthawks offense. But Basped tackles Shipp in the backfield. The Locos settle for a field goal. They now lead 13-6 with five minutes left in the game.

After a quick possession, the Nighthawks punt back to the Locos. Clement leads Vegas to the Omaha 20, where they face a fourth-and-one. Fassel, looking to end the game, decides to go for it. Joe speaks through his headset to Olivadotti in the coaches' box: "One more stop." They get it. Omaha has the ball back with two minutes to go. Masoli completes a pass, then scampers for twenty yards. The ball is on the Locos 33. But on fourth down, Masoli overthrows his receiver. The Locos take a knee. And somehow, the Nighthawks have lost.

Despite the devastating loss, Olivadotti and his defense have redeemed themselves, holding the Locos to 283 yards in total offense after giving up 401 the week before. "I couldn't have been prouder of the effort you gave tonight," Joe tells the defense. "You were physical, tough, and aggressive, and you made plays again and again and again."

The special teams, too, have done their jobs. Kent, after a tough start to the season, has improved his unit dramatically. Wolfert's misses seem an anomaly. "Jeff, you won us the game in Sacramento. You had an off night tonight. I still have faith in you," Joe says.

But regarding the offense, Joe is mum. Masoli was off-target all night. The line had regressed. The offensive stats on the game were brutal. Omaha had gotten the ball in the red zone five times (three times, they had been handed the ball there by the defense and special teams). They'd had the ball within the 5-yard line on three different occasions. And they came away with only six points. "The absolute worst display of offense I've ever witnessed" is what Joe will call it later. Adding to his frustration was the fact that powerball—which employed exactly the type of scheme and play calls that put the ball in the end zone from the 2-yard line—still had not been fully installed by Andrus and his staff.

The dark mood in the Nighthawks locker room is brightened slightly by the news that in the other UFL game that night, Sacramento had upset Virginia. With two scheduled games remaining, Virginia and Las Vegas were both 3-1, and Sacramento and Omaha were 1-3. All of the teams are mathematically still alive for the championship. That is, if the owners decide to finish the season. The players and coaches are sure there's no way they can call off the season now.

But any hopes Joe has of a continued season are dashed immediately. As he walks out of the locker room to go address the media, Huyghue—who had been waiting in the hallway—appears at his side. "It's over, Joe," he says as they walk down the hall. "Virginia and Las Vegas will play for the championship next week." Cutting the season short will save the owners $3.5 million. Joe nods and shakes Huyghue's hand. The bad news swiftly filters back to the Omaha locker room.

Later, as Huyghue stands in the elevator with a few others on his way out of the stadium, he shakes his head. "Man, they really pissed that game away, didn't they?" he says, to no one in particular.

The Nighthawks players and coaches all believe that this is it, the end of the season. They head out of the locker room and out on the town to try to forget the loss as quickly as they can.

But no one realizes just how unwilling Joe is to take no for an answer.

CHAPTER THIRTEEN

Somewhere in the Middle of America

Once upon a time in America if one wanted to trade a stock or a bond, one had to do it through a stockbroker, who had the exclusive power to trade securities, and the exclusive information on the securities upon which such trades were made. Wall Street firms like Merrill Lynch and Dean Witter, with their legions of stockbrokers across the country, were paid handsomely for that exclusivity, taking a whopping percentage of the money that changed hands.

Then along came a revolution, started by a reserved and pious man, who believed his employees should wear blazers and red ties, be citizens in good standing in their communities as members of Elks and Kiwanis clubs and, for damn sure, be nice to people on the telephone. The man was John Joseph "Joe" Ricketts, born and raised in Nebraska City, Nebraska. His first job was as a stockbroker at a Dean Witter office in Omaha. In his five years there, he learned their playbook, in and out, and proceeded to use that knowledge to turn the industry on its head.

In 1975, with $38,000 from his business partners and another $12,000 borrowed from family and friends, Ricketts founded First Omaha Securities. Despite some serious misgivings on the part of its own founder, and some near-death experiences along the way, it would one day become the $10 billion company known as TD Ameritrade.

What Ricketts had figured out was that by using technology, there was a way to deprive Wall Street of its exclusivity—and thereby make a ton of money. In 1988, just before another disruptor named Charles Schwab would effectively do the same thing on the West Coast, Ricketts introduced automated securities trading via touch-tone telephones, knocking out the high-priced Wall Street middleman. For a fee of a mere three cents per transaction, anyone could now do a stock trade without handing over a good percentage of the money to a stockbroker. (Ricketts's clients pressed "1" to sell and "2" to buy.)

What individual investors still lacked was the ability to access vital information on stocks and bonds—historical data, earnings forecasts, and market color. The Wall Street banks maintained a tight grip on that information. It was the last advantage they had.

Until the Internet came along. Ricketts saw the electronic wave coming. In 1995 he bought a stock-and-bond trading website called WealthWeb. The next year, he changed the name of his company to Ameritrade and began offering low-cost trades *and* online research tools. The power of investing had shifted away from Wall Street and to the individual. The boom in discount online trading was on.

Charles Schwab, E-Trade, Fidelity, Waterhouse, and hundreds of smaller firms joined Ameritrade in the frenzy. E-Trade went public in 1996. Ameritrade followed suit in 1997. "We were all going like crazy," says Frank Petrilli, then the chief executive of what would become known as TD Waterhouse. "Customers were coming in droves, the market was rocking, the parties were fun. And everyone—I mean everyone—was making money."

To get an idea of just how fast the industry was growing, consider this: It took Ameritrade twenty-five years to reach half a million customers. It took just one year (2000) to triple that number. The polite, family-owned company in sleepy Omaha—well off Wall Street's Manhattan grid—had become its own power source.

But the online discount brokerage industry would quickly prove that it was not immune to the excesses and follies of the financial industry that it was disrupting.

By the late 1990s the Internet and technology boom was at full roar. Online brokerages became hot stocks and irresistible investments for venture capital firms. The stock market had become a leading topic of conversation in American households and in the media. Suddenly it was perfectly socially acceptable to mention your stock portfolio at a cocktail party, if for no other reason than that a stock tip might be gleaned from the subsequent discussion. Fueling the mania was a new type of homemade entrepreneur: the day trader. In the late 1990s it became cool to sit in your house all day in front of your computer, keeping one eye on Yahoo.com's financial chatboards and the other on the ticker crawl at the bottom of CNBC, while trading your own assets through a company like Ameritrade. Individual investors had become one-person Wall Street brokerages, achieving some sort of simulacrum of the American Dream.

These day traders—who made multiple trades every day—were gold to Ameritrade, which collected money on each transaction. With hundreds of online brokers essentially offering the same service, scale became key. Ameritrade spent lavishly to attract new customers. By 2000 the company's marketing budget was $200 million, a whopping one-third of the company's revenues. That imbalance was just one sign that things were getting out of hand.

Somewhere around 2000, investors began to realize that money plowed into Internet companies and tech firms with no real business plans and no real revenues was perhaps not a great idea. The spigot ran dry. The stock market sank. Though it remained the prevailing topic in American households, it was now a conversation that was all doom and gloom. Almost overnight, day trading lost its appeal, looking more like folly than the future.

All of the major online discount brokers got hammered, but none quite so forcefully as Ameritrade. The company lost $14 million in 2000, despite, or maybe because of, its huge marketing splurge. That was nothing compared to what was to come. Ameritrade lost another $91 million the following year. It suffered the double whammy of having customers who were trading less yet were becoming more expensive to attract and retain.

Ricketts's twenty-five-year-old company, which had risen so fast and spectacularly during the dot-com boom, looked like it might go out of business, a crisp cinder falling back down to earth after the big fireworks show. In order to save Ameritrade, Ricketts realized he had to look outside the company. Even the most successful insurgents rarely make for good leaders after the revolution.

What he needed was a motivational leader who had a strong background in traditional finance. He needed that someone fast. Ricketts looked for salvation from among the ranks of one of those old-school Wall Street firms that he had been trying to destroy.

By 2001 Joe Moglia was maybe one rung below Merrill's top level, and just beginning his seventeenth year there. But despite his accomplishments and his proximity to the top, Joe wasn't going to be Merrill's CEO anytime soon. Entrenched above him was a group of executives with twenty-plus years at the firm, guys like Herbert Allison, Tom Davis, Win Smith, Jeffrey Peek, and Stanley O'Neal (who would in fact become its CEO in 2003). "I don't think Joe was on the CEO track," says Roger Vasey. "Joe had a very strong following at Merrill, but the board was too obsessed with moving Stan into the [CEO] role."

And anyway, Joe's philosophy may not have fit in with Merrill's gradual shift away from a teamwork-oriented firm to one that rewarded individual glory and increasing greed. "Joe had integrity and he treated people well. He was a team guy," says Mike Quinn. "He wouldn't have thrived or enjoyed himself in the regime that took over under Stan O'Neal."

Still, Joe maintained excellent relationships with upper management, including O'Neal. By 2001 it looked like Joe could have worked at Merrill, or at a comparably high position at another financial firm, and made millions a year for the rest of his working life. Many people would have been very happy with that career.

Joe wasn't.

"The bottom line was that I always wanted to be the leader," he says. And that desire didn't look like it would be fulfilled at Merrill anytime soon.

After a series of three interviews with Ricketts, Joe was offered the CEO job at Ameritrade in 2001. Joe realized that the company was in serious trouble. But he sold Ricketts a vision: the company could be not only the world's best online broker, it could become a place that long-term investors could call home.

Leaving Merrill, however, wasn't a slam-dunk decision. First there was the family component. Joe and Amy had been married for six years at the time. They lived in Chatham, New Jersey, with Amy's two sons, John (15) and Jeff (12). Amy liked the East Coast. Having seen the cost of what he'd put his family through during his coaching days, Joe was a bit gun-shy about how the move would affect his marriage, and his stepsons. Amy had her reservations, too. "At the time Joe was getting offers from everywhere," she says. "They were raining down. I just didn't think he was serious at first about Ameritrade. But when he told me that he was starting to get serious, I asked, sort of in an offhand manner, where it was located. He said 'Omaha.' I said, 'Um, where?'"

But Amy knew that this was Joe's shot—Ameritrade was the only CEO job he'd been offered. "It took a little while to adjust to the idea, then I thought, *Well, if we go there, what the hell. This will be an adventure.*"

Then there was the career side of the equation. Executives that far up the food chain at Merrill rarely, if ever, left for such risky propositions. "Make no mistake, leaving Merrill was a huge decision," says Waterhouse's Frank Petrilli. "Ameritrade was on the balls of its ass. No one thought they would make it."

The fact that Joe was even considering the challenging move was no surprise to those who knew him well. "Joe loves to put himself in situations where he has to pull a rabbit out of his hat," says his brother Johnny.

Some of Joe's coworkers were supportive. "Joe knew there was a huge risk in giving up the certainty he had at Merrill. But he was just so damn enthusiastic about the Ameritrade thing. I encouraged him, though he really didn't need it," says James Gorman, who ran the retail sales force at Merrill then.

Others were less sanguine. Dave Komansky, then the Merrill CEO (preceding O'Neal), was shocked. "I didn't like their business model and I couldn't fathom living in Nebraska. I mean, Omaha? I thought he was crazy." But Komansky believed Joe had handled the Ameritrade job offer in a totally honorable manner. "He was very upfront about it right away. Most guys will sneak around then surprise you with something like that," he says. As a reward, Komansky decided to give Joe all of his restricted stock in Merrill (worth millions), an unusual parting gift for an executive who was leaving for another firm. "I appreciated what he'd done here and how he handled the Ameritrade thing, so I arranged that he would get every single penny."

But before Joe made his final decision, he made a last-minute call to Randy MacDonald, who, as Ameritrade's chief financial officer, knew the company's books better than anyone. Joe had one more question: is this company going out of business?

"I don't think so," answered MacDonald. He didn't sound entirely convincing.

Joe took the job anyway.

Joe arranged for his salary to be based 85 percent in Ameritrade stock. He would sink or swim with the fortunes of the company he was now charged with running.

He moved to Omaha in April 2001, a few months before Amy and her kids would arrive at the end of the school year. One of his first acts as the CEO was painful: he laid off 40 percent of Ameritrade's employees, most of whom worked in divisions, like the overseas and real estate offices, that Joe didn't consider as part of the core business. "We had to do it merely to survive," says Joe. "But no one likes to come in and be the hatchet man." He also shut down the geyser that had been the marketing budget, cutting the spending down to one-fifth of its total the year before.

With expenses cut, Joe went on the offensive. The company's old model—offer the lowest price on trades, then market the hell out of it—worked well in a bull market, but was a loser in a serious bear market. Joe decided to focus on what he saw as the company's core strength—its transaction model. "We had an efficient engine already in place. We just needed to all be concentrating on that one thing that we did well," he says. "The question was how to get more business running through it." The answer was to get more accounts by buying up other companies.

Joe says the Ameritrade job appealed to him for four reasons: he liked both the brand and the technology that Ricketts had acquired for making customer transactions; bad as they seemed, he thought the financials were still strong enough to give him access to money to buy up some of the smaller online brokers; and no other big competitor in the space had embarked on such a consolidation strategy.

"I guess two out of four ain't bad," says Joe in retrospect. The brand was solid and the transaction technology did indeed turn out to be great, one of the best and most efficient in the industry. But the financials of the company were worse than Joe had believed. By the time Joe took over in the spring of 2001, the company was on track to lose $100 million in that fiscal year. There was no cash on hand, and Joe didn't want to take on more debt at crippling lending rates. Any acquisitions would have to be financed with Ameritrade stock, which put the risk solely on the shoulders of the company's shareholders. To top it off, competitors like Waterhouse and E-Trade had also begun making noises about buying up some smaller companies. Suddenly, Joe's consolidation plan had some competition.

The online brokerage industry by early 2001 was littered with failing companies that were too wounded by the dot-com bust to carry on by themselves. All of them could be had for cheap. Some of them even had good accounts. The key for Joe and his team at Ameritrade was to find the best one, buy it, then add its accounts to Ameritrade as seamlessly as possible. This was easier said than done.

At the time Ameritrade had no cachet with Wall Street analysts. The same folks who'd been touting Ameritrade stock a year before wouldn't even deign to talk about it now. As its new CEO, Joe first sought to restore Ameritrade's credibility. He went to Wall Street and met with a group of analysts who covered the online discount brokerage industry. Part of Joe's challenge was to convince those outside of the company—and especially those analysts whose job it was to cover Ameritrade and predict its future—that Ameritrade would not fail. It helped that Joe was a natural storyteller. He told them that once he got Ameritrade's act together—and he was sure he would—he would start to consolidate the industry. "He was really different from most CEOs," says Richard Repetto, a stock analyst at Sandler O'Neil. "He had this friendly manner about him. Still, what he was talking about seemed like a stretch at the time. It was a long shot."

But Joe went even further than that, and told them about his plans for the future, for turning Ameritrade into a place where investors would bring their cash and manage it for the long term. "Then they thought I was out of my mind," Joe says.

In late July 2001 Joe made his first move. Concerned as he was about the risk to the company's shareholders, he decided it was in their best interest to expand, and with $154 million of his company's stock, he bought National Discount Brokers. The deal added 316,000 accounts to Ameritrade's stable of 1.5 million. Joe got NDB for dimes on the dollar. Just nine months earlier, Deutsche Bank had purchased 85 percent of NDB for $850 million. Still, $154 million was a lot for Ameritrade to spend, especially since the company was still losing money. And the real work would be in the integration. They had to hang on to those NDB accounts. "If we don't get the integration right, right in the middle of a recession, we lose our marketplace and we go out of business," says Joe. He put together a team to work on the integration and told them they had only one job: make it work.

On September 6, 2001, Ameritrade closed the NDB deal. Though the integration had already started and was moving in the right direction, Joe felt he had to keep pressing and keep looking for more acquisition targets. NDB gave him a few months of breathing room. But he needed to make a bigger splash with his next purchase.

Cornhuskers football is a religion in the state of Nebraska, and as a new arrival, Joe had to pay his respects at the state's high church: Memorial Stadium in Lincoln. To turn down an invitation to a Nebraska football game would have been viewed as aberrant behavior at best, and flat-out rude at worst—especially for a former coach.

On September 8, 2001, some Ameritrade colleagues insisted that Joe accompany them to the Notre Dame–Nebraska game in Lincoln. He had no idea how he would feel. It was literally the first football game, other than some of Kevin's high school games, that he had been to in person since that long-ago game back at Dartmouth in 1984. Joe had successfully blocked out football from his consciousness. "It was a survival thing, really," he says. "I needed to maintain full concentration on my business career. I was a little scared of what even seeing football would do to me, what emotions it would bring up."

Joe remembers walking into Memorial Stadium that afternoon, thrilling to the energy of what was an ocean of red-clad fans. That old excitement hit him. His stomach did flip-flops, like it always did just before game time. As the game started, Joe began to feel a pang, a yearning for the road not taken. "I remember looking down at the field at [Frank] Solich [then the Nebraska coach] and thinking, *That could be me there on that sideline,*" he says.

But he had chosen another path. And in his latest move, he had committed himself to Ameritrade, which would die a quick death if he didn't quickly turn things around. Maybe this wasn't the path his heart most desired, but it was the one he was on for now, and he knew he owed it to his new company to dive in with everything he had.

Watching the game turned out to be a painful experience for Joe, just as it had been in 1984. He squirmed in his seat. He was ready to leave after the first quarter and to start trying to forget football again. He managed to make it through the game, but he vowed to do his best to avoid having to attend another one. And sure enough, he would be more or less successful in doing so for the duration of his time at Ameritrade.

The game itself turned out to be an easy 27–10 win for Nebraska. Eric Crouch, in what would be his Heisman Trophy–winning season, had a relatively quiet game, passing for one touchdown. There was no way of knowing then that eight years later, Joe would become a member of the Cornhuskers coaching staff working as an unpaid assistant. And that exactly ten years later, he would be on the sidelines in a different stadium sixty miles to the northeast, a head coach again, running another Nebraska team, which would be led by none other than... Eric Crouch.

Three days after Joe attended the Nebraska game, the world came to a complete halt. When Joe flipped on his television that morning, he saw the Twin Towers, once described by Ian Frazier as the city's "exclamation points," in flames. New York City was his hometown. He'd grown up there and still owned that small studio apartment in Battery Park City just a few blocks away from ground zero. And Kara and Kevin were still working at Merrill Lynch in the World Financial Center, across which, on sunny mornings, the towers cast their long shadows.

As the towers burned, Joe received a phone call from Kim, who was then living in Brooklyn. She told him that she'd spoken to

Kara and Kevin and that they were both okay, and that the Merrill Lynch building was being evacuated. Joe worried about the many people he knew who worked in the towers, but was relieved that his kids seemed safe. Meanwhile, Ameritrade was in emergency mode. Joe spent the early morning running around the offices, ordering associates to reach out to their clients to assure them that their money was safe.

Then Joe heard muffled cries coming from Ameritrade's main floor, where people had gathered around the television. When he went to see what had happened, he discovered that somehow, the south tower had collapsed. Half an hour later, the north tower went down, too.

Joe's secretary, Peggy Henderson, told him that Kim was on the line again. Joe raced to his office to pick up the call. Kim told him that Kara was safe in New Jersey. Then she paused for a moment that seemed to go on forever. "Dad, have you heard from Kevin?" she asked. The last time anyone had seen him, he was headed to the towers to help out. And now they were both down.

Joe sat in his office alone, stunned. He and Kim continually tried Kevin's cell phone but got no answer. It hit him that there was a real chance that he had lost his son. "I felt helpless. I was in Omaha. There was nothing I could do," Joe says.

One thing gave him solace. Thanks to that moment in his childhood when he had realized how important it was to tell his mother how much he loved her, he had made sure that his children knew how he felt about them. So as he sat in his Ameritrade office in the hours after the towers fell, trying his best to push his worry about Kevin back into some box in his head where it could be contained, it comforted him to remember that he had made his feelings known to his son: "I had told Kevin everything I needed to tell him. Kevin knew that I loved him."

At 5:00 p.m., six long hours since learning that Kevin was missing, Joe's cell phone rang. He was sitting by himself at his desk in his Ameritrade office. "Dad, it's Kevin. I'm fine." He had been near the towers, but when he saw he couldn't help, he'd walked home. His cell phone, like many New Yorkers' phones that day, didn't work.

Tears streamed instantly down Joe's face. "I love you, Kevin."

"I know. I love you, too, Dad."

The rush of relief Joe felt when he heard Kevin's voice took everything out of him. But he would have little time to recharge. He still had to figure out how to save his company.

⊢+++⊣

Ameritrade was in dire trouble. At the height of the tech boom in 1999 and even into 2000, the company was netting good money on trades, an average of $1 per every $10 traded. But in 2001, due to the drop in trade volume and then to the aftereffects of 9/11 on the stock market, Ameritrade began to *lose* 80 cents for every $10 traded. This was alarming news, especially given the fact that the union with NDB had been nearly flawless—a stunning 98 percent of NDB customers stayed on with Ameritrade after the merger.

Joe needed to stick to his game plan and needed to buy another company. And this one needed to be big.

⊢+++⊣

Datek Online was a privately held online discount broker known for its proprietary technology, which conducted superfast, superaccurate web-based stock trades (the technology is what basically runs the NASDAQ today). Because of that technology, Datek had the most desirable group of clients in the entire online brokerage industry: 250,000 savvy, wealthy folks who made a lot of transactions.

Joe wanted Datek and its accounts, but unfortunately, so did everyone else. Competitors E-Trade and TD Waterhouse were making bids. So were Wells Fargo and Bank of America, big banks looking for an entrée into online trading. The problem for Joe was that no one was taking Ameritrade seriously. "Datek's investment bankers wouldn't even give us the books to look over," says Randy MacDonald, Ameritrade's CFO. "They didn't think we were legit."

Joe wasn't deterred. Datek was owned by a group of private equity firms at the time. Joe correctly assessed Bain Capital and Silver Lake Partners as the company's most influential owners. He badgered them. As always, he felt that if he could just get in front of them and sell them his plan in person, he could win. Joe finally got Steve Pagliuca, a managing partner at Bain, on the phone, and talked him into having dinner with him in Bain's hometown of Boston.

Joe met Pagliuca at Legal Sea Foods on Boston's Long Wharf. He told Pagliuca of his plan to become the biggest player in online trading, then to begin to transform the company into an asset gatherer. He sketched out an outline on a paper dinner napkin. "He was pretty passionate," says Pagliuca, now an owner of the Boston Celtics. "That certainly got the ball rolling."

Next Joe met with Glenn Hutchins, a cofounder of Silver Lake. He gave him the same pitch. Hutchins, too, was impressed with Joe's fervor. "I wasn't sure I agreed with Joe on the asset-gathering strategy. I didn't really find it that compelling," says Hutchins. "But I did find Joe compelling."

In April 2002 Ameritrade acquired Datek Online for $1.3 billion in stock. The combined company, with three million accounts, became the biggest online broker in terms of trade volume. Best of all, the quality of the Datek customers meant that Ameritrade—if all went well—would start making money again on trades.

Ameritrade had taken the other bidders totally by surprise. "Honestly we didn't even consider them a competitor at first," says Frank Petrilli from TD Waterhouse. "We thought they weren't going to do anything, since they were losing so much money."

But Silver Lake and Bain and the rest of the private equity folks liked what they saw in Ameritrade, and liked where Joe intended to take it, so much so that instead of going the usual route and cashing out after the sale, they decided to roll over their shares into Ameritrade. "We believed in Joe," says Pagliuca, and they wanted to participate in his long-term asset-gathering plan.

The purchase of Datek made perfect sense for Ameritrade. It combined the best customers and technology with a great brand name and distribution model. It was a necessary move for Ameritrade to ensure its survival. But there was significant danger in the deal: as with the NDB purchase, Ameritrade had to be able to fully digest Datek, or it would kill its host.

Joe brought together the same team that had handled the NDB integration so well. Merging the two companies' tech platforms and accounts would be arduous, but not impossible. The bigger challenge had to do with a culture clash: although the people in the two companies did basically the same thing, they came at it in very different ways and had completely different work environments.

Datek was a hip, urban company, based in Jersey City, just across the Hudson River from Manhattan. "A lot of these folks were in their twenties," says Asiff Hirji, a technology expert from Bain & Co., whom Joe would eventually hire as Ameritrade's chief operating officer. "They had body piercings and tattoos and rode skateboards to work."

Ameritrade, by contrast, was still very much Ricketts's vision of the "pride of the community" company, its employees gushing with Midwestern politeness and wearing blazers and ties and sensible shoes. Its headquarters, then and now, are located in an industrial park in southwest Omaha, right next to a Kellogg's cereal plant. An east wind carries the scent of Frosted Flakes. A west wind is not so sweet: Ameritrade is also down the road from a pork-rendering plant.

Joe realized that he had to make an emotional connection with the Datek troops or he would risk losing them and put the integration in jeopardy. He traveled to Datek's Jersey City offices and called all of the employees together for a meeting.

They were expecting an "aw-shucks" Midwesterner. Instead what they got was a passionate plea from a man whose speech was laced with the strong, never-to-be-lost traces of his New York City upbringing. Joe talked to these tattooed, twenty-something hipsters about his childhood in the inner city. He talked about his two friends who died and the others who, through their life choices, didn't make it out of the 'hood, about how he had had to take responsibility for himself to make something of his life. "If you don't want to work here anymore, that's fine. I respect that. But if you do, you have to take responsibility to help make this work," Joe told them. In other words, "be a man."

Hirji was there that day. "Joe has that gift that the best politicians have. He shares very personal pieces of his back story and makes it relevant, interweaving it into a bigger narrative," he says. "He's talking to a big group, but somehow you feel like he is talking to you and only you."

By Christmas 2002, the integration was moving along, but slowly. People on both sides of the deal were tired and short-fused, which resulted in bickering stalemates. Joe decided to have a Christmas party at his house in west Omaha. He invited all of the senior leadership from both Datek and Ameritrade. Most of the

Ameritrade folks had their spouses with them. The Datek folks, primarily from the east, did not. Joe had hired a band. After dinner, the band started playing and people began to hit the dance floor. None of the Datek leadership was dancing. Instead, they sat around the tables and gossiped with each other. Joe knew he had to do something.

With a grand flourish, he walked over to the tables, grabbed Hirji and pulled him onto the floor. He started dancing with him, violently twisting to a Chubby Checker tune. The Datek folks, as embittered as they were, couldn't help themselves. They cracked up in laughter at this red-haired nut who was concentrating so hard and working himself up into a serious sweat. Joe had no problem making fun of himself to help a greater cause. "The mood of the party changed instantly," says Hirji. "Also, it was the first time I'd ever danced with a man."

A few months later, the integration of Datek into Ameritrade was basically done. "This was a transformational deal and integration," says Roger McNamee, a cofounder of Silver Lake and the venture capital firm Elevation Partners. "Datek took Ameritrade from being one of a bunch to being *the* one."

After losing money for two straight years, Ameritrade finished 2002 with a net profit of $131 million, a spectacular turnaround for a company that had been left for dead eighteen months before.

With the Datek acquisition, Joe had pulled off something even bigger in the boardroom. He had turned Ameritrade into a real public company, with a real board and a more diversified group of shareholders. The acquisition meant that Ricketts's share in the company he had founded went from 56 percent down to 32 percent. He was still the largest single shareholder and the chairman of the board, and still controlled three of the board's eight seats. But the private equity folks, combined, matched his 32 percent share and had two seats on the board (while the remaining three seats were held by independent members). Joe had, in essence, convinced Ricketts to give up a degree of control of the company for the betterment of himself and the other shareholders.

Joe kept pushing consolidation. From 2002 to 2005, Ameritrade snapped up four smaller companies with a combined total of 175,000 accounts. These purchases were important because of what they represented in sum, which was somewhat akin to what John D. Rockefeller had done 125 years earlier in buying up dozens of small oil refineries in Ohio and Pennsylvania to build up Standard Oil.

Each of these small fry was easily absorbed by Ameritrade, which no longer had to worry about choking on its food. Joe could now begin setting the stage for the next phase of the company, part two of the game plan he had sold to Ricketts in late 2000.

Joe was only halfway to his goal at Ameritrade when football reared its head yet again. This time, though, it wasn't a coaching job that was being dangled.

In 2004 Joe got a surprise call from a well-connected friend who told him that the National Football League's commissioner, Paul Tagliabue, was going to retire in 2006. The friend thought that Joe might be a good candidate for the job.

Joe, of course, had never shaken the football bug. He'd been tempted to go back to coaching on a few occasions, especially when he got the call about the University of Buffalo job while at Merrill a decade before. But each time he'd decided he'd not quite played out his business career to its full extent. Head over heart.

He'd always believed that if he were ever to return, it would have to be as a head coach. But the NFL commissioner job intrigued him. It seemed like a way to get back to football and use what he'd learned during his business career. His contract with Ameritrade was supposed to end in 2005. Though Joe believed he would be able to work out an extension if he wanted, the exit door was ajar. The question was whether he wanted to walk through it.

But just as Joe started to put together a plan for pursuing the job, an opportunity presented itself. It was too good to pass up. It would give him the chance to complete his original mission at Ameritrade.

By 2004 the online brokerage industry had undergone so much consolidation that it was now limited to basically five big players: Ameritrade, Charles Schwab, E-Trade, Fidelity, and TD Waterhouse. All of them save for Ameritrade now had banks and thus were already asset gatherers and not just online brokers. Ameritrade did have one advantage over its peers. It was far and away the best online broker. But if it was to take the next step toward becoming a financial superpower, Joe needed a bank.

Joe put aside the idea of becoming the NFL commissioner. Instead, he signed a new contract with Ameritrade, one that would allow him to stay on long enough to accomplish his final goal. The most logical way to do that would be to partner up with one of the other big players in the industry. Over dinners and through countless hours of discussions, Joe learned that neither Schwab nor Fidelity, a private, family-run company, was very interested in partnering up. That left TD Waterhouse and E-Trade.

E-Trade was run by Mitch Caplan, who, like Joe, had rescued his company from the dot-com meltdown. But unlike Joe, he had accomplished this in large part due to his company's bank, which by 2005 had begun to purchase third-party mortgages.

TD Waterhouse was run by Frank Petrilli, who had been a year behind Joe at both Fordham Prep and Fordham University (though the two had not known each other at either school). Waterhouse's brokerage department seemed to be falling behind a bit in the online transaction race and its parent company—the Canadian bank Toronto-Dominion—appeared eager to do a deal, and had been impressed with how well Joe had delivered results in the Datek deal.

Either of the two companies, because of their banks, seemed able to provide Joe with what he was looking for. The three companies soon embarked on what would turn into a wild, partner-swapping dance. First it looked as if Ameritrade and TD Waterhouse would link up. Then it was E-Trade and TD Waterhouse. Then it again appeared as if Ameritrade would be paired with TD Waterhouse.

That company was Joe's preferred partner. E-Trade had the better brand name, but after doing due diligence on the company, Joe was scared off by some of the assets held by E-Trade's bank—specifically its third-party mortgages. "I had no idea at the time what a ticking time bomb those mortgages actually would turn out to be," says Joe. But he knew enough to be wary.

So Joe started negotiating with TD Waterhouse. However, he had serious problems back at Ameritrade. His board was not all aligned in its preference for Waterhouse. In particular, the founder and owner of the company wanted to pair up with E-Trade instead.

Up until then, Ricketts had been willing to give up ever-escalating increments of his control over the company. With each company that Joe had bought from 2001 onward, Ricketts's share of the company had shrunk.

But now Ricketts had had enough.

According to MacDonald and Hirji, Ricketts did not want to

do a deal with TD Waterhouse because it was so large that it would dilute his shares to the point where he would no longer be Ameritrade's largest shareholder. Ricketts believed that he could maintain his dominant position if Ameritrade went with E-Trade instead. "It was never really about the money for Ricketts," says MacDonald. "It was always about control. Ameritrade was his baby."

MacDonald also says that Ricketts wanted his son, Pete, who was then chief operating officer at Ameritrade, to eventually take over the company. In a TD Waterhouse deal, that ascension seemed highly unlikely. As a result, Joe had some very dangerous shoals to navigate.

In the spring of 2005, after tense back-and-forth negotiations, Ameritrade and TD (the parent bank) had worked out a deal for Waterhouse. TD would be effectively buying Ameritrade, becoming the company's largest shareholder, grabbing seats on the board and paying Ameritrade's shareholders a $2 dividend per share. Ameritrade—and Joe in particular—would remain the leaders of the new company. "That's the way we wanted it," says Ed Clark, the CEO of TD. "We believed in Joe."

But back in Omaha, Ricketts had been busy negotiating his own deal with E-Trade, undermining his CEO. According to Randy MacDonald, Joe was hurt by Ricketts's actions, but continued to play the good soldier, trying to determine what was best for the shareholders.

Ricketts eventually brought the deal he had negotiated with E-Trade to the table. It would allow him to remain the company's largest shareholder.

The board now had a clear choice.

In the end, the board decided that E-Trade's assets were just too risky, and they were set to vote for the TD Waterhouse deal. But the drama didn't end there. At the last minute, E-Trade submitted a $5.5 billion hostile takeover bid for Ameritrade.

Joe had expected the move from Caplan. He had remained in contact with him throughout the process. "We took a walk in Central Park one day and talked about it," says Caplan. "Joe made it clear that he preferred TD Waterhouse, but if I were to win the deal, he just asked me to take care of his guys."

Joe still believed the TD Waterhouse deal was the right one for the long-term interests of his shareholders. His position was helped by the fact that E-Trade's hostile bid scared TD into sweetening its own offer to Ameritrade. Clark boosted the dividend amount, from $2 to $6. Ameritrade's shareholders would now be getting a lot of money upfront. "It was a safety valve for the shareholders," says MacDonald. "If the marriage failed, they had a prenup in place." But the decision was ultimately left to the board.

This constant seesawing made Ameritrade a tense workplace. Though the employees knew nothing of the back-room dealings, they were aware that something big was happening that would affect their lives.

Joe decided to take it upon himself to break the tension. He turned to attempts at levity. He did back and hamstring stretches on his office floor while meeting with his management team. During one particularly tense conference call with Wall Street analysts, Joe, unbeknownst to the others in the room, pushed the mute button on his phone. Then he started yelling: "We're buying E-Trade! Woo-hoo!"

"We all turned ghost white," says Katrina Becker, the company's media strategist. That is until Joe stuck out his index finger for all of them to see, then pushed the mute button off, and spoke calmly to the analysts. "We were all giggling like mad," says Becker.

And Joe liked to sing, just like his mother. But unlike his mother, he was not always in tune. A couple of times a week, his voice would boom from his office. He sang Cher show tunes at the top of his lungs. He would pop in a CD and sing along to one of his favorite artists, Patrizio Buanne, an Italian baritone. He seemed to embrace Melville's sentiment in *Moby-Dick*: "I know not all that may be coming, but be it what it will, I'll go to it laughing."

After a few back-and-forth meetings, the Ameritrade board finally voted to go with TD Waterhouse. The $3 billion deal was made in June 2005. The new company would be called TD Ameritrade.

On a conference call with those formerly skeptical analysts announcing the deal, Joe serenaded them with an Italian love ballad that began: "Your eyes shine like the stars." This time, he did not hit the mute button.

After the deal, a reporter from the *Globe and Mail*, a Toronto newspaper, asked Ed Clark about the negotiations. Clark replied: "You have no idea what a son of a bitch Joe Moglia is."

He meant it as a compliment. "Joe obviously preferred the deal with TD Waterhouse, but he never lost sight of who he worked for," says Clark. "He was a tough negotiator. He did the right thing for his shareholders."

The largest single shareholder had been Joe Ricketts. The deal left him with 20 percent of the shares; TD was now the biggest shareholder, with 32 percent (with the rights to eventually go up to 45 percent). Ricketts's son, Pete, resigned from the company shortly thereafter and went into politics.

"Joe's magic was getting the board to agree to this deal," says David Livingston, who was the head of corporate development at TD. "He just gradually convinced Ricketts that this was the best deal for him, even though he'd no longer be the largest shareholder."

Says MacDonald: "Joe brilliantly maintained the ship while never publicly calling anyone out."

And he hasn't to this day. Joe refuses to talk about any friction there may have been between him and Ricketts, though it had to sting that his chairman had tried to go against him on the company's biggest deal. "I will always be thankful to him for giving me a shot to run this company," he says diplomatically.

By 2006, Joe's vision for the company was complete. TD Ameritrade was still the leader in online discount trades. But now it was also a company for long-term investors, the "mass affluent" market (people with between $100,000 and $1 million in liquid assets) so coveted by financial services firms. TD Ameritrade had more than one hundred branches and investment advisory services for its six million customers. It was essentially Charles Schwab with better technology.

In the fall of 2006, the integration of the two companies was nearly complete. One night Joe invited his top three lieutenants—MacDonald, Hirji, and Chris Armstrong, the product and marketing director who had come on board to help with the TD Waterhouse integration—to dinner in order to celebrate their achievement. He invited their wives along as well. There Joe told the three men how much he appreciated the sacrifices they'd made, the late nights and early mornings, the missed Thanksgiving dinners.

Then he turned to their wives. "I also want to thank you for your sacrifice. I know it wasn't easy on your family life," he said. Then he pulled out three stunning diamond tennis bracelets and presented them to the wives. "Our wives were speechless," says Hirji. "I know it's just a gift, but it made our wives so happy. He built a huge amount of loyalty and dedication from us that night because of that happiness."

The company ended 2006 in great shape, recording its fourth

straight year of record revenues and profits. TD Ameritrade's stock had outperformed the Standard & Poor's index—the benchmark against which all stocks are measured—by 250 percent. Joe thought he would stay on for two more years to oversee the new company, to help get the best out of the employees and encourage them to concentrate on the things that mattered.

There would be one more huge hurdle to get over, though, one that involved the largest financial calamity since the Depression.

By late 2006, many financial firms in the United States were flying high, recording record profits, inflated by the global housing bubble. With low interest rates, mortgages—and in particular, bundled third-party mortgages—became all the rage.

Joe had seen this before. While at Merrill, he had lived through a few financial crises that were in one way or another caused by risky leverage: the Savings & Loan crisis in the 1980s; Merrill's own Orange County debacle; and the failure of the hedge fund Long Term Capital.

The real estate boom seemed to Joe like another bubble underpinned by shaky leverage. He didn't want any part of it. "I've just seen the smartest guys in the world get a little bit greedy. Money gets in the way. They get undisciplined. In this case, they thought they'd be smart enough to get out when they saw the real estate market start to crack. But it became like a gambling addiction, like they thought, *One more $100 million bet on black and I'll get out.*"

Around this time TD Ameritrade began to get hammered by the media, and by analysts who were wondering why in the hell Joe wasn't levering up and getting a piece of the hot action.

There were essentially three different ways Joe could have gotten into the mortgage game: he could have started buying the mortgage-backed securities himself, as his old company, Merrill, was doing; he could have bought a company, like E-Trade, that had some of them on its books; or he could have leveraged his own balance sheet. "We were under severe duress to get into the mortgage business somehow. I just never thought it was our strength. It was just too risky," he says.

But others, in particular two very powerful hedge funds named SAC Capital and JANA Partners, didn't see it that way. The two firms—led by, respectively, Steve Cohen and Barry Rosenstein, two giants in the financial world—owned 8.4 percent of TD Ameritrade's stock, enough to be able to make their opinions heard.

In late 2006 and early 2007, Joe had informal talks with Charles Schwab, and floated the idea of a possible merger. Joining Schwab would have made a certain strategic sense. Counting E-Trade, there were essentially three big players left in the space. Combining two of them would have created one of the biggest non–Wall Street–based financial services companies in the world.

Schwab decided that it was still not interested in any sort of merger. Joe had continued, off and on, to talk with Caplan at E-Trade. But by 2007, Joe was getting even more worried about the mortgages on E-Trade's books. Unlike in 2001, Joe now had the luxury of staying put. He didn't have to do a merger or an acquisition to survive or even thrive.

SAC and Jana did not agree. The hedge funds are both known as "activist" shareholders; that is, they seek to identify hidden value in a company, then through either accumulating shares in the company or using public pressure (or most of the time, both), they try to push the company into action.

In this case they wanted TD Ameritrade to combine with either Schwab or E-Trade. On May 29, 2007, the activists sent a letter to TD Ameritrade's board urging that course of action because of the "massive value creation opportunity." After sending the letter, the activists began a full-scale assault on the board, calling each of the members individually, writing e-mails and more letters. "There was no technique they didn't use to get at us," says board member Ed Clark.

Their cause was helped by the fact that, according to MacDonald, the hedge funders had one key TD Ameritrade board member in their corner: Ricketts. He again wanted to pair up with E-Trade and regain some of the control that he had lost.

But both Joe and Clark agreed that a merger with E-Trade would be a very bad idea. Not having Ricketts in their corner was troubling, to say the least. But Joe started to fret about the other board members, too. "They were under tremendous pressure and I was worried that they would crack," says Joe.

He called an emergency meeting in New York. At that meeting, he and his management team hit on a bold plan. They didn't have anything to hide. Why not go public with the whole thing?

And that's just what they did. TD Ameritrade released the letter from the activists to the media with a response from Joe in which he pointed out that his company hadn't exactly been sitting on its hands for the last six years. They'd done eight deals. And if something ever made sense for their shareholders, Joe wrote, he'd do it in a heartbeat.

The press loved his gumption. Joe did the business TV show circuit where his blunt, no-BS style was particularly effective. On each show, Joe reiterated what he had said in his letter. Then he would tack on his masterstroke, saying: "Look, SAC and JANA are just doing their jobs. They want us to merge, they want a pop in the stock, then they want to get out. That's fine. That's their job and I respect that. But my job is to do the right thing by our shareholders. If we thought E-Trade was a good combination and would be good for the long-term interests of this company's shareholders, we would do it. But we just don't believe it is."

With that, it was all effectively over. By going public with the letter and the response, Joe had accomplished three critical objectives: He had framed the debate in his favor. By alerting the public that these two activists were interested in TD Ameritrade, he had made the stock price rise—which, of course, prevented SAC and JANA from buying any more shares. And he'd successfully nipped in the bud—once again—a possible board insurgency.

Game. Set. Match.

(Both SAC and JANA would sell their shares later on for handsome profits.)

Not doing a deal with E-Trade turned out to be one of the best moves Joe ever made. As it developed, in late 2007, E-Trade became one of the first financial firms to be hit by the bursting of the housing bubble. Caplan left E-Trade that November. "I have nothing but nice things to say about Joe. He was always honest and straightforward with me. We remained congenial throughout," Caplan says. Joe called him the day he resigned to wish him luck.

In 2008, when the world's debt bill finally came due, the overleveraged world economy was brought to its knees. Americans saw more than a quarter of their net worth wiped out in a flash. Lehman Brothers failed. Joe's old company, the once-conservative Merrill Lynch, lost an almost inconceivable $28 billion because of its gamble on subprime mortgages, and was sold on the cheap to Bank of America. E-Trade lost $1.3 billion and nearly sank.

But TD Ameritrade prospered. In 2008 the company had its sixth straight year of record growth. As the rest of the financial world crumbled, TD Ameritrade made a *profit* of $800 million, its record. Its performance during that time remains one of the most underreported success stories from the 2008 financial crisis. The old mantra stands true: you don't get credit for not doing something stupid.

What happened during the financial crisis, especially at Merrill, with which he still felt an emotional connection and where he still had many friends, hurt and angered Joe. His old firm essentially went under because its leaders forgot for whom they worked: their shareholders and their employees. "Merrill had something like eighty thousand employees," says Joe. "Many, if not most of them, had their hard-earned money in the company's stock. That all just disappeared. That's just not right. Those leaders, at Merrill and elsewhere on Wall Street, were never really punished for what they did. There should have been consequences. They should have given back the money they made on the bubble. Or there should have been some sort of legal ramifications."

Joe never took his eye off what he believed was his fundamental duty at TD Ameritrade: to take care of the shareholders and the employees.

During his tenure at TD Ameritrade, client assets grew from $24 billion to $300 billion, and the market cap went from $700 million to $10 billion. And the company grew its revenues every year.

"What Joe did was unbelievable. Under his guidance, the company followed the best possible path it could have followed," says Silver Lake's Roger McNamee. "I give a lot of credit to Ricketts, too, for hiring Joe and for listening to him even though his instincts might have told him not to."

The Ricketts family even gave Joe his due. "He was critical to our success during that time," says Pete Ricketts.

After all, despite their differences, Joe's tenure at TD Ameritrade paid off with a very tangible benefit for them. In 2009, the Ricketts family bought the Chicago Cubs, one of the sports world's most recognizable franchises, for $845 million, the largest amount ever paid for a baseball team. A lot of that money was the fruit of Joe's vision and work. (In 2011, J. Joseph Ricketts resigned from the board of the company that he founded in 1975.)

In late 2008, Joe retired from the CEO post and became TD Ameritrade's chairman. His work there was done. In his last year Joe made $21 million, 90 percent of which was based on the performance of the company's stock. He also owned $121 million worth of TD Ameritrade stock. "Joe created wealth for himself and for his shareholders," says Caplan. "Not every CEO does that."

What Joe loves and craves most of all in his work life is intensity. He finds it quite rapturous. It allows him to blaze each day rather than shuffle along, to be acutely aware that he is alive. He has sought out and achieved this intensity all of his life, starting in his childhood, when he worked hard to become a good student and athlete while also pushing the extracurricular "bad kid" stuff—the drinking, the fighting—right to the edge.

Some people shrink in the face of such intensity. Joe thrives under it. He can get anxious and emotional, sometimes even short-tempered enough to raise his voice, in the days and weeks leading up to an event. But when the moment arrives—during an earnings call, or a critical moment in a football game—something comes over him, some sort of serenity. That calmness and cool filters down to others. It is the true key to his uncanny ability to lead.

To invoke an old cliché, Joe loves the journey, not the destination. When a destination is reached, Joe then gets restless, bored. At Merrill, he seemed to have peaked in 2001. So he sought out another challenge, and found it at TD Ameritrade. In 2008, with his goals accomplished, and with the company enviably situated after the financial crisis, that journey, too, had come to its end.

And so he stepped down, intending to relax and enjoy some free time. Instead he was soon to resume the journey he had never completed—as a football coach. Finance has its intense moments, to be sure: the daily eye on the company stock price, the quarterly earnings calls, the deal making and deal breaking. But coaching was king. "Nothing is more intense than in-season football," says Joe.

He had no idea how intense it was going to turn out to be—both on and off the field.

CHAPTER FOURTEEN

Endgame

The Nighthawks' end-of-the-season gathering starts out slow, a subdued affair at a local sports bar not far from the stadium. Players stand next to each other, staring into space, nodding, in mourning. Nearly all of the players are in attendance, even the teetotalers. Joe's not there, but a handful of his coaches are.

But the night eventually gains in volume and momentum. The next stop is a crowded nightclub located in a strip mall in west Omaha, and when that shuts down at 2:00 a.m., a group of twenty or so players and coaches ends up at center Donovan Raiola's house for the after-after party. There, the tone is different. Eyes are off the rearview mirrors. The past is forgotten, at least momentarily.

The party goes on well into the morning. An hour or so before sunrise, Jay Moore, who is living with his parents, calls his mother, and she comes to pick him up, still in her pajamas. The other players present seem to take that as some sort of sign, and gradually they all begin to drift home, disappearing into the lifting darkness.

But while the team has been out, and even while they're sleeping off the night the next morning, Joe has been planning. He's been on the phone with Hambrecht and Huyghue. He can't accept the season ending the way it has.

ᚎᚎᚎᚎᚎ

At 3:00 p.m. the next day, the players amble into the Kroc for a meeting called by Joe. They are all expecting official word of the end of their season.

"Stewie," says Joe to Schweigert. "How was the party last night?"

"Still going, Coach."

Joe smiles, then pauses a moment. "Okay, guys, listen up. Here's why I brought you in today. I know last night you heard that Virginia and Vegas are playing next week in the championship game and that we are done," he says. Then he adds: "But that might not be the case."

Joe explains that he has worked out a scenario with the owners wherein the Nighthawks would play once more, a sort of UFL consolation game, against Sacramento. The game would be in Omaha.

"I want to play Sacramento," Joe says loudly, maybe the only one in the room with any energy left.

He surveys his troops, clearly expecting them to jump to their feet and erupt with excitement. But there are no cheers, only a general murmur. Joe looks stunned.

"Wait, don't you guys want to play?" he asks.

"I do, Coach. I want to play," says Schweigert.

Joe looks around the room. "How about the rest of you guys?"

There are a few garbled words in support of the idea, but the players remain in their seats, talking quietly among themselves. They don't seem overly enthusiastic, especially the veterans, who seem emotionally and physically drained. They tell Joe they'd like to discuss the matter privately. Joe and the coaches leave for their own room. It turns out that they, too, are divided, roughly along offensive and defensive lines.

There is a concern among some of the coaches about the players' state of mind. "The players assumed this season was over, Joe. Some of them have already made plans to go home," says Olivadotti. "They're sick of being yanked around by this league. They may have already checked out. And we really don't want to play a game with guys who don't care anymore." He'd seen plenty of NFL teams quit on a season, and it was never pretty.

Andrus has a different take. "Don't you think these guys want another chance to get on film for the NFL? Don't you think they want to redeem themselves? You don't think Masoli wants another game? Or how about Wolfert?"

The division among the sides is perhaps predictable. The defense has just played a game for the ages, and firing up the engine again for one more performance like that may prove difficult. The offense, of course, wants one more chance to prove itself.

Joe listens, takes it all in. "Let's see what the players say."

Minutes later, the coaches head down to the players' room. The players have decided they do want to play, but they have a serious concern: will they be paid? They are wary of a league that has had trouble paying off its own bills and, as they've recently learned, is currently being sued by its own chief operating officer—the man in charge of paying the league's bills—for failure to be paid himself. (The case would eventually be dismissed.)

Joe tells them he will make sure the league pays their $5,000 game check, and that he will throw in an extra $1,000 if they win. He also tells them that the team will cover their expenses to get home.

"The only thing I ask from you guys is that you not just go through the motions in this game," he says. "I want you to treat this like the championship game."

Suddenly, from the back of the room, Don Lawrence raises his hand. "I have something to say," he yells as he makes his way toward the front, teetering a bit, like an ocean buoy. "Do you guys hear what this guy is saying? What he's going to do for you?" This is not the usual mild-mannered Lawrence. He is almost seething. "If you guys don't appreciate this guy you are a bunch of freaking dumbasses."

Then he puts his head down and retraces his steps to the back of the room.

The Nighthawks are in. Joe gets his wish. But he worries: Has he put his own desires over those of others? And if so, will that come back to haunt him?

He also has another issue to worry about: his completely inept red-zone offense.

The discord that has been brewing between Joe and Andrus since the first Vegas game is finally coming to a head. What happened during the second Vegas game, when the offense couldn't score a touchdown in five trips to the red zone—three of which were within the 5-yard line—is inexcusable, Joe believes. He blames this partly on the fact that Andrus has never installed powerball, the short-yardage and changeup scheme, to his satisfaction.

Andrus doesn't see the offensive woes as a failure of scheme. He sees it more as a failure to execute, like Orton's drop of what should have been a sure touchdown. "These players are inconsistent," he says. "That's why they are here in the UFL." If they were consistently good, they'd be in the NFL. If they were consistently bad, they'd be out of football.

Joe understands this, but argues that since Andrus and his staff have known the shortcomings of their players since minicamp, they should have adapted the scheme to the players' strengths and weaknesses.

"We have to find a way to punch the ball into the end zone

from inside the five," says Joe. "We just have to." There'll be a team-wide mutiny if Andrus and his staff don't figure that out. He once again asks Andrus to install a set of short-yardage plays based on power running. He also asks him to use Clarett and his 230-pound body on the goal line. Through the first four games of the season, Clarett has gotten just five carries on offense, and been relegated to the kickoff coverage teams.

Everyone is edgy. The week has already been incredibly draining. Andrus briefly considers Joe's propositions, then says, pleadingly: "We'll do it, Joe. We are trying to give you what you want."

Joe stares back at him for a silent moment. His electric blue eyes are surrounded by blood red. In those eyes there is a brief flash of the past, those hard concrete streets from his childhood that are still a part of him, those flurries of fists. Andrus shifts his body around in his seat, looking uncomfortable.

"Bart," he snarls, his voice rising. "I want *you* to want it. *You* have to want this. Don't you want to score from within the five?"

It's the first time all season that Joe has yelled at anyone on his staff.

At the beginning of the first practice of the week, the players dawdle onto the field without any discernible energy. That lack of enthusiasm in the Kroc has been carried with them. The weather doesn't help: it is cold and windy, and the sky is leaden. The coaches had hoped that a few changes would help provide a spark for the team. Troy Smith will replace Masoli, whose inaccuracy has put him on the bench. Masoli takes the demotion in stride and without complaint. And Maurice Clarett is made part of the offensive game plan for the first time all season, getting snaps with the first team in practice.

But the practice is wretched from the start. Individual drills are rife with dropped passes and lethargic blocking. The players seem to be just going through the motions, as Olivadotti had feared. The decision to play the last game seems like an impending disaster.

But some sort of transformation takes place on the field during the team drills when Clarett first touches the ball. He runs through his plays with determination and quickness. He crouches low and bursts through the line, as if it was a live game. He is vocal, exhorting his teammates to play harder, patting them on the shoulder pads. Heads turn. "My God, what the hell got into him?" says running backs coach Brock Olivo.

Clarett's teammates and even the coaches feed off his radiating energy. The practice takes an immediate turn, becoming crisp and full of enthusiasm. The following two practices, the last of the year, are equally sharp. The team is working hard and having fun. The Nighthawks, it appears, will indeed give it their all in this game. And the one player whom Joe had protected against nearly everyone else's wishes is the catalyst. At last Clarett has been given an important role on the team. He is needed. Clarett has paid Joe back for his loyalty, in kind.

"I learned a lot from this Clarett thing," Olivo would say later. He'd been one of the doubting coaches. "I learned about the game, about myself, about people."

"Since minicamp, we've said there is more to life than this game. It is only a game, but while we're playing it we will give it our all. If you leave this season without that in your head, I have absolutely failed," says Joe. It's the day of the game, the team's last in-season meeting.

"I love this team. The defense has played its heart out. The special teams have gotten better and better each week. The offense has had its moments, but it has not had a great season. That is totally my fault. But we have one more game, our last together. Let's play the game we haven't yet played. I'm not talking about playing over our heads. I'm talking about playing up to our capabilities. You've had a great week of practice. Let's take that to the field. All I ask is that you do this, for me and for yourselves."

Then he pauses, stares at the floor, and takes a few steps forward.

"For a lot of guys, including me, this may be our last game. For me, this is my career. People have been cynical about me, about my attempt to get back into coaching. My career could be over. But this is a chance for all of us to end this on a high note, to get more film for the NFL, to win. Let's make this our best game."

Just before the pregame meal, Olivadotti takes his defense aside. There is no game planning left to do. He just wants to address them one last time. "This game means absolutely nothing," he tells them. "But it could be the most important game of your lives. You could quit if you wanted. But remember this: The first time you quit is the hardest. After that, quitting gets easy."

A few minutes later Olivadotti is sitting at a lunch table, staring into space with his doleful eyes, one leg crossed over the other. He's chewing his food carefully, slowly, trying to kill those painful hours leading up to kickoff. "This is the first time in my career that I don't want to win for me. Even when I was with Shula, I wanted to win for me. I'm a selfish guy. But now I want to win for him," he says, pointing to Joe, who is at a table with a handful of players and interns. "He is a great coach."

In the locker room, Joe does his hybrid pregame prayer/pep talk.

"Lord, we ask you first to keep every player on our team and theirs from serious injury. Help us maintain our composure. Do not let us be discouraged when there's a problem. Help us let the problem go, get it solved, and go back out there and give it our best shot. If we are ahead, we're not going to let up. If we are behind, we're not going to give up. Help us with that. Lord, we are a group of men who have come together for a common goal. Lord, we are the 2011 Omaha Nighthawks. We have worked hard. Help us to give the very best we've got every second we are on the field. Help us be men."

In front of a crowd of ten thousand on a frigid night, the players stream through a large, black inflatable Nighthawks helmet onto the field. Dvoracek hobbles out, in uniform. Despite the fact that he has sustained even more damage to his knee, he is playing yet again tonight, not able to give it up. Smith confidently skips and points to the crowd, ready for his first game of the season. Schweigert sprints to the far end zone to greet some fans who have hung a banner that reads: "Stu's Crew." Clarett jogs on his toes, head down, his eyes never lifting from the turf. Joe runs out last, accompanied by his son, Kevin, who was too young during his father's previous coaching career to remember it.

Dennis Green's Mountain Lions are now led by quarterback McLeod Bethel-Thompson, who began the year as the backup. He's a rookie who had been in the 49ers camp with Masoli. He goes by "Macbeth" for short, perhaps a fitting moniker for a second-stringer who has overtaken the incumbent in the dog-eat-dog world of professional football. He leads Sacramento on a long drive to start the game. They get a field goal. They get another one a few minutes later when Smith tosses an interception on his second pass of the game. The Nighthawks respond with a Wolfert twenty-five-yard field goal. The game, only in its first quarter, has the same seesaw feeling as the first one.

Then Macbeth makes a mistake, fluttering a pass down the right sideline that Schweigert, with his uncanny nose for the ball, picks off and runs back to the Sacramento 7. The Nighthawks are in business. But they're also in that area of the field where time after time they have foundered.

Clarett is in the backfield and gets his first carry since the first game of the year. He powers the ball down to the 2. He gets another carry and is stopped at the 1. He hurts his shoulder on the play and is more or less done for the game, but he had done his part earlier in the week. Smith then throws an incomplete pass.

It's fourth and goal. Without hesitating, Joe decides to go for it. The game feels like it is on the line with this call, that failure to score would ruin everything. Smith takes the snap and is flushed from the pocket and scrambles to his left. The play looks eerily similar to the Masoli-Orton errant connection from the game before. But Smith throws a chest-high bullet to Andrew Brewer for a touchdown. The Nighthawks rejoice. A demon has been slain. They are up 10–9 deep in the second quarter.

The defense is standing tall, thanks in large part to Dvoracek, who hobbles to the sideline after a defensive stop and gently lowers himself onto the bench. He's clearly hurting. Joe goes to him and puts a hand on his shoulder.

"Dusty, don't go back out there if you can't do it," he says.

Dvoracek slowly lifts his head. "Coach, I want to."

On the field, Smith has found his passing groove. On the Nighthawks' next possession, he hits Chad Lucas deep for an eighty-one-yard touchdown. Finally the offense is working as it was supposed to all season. At halftime, Omaha is ahead, 17–9.

There is one half of the game left, one last chance to leave on a good note. "Let's finish this," Joe says in the locker room.

But worry and uncertainty resurface on Omaha's first drive of the second half. They get down into scoring position and Wolfert comes on for a forty-one-yard field goal attempt. He pushes the ball badly to the right. He is a golfer with the yips. Sacramento drives for another field goal. It's 17–12, Omaha.

The defense pins Sacramento deep in its own territory. Omaha's Sam Aiken, a rangy wide receiver, blocks the Mountain Lions punt. The Nighthawks' special teams, with the recent exception of Wolfert, have become an elite unit. The ball bounds for the end zone. Several Nighthawks chase it, but it ends up out of the back of the end zone for a safety.

"Damn it," Joe yells. A safety is nice, but a touchdown might have clinched the game.

The Nighthawks' next drive ends at the Sacramento 34. Wolfert is sent out again to try to put the Nighthawks up by 10 with just four minutes to play. But his fifty-two-yard attempt is well short. He has now missed four of his last five field goal attempts. It would appear that his NFL dreams are over.

Macbeth calmly leads Sacramento down the field for the tying score with just 2:39 left on the clock. Omaha goes three and out. Macbeth leads Sacramento into field goal range with three seconds left. But, incredibly, the Nighthawks block the kick.

The game goes into overtime. Both teams will get a possession before sudden death. The teams take turns punting it to each other. The players on both teams are weary, strung out from the physical game as well as the emotional swings of the UFL's troubled third season. Smith hurts his ankle on a sack. Masoli comes back in with a chance to redeem his season with a game-winning drive. Instead, he goes three and out.

Macbeth leads Sacramento down the field, a methodical drive. They reach the Omaha 23-yard line with 1:30 left in overtime. It is 10:30p.m. A cold prairie wind whips through the stadium. Cody Ross, a diminutive back who's been overlooked by the

NFL, bursts through the line and runs, untouched, to the end zone.

The game—and the season—are over.

As Joe walks slowly off the field, Kevin runs up to him, whispers something into his ear, then puts an arm around him. From a distance, it looks like the son is holding his father up.

⊢+++⊣

This game was a gamble for Joe. He rolled the dice because he felt he really didn't have any other option if he wanted to get back into coaching. He absolutely knew what the stakes were, knew that the possibility of failure was there.

He'd believed that 1-3 was a bad record for him to carry forward. He fought hard to play the last game. He went for it, for something that would look and feel better.

He didn't get it. 1-4.

⊢+++⊣

"It's a difficult thing to explain," Rik Bonness, the former Raiders linebacker and friend of Joe's, had said when he stopped by to watch a Nighthawks practice in August, back when all of this was just beginning. "But he can win here without winning."

And he did, in some important ways. Joe showed Hambrecht and Huyghue how to run a professional football franchise. He restored the Nighthawks' credibility in the community by not taking his salary until all 2010 bills were paid. He halved their loss of $11 million and established what Hambrecht called "the league's best business practices."

Having inherited the UFL's worst team, Joe improved it, at least statistically. Omaha led the league in passing, sacks, and tackles for a loss, and had by far the best special teams, averaging a blocked kick per game. In Schweigert the Nighthawks also boasted the UFL's defensive player of the year.

But more than that, and more to Bonness's point, Joe won over the players. On losing teams, the players are almost expected to be miserable and mutinous. But the Nighthawks weren't. "He never lost the team," says Dvoracek. "Never. We'd run through a brick wall for the guy."

Joe's willingness to remain loyal to players like Crouch and Clarett was noticed. Little things—like the "Life after Football" sessions, and having the team pay for the players' trips home—endeared him to them. He'd established a bond.

And even the "Be a Man" drumbeat worked. Joe's central message is probably better suited for the college game, where the kids have had neither the time nor the experience to become jaded, where "be a man" is about transformation, not rediscovery. But what seemed like something more relevant to college students—all of that emphasis on what appeared to be non-football matters—did actually work with these pros. By and large, they bought into the "Be a Man" concept. It helped that Joe repeated it often and that he did so with such conviction. His success in business carried weight, too. He lived up to his own mantra. It was fatherly. With its masculine simplicity, it resonated.

Joe had the coaches, too. "Joe could coach in the NFL if he wanted. He's as good as anyone I've seen," says Olivadotti. "He's particularly great at handling people, at communicating with his players."

This may sound like a friend sticking up for another friend. And perhaps it is. But, surprisingly, Andrus very much felt the same way about Joe, despite the tension between the two. "I think he's a really good coach," says Andrus. "I would work for him again for sure."

Andrus's only complaint was that Joe didn't spend enough time with the offense, wasn't present enough to make sure he got what he wanted.

And time may have been at the root of the problem. Eight weeks was all Joe had, including training camp. Eight weeks to turn around a franchise with a totally new staff and mostly new players. Five games to prove he could coach. That was it.

Hambrecht says that the UFL got a two-for-one hire with Joe—they got a coach, but they also got a superb businessman. Joe never said no to Hambrecht and Huyghue when they called and asked him for advice. He was the only coach in the league on those conference calls where the fate of the league hung in the balance. Joe wouldn't have had it any other way, since he wanted the season to be played. But that time away from the team took a toll. It robbed him of time as a coach, time which was especially precious for someone who'd been away from the game for so long. In his business career, Joe had always, somehow, been successful at pulling the rabbit out of the hat, as his brother Johnny put it. But this time there was no rabbit.

There were no excuses, though. "I just didn't get it done, plain and simple," Joe says. "At the end of the day, in my one shot, I had a losing season. Regardless of any factors, I'm 100 percent responsible for that."

"I want to tell you guys how much I appreciate your effort out there tonight and during this entire season," Joe tells the team in the locker room after the game. "We talked about this before. We said we were never going to give up. I believe we gave it all we had out there. That's the only thing I asked of you all year long. I asked you to do it one more time tonight and you did it. And from the bottom of my heart I want to thank you for that."

Tears begin to form in his eyes. "We've talked about being a man, standing on your own two feet and accepting responsibility for your own actions. I want you to know this. We might have lost, but I've never met a better group of winners and a better group of men. And in life, it's all about being men. I am proud to be associated with you. You can count on me down the road for anything. This loss hurts, but let's keep our heads high. I love you guys."

Then, from around the room, players seated at their lockers, in grass-and-dirt-stained uniforms, say: "We love you, too, Coach." It becomes a chorus.

As Joe starts the Lord's Prayer, he is openly, nakedly, weeping.

Football is an unbearably cruel game. The line between winning and losing is ultrathin. A difficult-but-not-impossible catch in the end zone. A made field goal. A blocked punt that's recovered in the end zone instead of rolling right through it. Any one of these plays might have made a difference for Joe, might have made for a more palatable 2-3 or even 3-2 record. Then again, any one of them might not have.

But the football world is black-and-white. You are not given credit for how you play the game. Joe went 1-4 on the season. "You are what your record says you are," Bill Parcells once famously quipped.

But records still don't account for everything. Bill Belichick went 37-45 in five seasons with the Browns before taking over the Patriots and winning three Super Bowls. Gene Chizik, the Auburn coach who won the national championship in 2010, went 5-19 in the two seasons with Iowa State prior to taking the Auburn job in 2009. Both Belichick and Chizik have said that those losing seasons were critical to their later success. Joe feels the same way. "There is no doubt that I am a better coach today than I was before the season," he says.

Joe is not going to give up. He will make one more attempt at getting a college coaching job. And if he fails? "Well, I suppose I could come back here, assuming there is a UFL next season," he says. "But if the UFL doesn't make it and I don't get a college job..." His voice trails off. "Here's the deal: as much as I want to spend the rest of my life coaching, I do not want to spend the rest of my life *looking* for a job. If an institution doesn't appreciate what I can bring to the table, then so be it. I gave it my best shot. I put my heart—I put everything I had—into these last three years."

Joe doesn't need to coach. Not like he *needed* the Merrill Lynch job. But in some ways, that's what makes his quest—the pain, the sacrifices, the work—even more meaningful.

Joe leaves the locker room. A moment later he is outside of the pressroom, waiting for Dennis Green to finish up his interviews. But instead of standing outside the door, he walks behind a half-pulled curtain by himself. He sits uncomfortably on stacks of unopened, shrink-wrapped bottles of Gatorade, his head in one hand. He is no longer crying, but his cheeks are red, seemingly stained by the tears. He is utterly alone.

What happens to a dream deferred—and never attained?

Epilogue

The season is over.

The UFL still exists, for now. In the week leading up to the 2012 Super Bowl, Huyghue resigns as commissioner of the UFL, citing a desire to let "the owners figure out funding." Hambrecht says he's determined to play on, that he has new investors queued up. There's even talk about expansion. But as of early 2012, the UFL still has no national media contract and no true relationship, financial or otherwise, with the NFL.

In the UFL championship game, the Virginia Destroyers beat the Las Vegas Locomotives 17–3, giving Marty Schottenheimer his first professional football title as a head coach. In January, he has a chance to get back into the NFL, interviewing for the vacant Tampa Bay Buccaneers coaching job. He doesn't get it.

Tom Olivadotti heads to south Florida, back to a life of semiretirement. "But, dammit, I still find myself waking up in the middle of the night thinking about what coverage to play against slots or trips," he says. Olivadotti knows that if Joe gets a college job, he may ask him to come along to coach his defense. He has told Joe that he will do so only if he insists. Olivadotti no longer wants to recruit. He doesn't want to drag his sore bones across the country for several months a year anymore, chasing down high school kids.

Bart Andrus goes to Montana, where he has a house near a glacial lake. He awaits a call from someone else who is willing to take a chance on his offense. He is convinced it can work.

Richard Kent drifts down south by way of a few coaches' conferences and college all-star games. He carries with him now an impressive special teams coaching resume, which includes an advanced degree in the dark art of blocking kicks.

Don Lawrence shuffles back to the Kansas City area with his wife. The Nighthawks season may have been the last in his professional football career, which he started in 1959 as a lineman for the Washington Redskins.

Rick Mueller is hired by the Philadelphia Eagles as a player personnel executive.

Eric Crouch is done with football, having finally found closure in his final act as a professional player in his one game with the Nighthawks. "My mind is at peace," he says.

Jeremiah Masoli is still determined to make the NFL. He will try out for a team in the CFL, looking to use that league as another stepping stone.

Troy Smith signs with the Pittsburgh Steelers after their season and will compete for a job as a backup quarterback. He still throws a beautiful deep ball.

Maurice Clarett stays in Omaha with his family, though he sometimes pines for Columbus, Ohio. He says he will try to play again if there is a UFL in 2012. Encouraged by Joe, Clarett, Matt Overton, and wide receiver Chad Lucas start a year-round football academy called Led by Pros, which focuses on teaching kids how to handle themselves on and off the field. For Clarett, the mentoring is yet another step in his journey to become the man he wants to be—no longer a tale of caution, but one of inspiration.

Jeff Wolfert signs with the Cleveland Browns at the end of their season. He will enter 2012 training camp with the team, where he will attempt to forget the end of the 2011 UFL season and regain his confidence.

Stuart Schweigert, despite his excellent season, never gets a call from an NFL team. He lives in Saginaw, where he runs his professional indoor football team, the Sting, and a sports-oriented foundation for kids, to which Joe donates $10,000. "I still want to play football," Schweigert says. And he still wants a baby boy.

Angelo Crowell and his wife are looking to buy more Jersey Mike's Subs franchises. He retires from football. "I won't miss it. I did it for so long. It's time to start a family," he says.

Mike O'Connell starts to work out again once he's clear of his concussion symptoms. He's aiming for an invite to an NFL camp this summer. On the side, he is planning to start his own youth sports foundation, called Dare2Dream.

Dusty Dvoracek spends the offseason hunting deer and hosting a daily call-in sports radio show in Norman, Oklahoma. He claims he is done with football.

And then there's Joe Moglia. He is a man who has seemingly everything he needs—his health, wealth, a loving family. He has worked hard on the latter. For the last decade and a half, Joe's children feel that he has begun to make an earnest attempt to become more involved in their lives, to make up for his earlier absence. Joe has certainly succeeded beyond his wildest dreams in providing for them. His kids and even his grandkids are set financially, for life. And despite the rough patches they endured, the kids are all doing well. Kelly is a manager of a Head Start program in Vermont. Kim is a social worker. Kara worked at Merrill Lynch until she had kids. Kevin still works as an equities trader for Bank of America Merrill Lynch. Joe's stepson, John, works in mortgage servicing. Jeff is thinking about a career in finance.

"All Joe's done in his life is push, push, push. It's what's made him so successful professionally," says his sister, Mary. "But he's getting better at giving attention to his family. And he's good at it. He's giving and thoughtful and fun."

But Joe finds that he has one more professional push to make.

A week after the season Joe embarks on what is his last attempt to find a college head-coaching job. He knows that most athletic directors will reject him outright because of his record in the UFL.

But he believes, as he always has, that if he can just meet someone in person, to tell his story, to give someone a chance to actually *see* what they will be getting for a football coach...

He applies to ten schools. They run the gamut in terms of size and prestige. He sends resumes to, among others, Fordham, Columbia, Memphis and, yes, even to Penn State, which has just let go of another coach named Joe.

Four schools get back to him. Columbia, mired in a decades-long funk at the bottom of the Ivy League and in need of a radical change, conducts a quick phone interview with Joe. They never call back.

Joe is a finalist for the job at Florida Atlantic University, a Division I FBS program that was built from scratch by Howard Schnellenberger, Olivadotti's former boss at the Miami Hurricanes. But Joe is passed over for a familiar name: Carl Pelini, the Nebraska defensive coordinator, brother of Bo, and a man with whom Joe had worked closely during his two-year internship with the Cornhuskers. Pelini immediately hires Marvin Sanders, the Nighthawks' secondary coach, as his defensive coordinator.

Joe is also a finalist for the Fordham job. The school's athletic director, Frank McLaughlin, and president, Father Joseph McShane, were early supporters of Joe's attempt to return to coaching. Joe is an alumnus of the school. In 2009, he received an honorary degree from Fordham and was the commencement speaker for its business school. He is a New York City boy. The football team is coming off a 1-10 season and needs not only a new coach, but a brand-new start. It seems like a perfect match.

But the school seems hesitant. Joe has to practically beg for an interview. He eventually gets one, and the board likes him, but they still don't fully commit. He's one of two finalists. All coaching jobs carry with them an element of reciprocity: the prospective coach has to want the job—but the school has to want him, too. Fordham's recruitment of Joe seems almost forced, as if it's being done out of some sort of obligation. The vibes don't seem right to him. With a heavy heart, Joe withdraws his candidacy.

There is one more job opportunity. It's at a medium-sized university in Conway, South Carolina, a Division I FCS program. The Coastal Carolina University Chanticleers need a new football coach. They call Joe.

Surprisingly, the call doesn't come from the athletic director. It comes from the school president, David DeCenzo. DeCenzo, starting his fifth year as president, has a track record of looking at the world a little differently, especially when it comes to the school's athletic teams. In one of his first moves as president, he hired Cliff Ellis, a former Auburn and Clemson coach, to take over the Coastal Carolina basketball team. DeCenzo was widely ridiculed for the hire: Ellis had been out of basketball for three years and was perceived to be washed up. But DeCenzo's leap of faith was rewarded. Ellis has completely turned around the basketball program, winning 75 games in his first three seasons.

And now DeCenzo wants to take another leap.

He loves Joe immediately, loves "his drive and his passion and his uncanny ability to achieve his goals." He's not scared off by his long absence from the game or by his record in the UFL. "I believe in the *man*," he says, looking past the supposed credentials and pedigree, and sounding eerily like Mike Quinn at Merrill Lynch nearly three decades ago.

He offers Joe the job, a five-year contract with an annual salary of $175,000.

The job has everything Joe has ever wanted. A solid football program. Good academics. Top-notch training facilities. A firm commitment of support from both the president and athletic director. Brother Johnny lives fifteen minutes away. And Joe and Amy happen to own a beach house nearby.

The Coastal Carolina Chanticleers (the nickname comes from the clever rooster in Chaucer's *Canterbury Tales*) officially hire Joe as their head football coach four days before Christmas 2011.

The press conference is vintage Joe. He talks for a solid hour about his background and his desire to return to coaching. He talks, of course, about standing on your own two feet, accepting responsibility for your own actions, about being a man. He answers every question thrown at him by the assembled media.

"No, I am not a billionaire."

"No, I don't expect anybody to automatically and blindly accept me, but I would ask you to give me a shot, and I believe I'll earn your respect over time."

There are, of course, legions of doubters. People take to Internet chatboards and openly wonder why this school would hire a guy like this and not, say, the defensive backs coach from the University of South Carolina. They say Joe bought the job. They wonder what the hell DeCenzo is thinking.

Joe brushes it all off. Much of it is, after all, a very familiar echo of what he has heard all of his life.

It's a humid winter day in 2012. The clouds hanging above the sprawling Coastal Carolina campus are heavy with rain. Joe is in his new office in the Adkins Field House. A dozen unopened brown cardboard boxes sit on his floor. Various picture frames lean against the bare white walls. Joe is on the phone with a prospective defensive assistant. George Glenn, Brandon Noble, Mike Gallagher, and Brock Olivo have come with him to the Chanticleers from the Nighthawks (Joe has decided to let Olivadotti rest his bones). But he has many coaching holes to fill. And time is short: he is just a few weeks away from national signing day, when high school football recruits officially commit to a college. Joe is already putting in fourteen-hour days.

He hangs up the phone. For a brief moment, he casts his gaze out of the huge window in his office, which overlooks the football stadium. The grass is pale brown, dormant for the winter. Faded teal-blue letters occupy the end zones. But soon—very soon—that grass will be green again, and the seats in that stadium will be filled with thousands of fans who have come to watch his team play a football game.

Joe reins in his gaze, picks up the phone, and dials the number of another prospective assistant coach.

Against the odds, he has reached his goal, the one he held on to for forty-two years, the one that he thought, lying in that cold storage room three decades ago, was derailed for good.

But Joe doesn't have time to dwell on the achievement. The intensity is building again, another journey is beginning. He has a program to rebuild, staff to hire, schemes to install, boys to mold into men.

He has a team to coach.

Acknowledgments

My first thanks, of course, goes to Joe Moglia, who shared with me his life, both past and present. No topic was out of bounds; no question was left unanswered. Complete openness like this is such a rarity, and is to be cherished.

The Omaha Nighthawks coaches and players, also without reservation, took me in and immediately made me feel welcome.

I spoke to two hundred people for this book. Not every interviewee made the final manuscript by name. But each and every one of them helped.

Steven Bertoni first introduced me to Joe and his story, and for that I will always be thankful.

Peggy Henderson was an ever-smiling wrangler of facts, photos, and people.

Mike Hainen provided wise counsel.

Matt Boockmeier helped with accommodations.

My agent, Richard Pine, was my constant guide throughout this journey. I was—and remain—in excellent hands.

Rick Wolff and Jamie Raab made this project come to life. I owe them a huge debt of gratitude. Rick's fine editing touch is felt throughout these pages.

Beth Rashbaum and Charles Gaines read drafts of the manuscript. Their excellent edits, comments, and critiques were invaluable.

Linda Carrington, my babysitter extraordinaire, kept the little girls to whom this book is dedicated at bay just long enough for me to get it done.

My father's spirit hovers over everything I do.

My mother, Hansell, has always taken such incredible joy in her sons' lives. Like Joe, I too am my mother's son.

My wife, Heidi, held down the fort while I was in Nebraska, and was, as always, unstinting in her encouragement and love.

About the Author

Monte Burke grew up in New Hampshire, Vermont, North Carolina and Alabama. He has been a staff writer for *Forbes* magazine for the past twelve years, covering sports and business. He has also written for the *New York Times*, *Men's Journal*, *Outside*, *Field & Stream*, *Town & Country*, *Golf Digest* and *Garden & Gun*. His previous book, *Sowbelly*, was named one of the best books of the year by *Sports Illustrated* and was chosen for Barnes & Noble's "Discover Great New Writers" program. He lives in Brooklyn with his wife and two daughters.